To Deborah

   May you find much insight
and beracha from the rich
illumination of the Torah, & the
words of Chazal — its profound
spokespeople.

בברכת אותך הכל נא ניב גם

מאתתר

ArtScroll Judaica Classics®

Rabbi Nosson Scherman / Rabbi Meir Zlotowitz

General Editors

A PROJECT OF THE

Mesorah
Heritage
Foundation

=== *Maharal of Prague* ===

באר
הגולה **BE'ER**

Published by

Mesorah Publications, ltd

HAGOLAH

THE CLASSIC DEFENSE OF RABBINIC JUDAISM THROUGH THE PROFUNDITY OF THE AGGADAH

Adapted by

Rabbi Yitzchok Adlerstein

FIRST EDITION
First Impression … January 2000

Published and Distributed by
MESORAH PUBLICATIONS, LTD.
4401 Second Avenue
Brooklyn, N.Y 11232

Distributed in Europe by
J. LEHMANN HEBREW BOOKSELLERS
20 Cambridge Terrace
Gateshead, Tyne and Wear
England NE8 1RP

Distributed in Israel by
SIFRIATI / A. GITLER
10 Hashomer Street
Bnei Brak 51361

Distributed in Australia and New Zealand by
GOLDS BOOK & GIFT SHOP
36 William Street
Balaclava 3183, Vic., Australia

Distributed in South Africa by
KOLLEL BOOKSHOP
Shop 8A Norwood Hypermarket
Norwood 2196, Johannesburg, South Africa

Typography by CompuScribe at ArtScroll Studios, Ltd.
4401 Second Avenue / Brooklyn, N.Y. 11232 / (718) 921-9000

Printed in the United States of America by Moriah Offset
Bound by Sefercraft, Quality Bookbinders, Ltd., Brooklyn N.Y. 11232

This attempt to present the thought of the Maharal
is dedicated to my Rosh Yeshivah,
the man who introduced me
to the world of such thought,
in its depth and grandeur,

הגאון הר"ד ר שמואל יעקב וויינברג זצ"ל
Hagaon Harav Yaakov Weinberg זצ"ל
Rosh Yeshivas Ner Yisrael

His breadth of knowledge, clarity of thought,
and greatness in Torah
molded generations of Talmidim.

יהי זכרו ברוך

Rabbi Yitzchok Adlerstein

Rabbi Nachman Bulman
Yeshivat Ohr Somayach
Ohr Lagolah

הרב נחמן בולמן
ישיבת אור שמח
אור לגולה

בס״ד

אור ליום ה׳ ב׳ כסלו תש״ס פה עוה״ק ת״ו

The remarkable revival of Torah-learning and practice in our times is obvious for all to see. The aspect of Halacha in that revival has attained monumental dimensions, and has acquired common denominator status, though its thrust is by no means monolithic.

Not so concerning the application of Torah values and norms to the societal frames of Jewish life.

With little exception, mussar, chasidic, and hashkafa writings deal with the inner life of the individual: with Faith rather than its intellectual foundations, with the refinement of character traits, rather than with the struggle to enthrone Torah in every aspect of life, whether outside or inside Eretz Yisrael.

But הנפש לא תמלא (the soul is not fulfilled). Some turn to Kabbalah, which elevates the mundane to the cosmic. Others turn to passionate precision in the deeds of Halacha.

A malaise of spirit persists for those who seek a unity between mind and heart, between the logistics of Torah law and its ethos, between the Jew as individual and Knesset Yisrael as a whole.

For them the works of Mishnah are bread and water, as well as wings to liberate the soul from enslavement to smallness and philistinism.

For those who are distressed by rational and scientific challenge to the teachings of our Sages in the Aggada aspect of the Oral Torah, the Be'er Hagolah of the Maharal, is vital and seminal, as an exposition of the grandeur of Torah in its non-halachic aspects.

R' Yitzchak Adlerstein has won wide acclaim for the eloquence and cogency of his public shiurim and letcures. But now he has finally authored a major study of Maharal's Be'er Hagolah. He has not been daunted by the abstruseness of Maharal's style of writing, and has succeeded in offering us a lucid exposition of the seemingly untranslatable.

With Hashem's help, many will gain access to the Divine light of Torah through R' Adlerstein's rendition of the Be'er Hagolah. In these times of the hiding of the Divine Countenance, such a work is a precious gift to our generation.

הכותב וחותם לכבוד התורה – לומדי ומרביצי״ –
ולכ׳ תורתו של גאון הדורות המהר״ל זלל״ה

נחמן בולמן

137/21 Ma'alot Daphna, Jerusalen 97762 Israel Tel: 02-5824321:טל 97762 ירושלים 137/21 מעלות דפנה

Moshe M. Eisemann   משה אייזעמאן

401 Yeshiva Lane Pikesville, MD 21208

Dear R' Yitzchak,

The other day I was listening to a tape of a recent Agudah convention and was inspired by the many speeches that mentioned the seventy-thousand Yidden, who took part in the most recent Siyum HaShas. A few days earlier I had read an article on the seventy-thousand Jewish young people who are currently in India and other countries trying to find spiritual content for their blighted lives at the feet of sundry gurus and other masters.

I wondered whether there was a connection. Were the seventy-thousand Shas-Yidden a kind of atonement for the seventy-thousand lost souls, or did the seventy-thousand seekers in India drain our wonderful accomplishment of some of its beauty?

What are our children doing out there? What drives them so?

It occurred to me that in a fiendishly brilliant stroke of genius the Satan had tapped into the יפרצו מעיונתיך חוצה longings which, according to the well-known tradition, are to herald the Messianic era, and turned it on its head.

We seem to have lost our ability to communicate with our children. Is it they who refuse to listen or is it we who have not cared enough to learn the language to which they are attuned?

Enter your really beautiful English adaptation of the Be'er Hagolah. We both know that on its own it cannot stem the dreadful tide, but it can help. Oh, how it can help! And what a job you did! You had to understand the material, you had to internalize it, you had to learn to love it enough to face the terrors of the blank page and, quite often the blank mind, when looking for the right phrase that would keep you talking English and still be honest with your readers.

A word about your English rendering of this awesomely difficult work.

There are many translations of many important works on the market. Many of them are wooden or turgid and sometimes both. Often they are boring. People are writing Hebrew in English words. But the languages are different. Structure, sequences, idioms and the like are all indigenous to the home-language and cannot simply be carried over.

While looking through your book, I came across the phrase, man ought properly find his niche in his own backyard, on planet Earth

My interest was piqued. Niche? Backyard? In the Maharal?

I could not resist taking a peek in the original, and found: כי יוצא האדם ממחיצתו להיות מחיצתו בין העליונים. That is an absolutely brilliant translation. מחיצה is one of those words with many different nuances (קל טוהו מחיצות, בשר שיצא חוץ למחיצו, and so on in many different variations] and here they all landed up as niches in your backyard.

R' Yitzchak, you have done a great job. May the book become as popular as it deserves to be, and may you have much nachas from your own wonderful children even as you have striven wondrously to let the Ribono Shel Olam have nachas from His.

Best wishes,
Moshe M. Eisemann

Table of Contents

Introduction ix

Acknowledgments xvii

The First Well: Appreciating the Fundamental Principle

Asmachta and Tumah of the Hands 3
Bishul Akum 7
Rabbinic Fences 9
The Severity of Rabbinic Law 11
"These and Those are the Words of the Living G-d" 15

The Second Well: Beyond the Obvious

False Witnesses, the Power of Thought,
   and the Limitation of Justice 24
The Unanimous Verdict 32
Magic and Manipulating the Divine 37
Zugos and Demons 41
Lost Property and the Value of Money 45
The Three Shabbos Meals 49
Scientific Knowledge: Unlocking the Secrets of Creation 54
Well-placed and Misplaced Love 59

The Third Well: Words' Deeper Meaning

Ears, Fingertips, and Self-Censorship 65
Yisrael the Unforgettable 70
Derashos and the Plain Meaning of Text 79
Sichon's Accounting and Scriptural Allusions 81
The Waning of G-d's Strength? 85
Organic Torah 89

The Fourth Well: Relating to G-d

G-d's Prayer 94
Rosh Chodesh and G-d's Atonement 101

The Victory Over G-d and the Achinai Oven 104
G-d vs. the Heavenly Academy 107
G-d's *Tefillin* 114
Earthquakes and the Fuzziness of Creation 122
G-d's Daily Schedule and the Leviathan 133
G-d's Moment of Anger 140
Dancing with G-d in *Olam Haba* 144
The Death of Sannacherib 147
Man's Blessing to G-d 153
G-d the Matchmaker 159

The Fifth Well: Taming the Extreme

Introduction: Open Debate and Closed Wisdom 164
Monsters and Freaks 169
How Good is *Olam Haba*? 177
Accusations Against Moses 180
Pharoah's Grotesque Stature 188
David, Bathsheba, and Sins that Weren't 191
Noah and the Curse of cHam 197
Mashiach's Birth in the Six Days of Creation 202

The Sixth Well: Reasons for Reasons

Chazal and Science 208
The Four Causes of Eclipses 211
What the Earth Rests Upon 220
The Value of *Aggadah* 227
The Gnat that Killed Titus 234

The Seventh Well: Specialness

The *Am Ha'aretz* 242
The *Am Ha'aretz* and *Olam Haba* 251
Relating to the Non-Jew 255
Heretics and Sinners 263
Evil vs. Evildoers 269
Suppressing Criticism 270

Introduction

৩৯ Crossroads

R av Nachman Bulman, once threw out a challenge to me. "How would you distill the Maharal's greatness in a single paragraph?" As I fidgeted and groped for both clarity and words, he let me off the hook by responding himself. The Maharal, he explained, stood at the crossroads of many different currents and streams of Jewish thought, and united them all. He brought together the worlds of the distant past, and the unforeseeable future. Through him, we span the distance between R' Saadyah Gaon, the Rambam, and R' Moshe Chaim Luzzatto. We can relate the ancient view of the natural world to the new science. He allows us to connect the rationalist *Rishonim* with *Kabballah* and *Chassidus.* He gave them all a common language and platform, so that we today can merge all of them into a useful and integrated Torah philosophy.

Having had some time since then to ponder the question, I would add that Maharal prevented the Balkanization of Torah thought.

No work of the Maharal positions the author at the crossroads as much as *Be'er Hagolah.* Maharal lived in revolutionary times for the Jewish community, and he took upon himself the challenge of facilitating the transition from old to new. He formulated *Be'er Hagolah* as a response to unfamiliar winds blowing through Jewish life, which threatened to spread confusion and doubt.

This was not the first time in our long history that new ideas threatened to unseat the old. Torah luminaries had responded in two very different ways. Some met the challenge head on, by exposing the flaws in whatever philosophy their contemporaries flirted with. Sometimes, they even went beyond this, by demonstrating that whatever advantage people sought in the new spirit was already offered by the Torah — only more so! The Rambam's *Guide to the Perplexed* is a good example of this approach. It provided answers to those who already had questions.

Other Torah giants did not so much venture out to the front lines, as shore up the structure of Jewish intellectual life from within. R' Yehuda HaLevi seemed to do this with *Kuzari,* as did the Ran in his *Derashos.* Rather than openly attack the competing philosophies of his day, they addressed a community in flux with incisive insights and definitions, strengthening Jews to resist the meretricious allure of the new and modern. By not leaving room for doubt, they denied a beachhead to insidious seepage of ideas from other faiths and from rationalist skeptics. Their words were addressed to all, including those who did not yet have questions, or didn't realize that they had.

Maharal uses both approaches in *Be'er Hagolah.* He explicitly inventories contemporary complaints against rabbinic Judaism, and answers them one by one. These grievances came at times from outside the community. Maharal frequently dialogued with officials of the Church, as well as the intelligentsia of Prague, such as the visiting astronomer Tycho Brahe. More troublesome, however, were barbs shot from within the walls of the Jewish community. The emerging Renaissance meant the revival of serious study of history and the sciences, often accompanied by a rejection of the old order, and an intoxication with the assumed power of the human mind to encompass everything worth knowing.

It would have taken a miracle for none of this spirit to work its way into the Jewish community. No such miracle was forthcoming. Instead, Divine Providence provided perhaps a more important miracle in the work of the Maharal. His contribution has not diminished over successive centuries. This owes largely to the fact that Maharal's answers were so important, that they continue to strengthen and illuminate, replacing uncertainties with reasoned strength of conviction, even for those who never grappled with the questions!

The questioning and the criticism found their way into the Jewish community within his lifetime. Much of *Be'er Hagolah* is a response to Azaryah de Rossi (1513 or 1514-1578, Mantua), often known by the Hebrew version of his name, Azaryah *min Ha-adomim.* He is addressed in *Be'er Hagolah* only as a nameless critic of rabbinic Judaism. However, in his *Chidushei Aggados, Gittin* (pg. 108), Maharal refers to his nemesis by name, adding that he had already done battle with him in *Be'er Hagolah.* DeRossi's most famous work is *Me'or Einayim,* in which he questions (or rejects) many statements of Chazal. The tenor of the work is uneasiness with the grasp that *Chazal* had on many areas with which they dealt. Although he paid full allegiance to Halachah, the upshot of his oeuvre is that outside of the actual fixing and interpreting of the law, Chazal had no more authority than their personal opinions. This, of course, was patently unacceptable to Maharal.

ৰ্জ The Structure Of Be'er Hagolah

M aharal organized his rejoinder into seven broad categories of criticism against rabbinic Judaism, particularly the work of the authors of the Talmud. He called each category a *be'er,* or well, alluding to the wells dug by the Patriarchs and early generations, which represent fonts of knowledge that were later covered over and sealed. *Be'er Hagolah* is a well for the community of the exile, a defense of both the Oral Law and the honor of the Sages (end of Maharal's introduction). Each Well was meant to draw from the earlier wells of Torah giants, and make their waters available to the contemporary student.

Each Well set forth its theme with a brief introduction in verse. Each theme was a complaint that some critics leveled at Rabbinic Judaism. Multiple texts from the Talmud and Midrashim illustrated the complaint, or served to answer it. These texts are the subtopics contained within each Well. Maharal provided the answers by demonstrating that the critics misunderstood the source texts, and by substituting his fuller explication and elaboration of their true meaning for the grotesque mistaken notions of the skeptics.

Maharal almost always adheres to this model. He almost never writes as if the ink flowed from his own quill. Rather, to each objection he counterpoises some citation from *Chazal,* and explains how they themselves anticipated the question and provided the answer.

This appears crucial to Maharal's success. He did not want his reader to digest his own defense of Rabbinic Judaism, regardless of how successful it would be. He wished instead that the reader understand how incredibly profound and complete our *Mesorah* was. He wanted to leave the student amazed at the discernment of *Chazal,* and not only restore them to their pedestal, but to raise its height well beyond the position in which the reader may have initially placed it.

◄§ What the Modern Student Gains

Two decades of teaching Maharal has shown me that the modern student of *Be'er Hagolah* undergoes the same transformation. I have puzzled over many passages with classes of yeshivah-trained students, and with curious newcomers who were very much at the periphery of Jewish practice and thought. Despite differences in background and orientation, their reactions are similar.

Students initially react with pained disbelief at many passages that the Maharal cites. How are they to make sense of them? Indeed, the question becomes part of the answer. The difficulties are often so great and dramatic, that even the non-observant skeptic quickly concedes that the authors must have meant more than the plain meaning of the words suggests. The passage becomes a puzzle, crying out for a solution. By the time the session ends, and the Maharal has spoken his mind, the participants are impressed by possibilities they never recognized. Even when they quibble over some detail of Maharal's explication, they nonetheless realize that his essential approach is liberating, and that the ancient Rabbis stored much wisdom in the space of few words and carefully chosen metaphors. Thus, the first reward for the modern student of this work is *emunas Chachamim*: a deeper appreciation of *Chazal,* the masters of our *Mesorah* who link us with Sinai.

The second dividend is an approach to difficult portions of the *Aggadah.* The importance of *Aggadah* in traditional Jewish life cannot be overstated. It is where we go — and where our *chachamim* have always gone — to determine how the Torah wants us to think, yearn, emote; how to relate to ourselves, our people, and our Creator.

Many passages in the *Aggadah* strain the credulity of the reader. (The problem was noted well before Maharal wrote, and is discussed within the pages of this book.) As R' Shlomo Carlebach, the former *mashgiach* of Yeshivas Rabbeinu Chaim Berlin, once told me, Maharal on *Aggadah* should be treated as a *Rishon.* We never attempt to understand a passage in the Talmud without *Rashi;* we ought not to enter the inner court of *Aggadah* without a door-opener like Maharal.

Maharal, more than anyone else who ever wrote, provides us with a methodology with which to approach difficult passages of *Aggadah.*

Be'er Hagolah is the best place to learn this method, because much of it collects the most recondite and opaque examples of such passages, and shows how they can be accessed. Once treated to the Maharal's approach, many people intuitively turn to his works whenever they study *Aggadah,* even before consulting commentaries closer to their fingertips.

~§ What This Edition Does

Maharal's style is individualistic and difficult to penetrate. He uses terms and phraseology that can be seen in so many different ways, that the student may be left frustratingly in the dark. The answer is close at hand, but eludes firm clutching. Sometimes it helps to compare parallel texts in which the Maharal uses the same phrase or argument. My own experience, though, is that finding three similar texts leaves me triply irresolute.

There are no classic line-by-line commentaries to Maharal that have become popular. I therefore attempted to storm the palace, and offer something other than a translation. In fact, I don't translate at all. I try to digest the Maharal's step-by-step development, and offer some understanding of what it may mean to us.

I have tried to steer a middle path between translation without comment, and complete modification and adaptation. These are not essays-based-upon. I have tried to remain faithful to the Maharal's own development of a topic. This means that more remains unsaid than stated, and this work is meant to be studied, not read. I've attempted wherever possible to convey the sense of each paragraph and argument, usually in the same basic order as the author. I have not held back in offering my own grasp of what he was getting at, but I have swallowed my words many times, and suppressed the desire to say much, much more. To do more would be imposing my own views more than tolerably.

I have not included every piece. I chose selections that I thought had the most interest to, and the most to contribute to, the contemporary student. Maharal at times maps out an approach to unlock a difficult passage of *Chazal.* He will next apply the same approach to similar passages, which he sees as variations on the same theme. Generally,

I have omitted the restatements, thinking the reader most interested in one strong presentation. Omitted entirely are the sections in the sixth *Be'er* that attempt to harmonize the astronomy and cosmology of *Chazal* with that of sixteenth-century Europe. While these sections are of immense interest to scholars of the period, I have not yet discovered how these passages would help today's student harmonize *Chazal* with today's science. (The passages that follow these skipped sections contribute wonderful tools to resolving the seeming conflicts between faith and science, and they are fully treated below.)

With considerable embarrassment I concede that I also omitted sections with which I struggled, but simply could not satisfy myself that I understood anything at all.

My approach will likely meet with responses in the extreme — either love or hate. Some will be offended at being offered less than a full translation, and the intrusion of modern idioms. If you are one of those, please accept my apologies, and give the book to your brother-in-law who may have different needs.

I hope that many will like the work, and find it a gateway to all the works of Maharal. I do not mean to present the definitive approach to any section of *Be'er Hagolah.* I do hope that it will show readers how the words of Maharal can be fleshed out to take a definite, cogent position. Readers who have little facility with Hebrew text will hopefully be inspired to study more, so that they can eventually handle the original. Those who already can will make the best use of it as a companion to the original. They should first find the matching text, and try to understand it on their own. If that fails, they should then read this edition. Hopefully, one of two things will happen. Either they will be pleased and enlightened, or challenged enough to go back to the original, and work on it until they come up with something better than I offer. Since my goal is have more people labor to understand Maharal, I win either way.

৺§ What It Doesn't Do

As in many other places, I find that the words of the Maharal himself are the best way to express my feelings. I close with a portion of his introduction to the Fourth Well.

I prostrate myself on the ground before the reader, with hands and feet outstretched, to ask and beseech two things. First: If you read what I have written and the words do not enter your heart, then read and study again. These ideas will not enter your heart without much deep thought. So it is with all words of Truth. Initially they seem remote, but in the end they are revealed and enlighten like the midday sun. Second: If, after everything, these ideas still do not enter your heart, consider them as if they were never said. Do not assume that since an explanation is offered, and that explanation is not appealing, that therefore there is no explanation at all. Do not attribute the fault, G-d forbid, to the words of the *Chachamim*! Then our attempt to enhance your appreciation of them will have accomplished the opposite — for you to find more fault with them. Rather, ignore my explanations, and treat the difficult passages as a closed book, just as they were before you began reading. Bear in mind the overwhelming majority of passages that you have seen, the wonderful, insightful instruction in wisdom, fear of Heaven, and ethical development that is incomparable to anything offered by all the sages of the world. . .

ACKNOWLEDGMENTS

If reading this work is meant to heighten appreciation for *Chazal,* writing it all the more so increased my appreciation to *HaKadosh Baruch Hu.*

Rhetoric and fine speech sputter when I try to thank Hashem for the merit of making a contribution to the world of Torah thought. Any insight I have been treated to, and any success I have in conveying it, are His doing, and part of my debt to Him.

I also thank Him for some wonderful agents He providentially sent my way at crucial times of my life, specifically those who shaped the creation of this work:

Mori Verabbi, Hagaon Harav Alter Chanoch Henoch Leibowitz. While others claim that we are what we eat, we know better. We are what we learn. The *Rosh Yeshivah* nurtured me during the crucial formative years. Part of that diet was an unbounded enthusiasm for *Chazal,* and an appreciation that no one and nothing could surpass the insight that could be gained from studying their words. My interest in and commitment to unlocking the greatness of *Aggadah* is built upon the platform that he erected. He has no other wish in life but to see the spreading and glorifying of Torah. May *HaKadosh Baruch Hu* give him the length of days to continue his incredible achievements.

Harav Nachman Bulman, *mashgiach ruchani* of Ohr Somayach, is responsible for far more than the opening theme of the introduction. Far more people than he knows look to him as a modern Maharal, blending, merging and integrating competing strains of contemporary Jewish thought. Decades ago, he opened me up to a much wider world of Torah thought than I knew existed, and would not let me go without a commitment that I would delve into it. Whenever my students hear me attempt to marshal Torah resources to address modern intellectual issues, they are really listening to the voice of Rabbi Bulman in the background.

Rabbi Peretz Steinberg, *mara d'asra* of Young Israel of Queens Valley, was my guiding light while still a child. No one more than he made the goal of becoming a *talmid chacham* the single most desirable one to pursue.

I have been privileged to supplement the wonderful guidance of my youth with new counselors in adult life. Chief among them is Rav Moshe Eisemann, *mashgiach ruchani* of Yeshivas Ner Israel. His incisive and profound thinking constantly enlightens, and his stunning artistry with words always prods me to try harder. Above all, his smile and support are immeasurably helpful.

Lehavdil bein chaim l'chaim, I would never have had the courage to attempt learning Maharal without the encouragement and steady guidance of Rav Aryeh Kaplan. Just why I merited being among the very small group of people that sought and received his counsel will always mystify me. Suffice it to say that no one in this century comes close to Rabbi Kaplan in making the abstruse accessible.

All my mentors are but add-ons to the energy that my dear parents invested in me. One cannot pursue knowledge of the unknown without a thirst for answers, an appreciation of products of the mind over products of the hands, and striving for excellence. All of these are the contribution of my father. They might all have produced a dour, bookish individual, were it not for the upbeat exuberance and constant love and attention of my mother. May Hashem give them both many years of health, happiness and *nachas* from the growing family they founded.

Few of us write books as our day-job. For over twenty years, I have had the privilege of working within the walls of Yeshiva of Los Angeles. There, I enjoyed the company of wonderful colleagues and friends, and could tell myself that I was still nominally a *ben yeshiva,* one of the greatest honorifics bestowed upon man. Even though I was often busy with less glorious things, maintaining the fiction helped my self-image. My thanks to all my close *chaverim* among the faculty and administration, and especially to one remarkable individual who not only made it possible, but who taught me the whys and hows of delivering one's message to the world at large — Rabbi Moshe Hier.

One day after the Los Angeles earthquake, I was licking my wounds. They had nothing to do with earth tremors, though, but rather the pain and embarrassment of serving as an honoree at a testimonial dinner. Uncertainty over where the earth was going to move next did not deter Rabbi Nosson Scherman from making the trip from the safety of New York to serve as the featured speaker. This should make it easier to understand the warmth and admiration I have felt for him for so many years. His help with this project is just part of a series.

I am grateful to Rabbi Meir Zlotowitz not only for making this work part of ArtScroll's magnificent library, but especially for transforming the Jewish world through the ArtScroll Series. My thanks go as well to Avrohom Biderman who shepherded the process of turning a manuscript into a book, and to all the other staff members who were part of the undertaking.

My greatest partner in this endeavor, of course, was my wife Reena. She both gave me the space I needed over the years that this book developed, and filled it with love, warmth, and cheer. While this book might increase my popularity, it will never hold a candle to hers. May we merit seeing much Torah *nachas* from all our children — Dovi, Rachel, and Eliyahu Moshe; Shevi and Moshe; Yehuda; Pesach; Yoni; Ari; Tzviki; and Akiva.

The final piece in the puzzle is the Maharal himself, whose works *HaKadosh Baruch Hu* put in my path when my *neshamah* needed them the most. I pray that he will forgive me for not doing justice (or doing injustice) to his words. And if there is some value in some of mine, I hope that he will act as an intercessor before the Throne of Glory, and push along my *tefillah* that *lo samush haTorah mipi, umipi zar'i, umipi zera zar'i ad olam.*

THE FIRST WELL

Appreciating the fundamental principle

The challenge:

Rabbinic law and interpretation changed and added to the Torah. This violates the Torah's own prohibition, "You shall not add to the word that I command you, nor shall you subtract from it."[1]

The response:

I. *Asmachta* and the *Tumah* of Hands

"Whomever the *zav* touches, without having rinsed his hands in the water . . . remains *tamei* until the evening."[2] R' Elazar ben Arach claimed, "Our Sages found in this verse (literally: *samchu* — supported their view from a Scriptural source) a basis for washing hands before eating." Rava said to Rav Nachman, "How is this implied? Because it says, 'Without having rinsed his hands in the water.' It is implied that if he had washed them, the person he touched would remain *tahor*. But one who is *tamei* requires full immersion in a *mikveh*! Rather, the reference is to another kind of person, [one who is not fully *tamei*,] who requires washing of the hands."[3]

C ritics of *Chazal* charge that our Sages made new laws, and then contrived far-fetched allusions to support them. In this passage, *Chazal* argue that the Torah instructs us to wash our hands before meals. In fact, of course, *Chazal* themselves manufactured this law, the critics charge.

---

1. *Deuteronomy* 4:2.
2. *Leviticus* 15:11
3. *Chullin* 106a.

·❧ Derashah and Asmachta

To understand the passage properly we must make an important distinction between two methods of connecting Torah text with laws derived from it. These methods are called *derashah* and *asmachta.*

Derashos find multiple layers of meaning in Torah text. They enable us to discover allusions and hints that Hashem deliberately placed in His Book. These allusions sometimes enable us to discover details of laws that had never been previously uncovered. At other times, they bridge the gap between the Written Law and points of Oral Law that had already been well established. *Derashos* can take practices that were long followed on the strength of oral tradition, and show how they are alluded to in the written text of *Chumash.*

Our *mesorah* is unequivocal about the origin and legal weight of *derashos.* We hold the conclusions that follow from them to be unmistakably part of the intention of the Author.[4] Clearly, what is at work in the passage we consider here, dealing as it does with a later, obviously Rabbinic law, is not a *bona fide derashah.*

Rather, the argument that links washing hands with this verse is an example of *asmachta,* as borne out by R' Elazar ben Arach's choice of language: "*samchu.*" Related to the word for "to lean on," some see *asmachta* as a remote allusion that tritely relates a rabbinic law to some phrase in the Torah.[5] This approach trivializes the greatness of our *Chachamim,* and fails to note the deep significance and profundity of their every remark. Each passage, each epigram, each comment of *Chazal* is redolent with wisdom. *Chazal* never engage in frivolous word games. They would never manufacture associations where they do not really exist.

Asmachta means something much more. It always points to a *kernel idea that Chazal discovered in a text,* not just a serendipitous resemblance of words. What you can expect to find in an *asmachta* text may

---

4. See *Sefer HaMitzvos* of the *Rambam,* second *Shoresh*, and the commentary of the *Ramban.* See also *Maggid Mishneh, Ishus* 1:2.

5. See *Moreh* 3:43. *Rambam's* position is one extreme: *asmachta* is a mnemonic device, without organic connection to the *pasuk.*

not prove the law, but it will provide the animating argument *behind* the law.[6]

"Whomever the *zav* touches, without having rinsed his hands . . . " does not imply that if he had merely washed his hands, the *zav* would no longer transmit *tumah*. By Torah law, immersion of part of the body alone is never effective. The halachic intent of this phrase is to demand immersion of the *entire* body in a *mikveh*. Why, then, does the Torah curiously choose the word "hands," when it demands much more?

⤳§ Gateways to *Tumah*

We can readily understand that the hands ought to be the parts of the body most susceptible to *tumah*. *Tumah* is not a natural state. We become *tamei* largely by making contact with the surrounding world. The hands are the typical instruments through which we meet up with the items that induce *tumah*. The laws of *taharah* teach us what Hashem expects of us as we engage the greater world at large. He demands that we exercise sensitivity and discrimination about what we allow into our personal orbits, even in regard to very mundane objects. We are to avoid contact with all items that conflict with our special holiness, that are abhorrent or unseemly to the Jewish *neshamah*. Hands, therefore, are appropriate symbols of what *tumah* and *taharah* are all about.

The special role of hands is borne out by halachah. Consider the parts of the body which typically perform in a manner quite the opposite of the hands. *Beis hasesorim* is the halachic term for parts of

---

6. There is an intermediate position, advanced by the *Meshech Chochmah* to *Deuteronomy* 17:11 s.v., *Vehinei matzanu:* The text contains an allusion to the law itself. This allusion was placed there by Hashem, Who knew what the *Chachamim* would eventually legislate, and left a hint that would strengthen their position of authority when they would introduce their new statute. *Asmachta* is no real *derashah,* and the allusion went unnoticed by the generations that preceded the rabbinic enactment. But once created, the *Chachamim* saw that their law explained anomalies in the text.

For more on Maharal's understanding of *asmachta,* see his *Gur Aryeh* to *Exodus* 19:15. Maharal likens *asmachta* to the work of a builder who leaves some of his work undone. A clever person, seeing the partially completed building, can see just what further additions were conceived by the designer, and realizes what must be done to complete the job. Credit for the total design, though, remains with the designer.

the body that are usually covered and ordinarily do not touch the external world. If, perchance, a person makes contact with something *tamei* through one of these body parts, he does not become *tamei*. *Tumah* cannot arise through contact very different from the way we most usually engage the world around us. The source of this law is a *derashah*[7] from no other than the word "hands"! Just as hands are generally exposed, so must be any part of the body that conveys *tumah* from a remote source. At the same time, though, by underscoring the word "hands," the Torah alludes to the special place they have in introducing us to the defiled, to the *tamei*.

By Torah law, it was chiefly the *Kohanim* who were expected by Torah law to guard themselves against *tumah,* at least if they wished to eat *terumah* or *kodashim*. At some point, *Chazal* sought to extend *tumah* awareness to the general populace, to make everyone somewhat responsible to value the difference between *tahor* and *tamei*.[8] They knew where to turn. The Torah directly pointed to the special affinity that hands have for *tumah*. So the hands became the object of *Chazal*'s scaled-down, rabbinically improvised legislation. Rabbinic enactment, not Torah law, makes washing hands mandatory before eating. But the reason for this washing stems from the root understanding of what *tumah* and *taharah* are all about. This understanding is the hidden jewel of the passage in *Chullin,* the real intent of its author. To treat it as a play on words misses the whole point.

---

7. *Niddah* 43a (See *Rashi, Niddah* 41b s.v., *tumas*).

8. The ordinary Jew would otherwise have to concern himself with *tumah* and *taharah* only when he wished to enter the Temple area, either voluntarily, or during the mandatory holiday pilgrimages.

II. *Bishul Akum*

Cooked foods [prepared by a non-Jew] are prohibited. What is the source for this? The Torah states, "Food you will sell to me for money, and I shall eat; and you will give me water for money, and I shall drink."[9] Just as the water they wished to drink was unchanged [at the point of sale] through heating, so were the dishes [that the Jews of the desert were prepared to eat] raw [when they were purchased from the non-Jewish providers]. Does this *pasuk* really say anything about cooking? Rather, the law is Rabbinic, and the source offered is but an *asmachta* . . .[10]

It is well known that food cooked by a non-Jew is prohibited rabbinically[11] and not by Torah law. How can the *Chachamim* justify this practice with a reference to a period of time well before the rabbinic enactment?

The Sages did nothing wrong. The Gemara does not imply that the Jews traveling through the desert observed a prohibition against food cooked by a non-Jew. This law, after all, was first promulgated centuries later. The Gemara does pick up on an assumption that Moses' flock made relating to Jewish identity and pride.

◄§ Jewish Pride: Doing it Our Own Way

All nations value their distinctive habits, customs, and way of life. The more unique a people is, the more distinctive its practices will be. A nation that sees itself completely set apart in its nature and its mission wants to keep its cultural distance from all others. It will

---

9. *Deuteronomy* 2:28.

10. *Avodah Zarah* 37b.

11. *Yoreh Deah* 113.

demonstrate its independence in spirit and goals by emphasizing its difference and separateness. It is quite probable that it will not be able to keep itself completely from the contributions of all outsiders. Few societies can be, or want to be, completely self-sufficient. They must often turn to others for some vital resources or products.

When it must depend on others, however, a proud people will take pains to accept only raw, unchanged materials. Substances common to everyone are not what make people unique. These, after all, are given equally to all. What people make of them is another matter. A distinguished and prideful people will insist on leaving its own distinctive mark on the raw stuff, on molding it and shaping it with its own character.

Food deserves special consideration and attention. We do not merely use food as a tool or building block, but realize that it sustains life itself. Precisely here, those who see a different, elevated quality in their life and mission will want to take full charge in preparing what they eat.

We now understand that it was not by chance that the Jews spoke of purchasing "food and water." The implied identity was intentional. "We will buy drink, and we will buy food comparable to that drink. Water is unprocessed, unrefined. So is the food we will purchase. Sell us some raw fruit and vegetables. Their preparation you can leave to us." The keen ear of *Chazal* heard this overtone of cultural pride in the words of the Jews of the desert. At the appropriate time they built upon it, molding it into formal legislation as an absolute halachic ban on the cooked food of non-Jews.

Once again we have demonstrated that *asmachta* is a valuable tool in exploring the foundational principles of a legal concept. Only those who turn a deaf ear to the truth will disagree. *Chazal* knew what they were doing. The same cannot be said for the critics.

The challenge: *Chazal* added a huge number of restrictions to Jewish law. This itself seems inappropriate, as they attribute legislative powers to themselves to mimic those of Hashem Himself!

The response:

III. Rabbinic Fences

> Six hundred and thirteen mitzvos were related to Moses: 365 negative commandments, corresponding to the days of the solar year, and 248 positive commandments, corresponding to the number of parts of the human body.[12]

The last part of this passage speaks of the correlation between organs of the body and mitzvos. *Chazal* understood that there was nothing coincidental about this. If there is correspondence, they argued, there must be relationship as well. We shall see that the relationship that they uncovered is a persuasive argument for building fences around the Law.

✒§ To Protect and Serve

Important organs are served by structures that protect and cover. The more crucial the organ, the more likely it is that Nature will have taken elaborate measures to protect it. The eye, for example, is clearly a significant organ. It is served by the eyelid, which reacts quickly to

---

12. *Makkos* 23b.

protect it against dust and debris — really, the penetration of any foreign material that can injure it.

In Nature, then, we find a correlation between importance and protection. Should mitzvos be treated with less concern and efficiency? Mitzvos are also designed by Hashem, and serve to make Man's entire existence worthwhile. Are they any less vital than body parts? Their importance implies — and demands — protection. Fences around the law, mitzvos *derabbanan,* afford this protection.

৵§ Nature is G-d's Subcontractor

We need one more subtle distinction to advance our argument to the next level. We must understand the different creative roles of Hashem on the one hand, and Nature, which He Himself endowed with the power to accomplish His bidding on the other.

It is clear to us what role must be assigned directly to G-d. We surely credit Him with the chief elements of design. Relating this to the human body, we would say that He willed, engineered, and created all of our important organs, all the equipment He felt we would need to do our human business.

We need not look at the creation of protective devices in the same way. It is more attractive to argue that it was *Nature* that spawned these secondary structures! To be sure, Hashem created and empowered Nature itself. But Nature is law-abiding, fixed, and predictable. Once eyes are created, its host organism *must* care for these organs properly in order for them to function effectively in a world where hazards to the eye abound. Nature can and must do its job. Nature looks over its shoulder to learn what to do. The design of the organ and its importance — precisely those things that are communicated by G-d Himself — dictate to Nature what it must provide

We showed before that mitzvos and body parts are related. So we should not be surprised to discover these same two distinct types of creation can be applied to mitzvos as well.

Just like body parts, mitzvos are important and vital. We know them to function in dangerous environments, too. The *Yetzer Hara* of man works incessantly to subvert their effect. They, too, require protection to survive, flourish, and accomplish their task. This is precisely what

Chazal did in building their fences, in surrounding Torah law with a layer of rabbinic legislation. Parenthetically, *Chazal* avoid building fences around fences,[13] just as eyelids are not covered with a second eyelid to protect them.

When we picture the eye, we do not think of the eyeball alone. The support structures are dragged along in our mental image, because we have come to understand them as part of a larger complex that enables us to see and continue seeing. We must understand mitzvos *derabbanan* the same way. The *gedarim,* the fences, are necessary add-ons. Once built, they become part of one large aggregate, not mere human inventions standing off to the side. The large corpus of rabbinic legislation surrounding Torah law complements, rather than subverts, its authority. Rabbinic fences are the "natural" — and essential — outgrowth of Torah law, the proper human response to the cues left by the Master Designer.

IV. The Severity of Rabbinic Law

"And more than these, my son, be heedful . . ."[14] Beware more of the words of the Rabbis than the words of the Torah. The words of Torah include both positive and negative commandments [i.e. of varying severity], while whoever transgresses the words of the Rabbis should be put to death.[15]

The Rabbis warn people to be more careful about violating their own laws than the laws of the Torah! Does this not smack of presumption?

Human beings are physical creatures. They must answer to the natural, physical laws that govern all worldly phenomena. Those who place their hands into fires suffer instant consequences. The "punishment" for their indiscretion is immediate, because the world is

---

13. *Beitzah* 3a.
14. *Ecclesiastes* 12:12.
15. *Eruvin* 21b.

precisely ordered, and fire and skin therefore behave in predictable fashion.

✲§ Of This World and The Other

We previously explained that rules laid down by the Rabbis are never arbitrary, but expressions of profound wisdom. It goes without saying, though, that their wisdom is still limited by human understanding. Their reasoning is of this world, unlike that of the Torah which transcends everything earthly. The laws that the *Chachamim* make belong to, and join with, the natural laws of our present world. Because these statutes belong to the here and now, their consequences are also felt in this world. This is clearly not true regarding Torah law. If a person eats *terumah* while *tamei*, he has not violated a natural law, organically connected to this world. His violation is appropriately dealt with in the World to Come. Should G-d address it in this world, the transgressor may still not feel the consequences immediately.[16]

In urging us to heed mitzvos *derabbanan*, *Chazal* do not imply any greater severity concerning them. Of course violating Torah law is more serious than ignoring a rabbinic precept! They mean to alert us

---

16. A number of explanations are possible. One is that a quick Divine punishment would preclude human free will. If a bolt of lightning struck every transgressor, there would be room for only two kinds of people: the perfectly righteous, and the dead! G-d must hide His reactions to leave room for our obedience and disobedience, without turning us into robots.

A second possibility, closer to the wording of Maharal, is that transgressions of Hashem's laws are violations of "higher," more sublime principles than those that govern this existence. However masterfully engineered our world is, the laws upon which it is based ultimately deal with a set of "givens." These givens are a group of fundamental interconnections between space, time, matter and energy. Just why these relationships are so is a mystery to scientist and non-scientist alike. Torah Jews understand them to be true not because they just are, but because G-d created these laws themselves in the first stages of Creation. He wanted them this way, so they were. They reflect the way G-d undertook a given project — the molding of a finite world. These laws are no more permanent and fixed than the rest of the macrocosm, which exists only through the sustaining will of Hashem.

Torah law, however, precedes Creation. Its principles are true because they lie within the nature and reality of G-d Himself (see *Nefesh HaChaim* 4:10). The world was modeled after the Torah, not the reverse. Any violation of Torah law is not just an inappropriate way to make use of the universe G-d gave us; it is an affront to princi-

in this passage to some practical advice for the here and now: Exercise caution regarding rabbinic law. Trample upon it, and you will suffer the consequences more quickly.

✑§ Rabbinic Laws Make Torah Law Viable

There is another argument to explain why less weighty rabbinic laws can carry the supreme penalty of death. Rabbinic law gives final, pragmatic form to Torah law. The restrictions the Rabbis added serve an essential role: They keeps us away from sin. In this sense, they are the completion and fulfillment of the law. Without the safety net of rabbinic proscription, we would lapse into sin all too often. While the mitzvos themselves would continue to exist, their intended impact upon our conduct and the course of our lives would be thwarted. So these fences around the law really make possible the law itself. Negating rabbinic law strikes at the core of what the law is all about.

In a sense, it is more dangerous than the violation of an individual precept. While we might violate a Torah precept because of some temporary weakness or backsliding, we will quite likely feel contrite later, and limit our misadventure. Taking liberties with rabbinic law, though, can lead us into a free-fall of transgression. When we ignore the sage advice of the *Chachamim* and the protective devices they understood to be vital to a halachic lifestyle, we can easily slip into a pattern of general violation.

Death, of course, is also a form of nullification, wiping out life itself. It is, therefore, an appropriate measure-for-measure punishment for negating rabbinic laws, our guarantors of halachic robustness. There is Scriptural allusion to this as well. Ecclesiastes writes, "He who breaks

---

ples that go far beyond the importance of this world. The proper place to address these laws is not in this ephemeral, changeable existence. It is in a "place" that is closer to Hashem's mode of existence: *Olam Haba.*

A similar argument might be made for the fulfillment of mitzvos. Here, too, one might argue that the world that we are conscious of is not the proper place to reward good deeds. Coming from a much higher place, they can only be properly addressed in the higher-order existence of the World to Come. Indeed, this is exactly the way we might understand the Gemara (*Kiddushin* 39b) when it argues that "there is no reward for mitzvos in this world." Interestingly, here too it has been argued that the strictly human contribution to the mitzvos, such as extraordinary zeal and esthetic innovation, are in fact rewarded in this world. See *Nesivos Shalom (Slonim), Leviticus,* p. 134.

down a wall will be bitten by a snake."[17] One infamous snake comes to mind. When we breach the walls that assure the integrity of halachah, we are met with the deathly venom that the primordial serpent first injected into humanity in the paradise of *Gan Eden.*

---

17. *Ecclesiastes* 10:8.

V. "These and Those are the Words of the Living G-d"

"The words of the wise are like goads, and like nails well planted [are the sayings] of the masters of gatherings, given from one Shepherd."[18] Why are the words of Torah likened to goads? To teach you that just as the goad directs the cow along its furrows, so too, the words of Torah guide their students from the paths of death to those of life. If so, [should we conclude that] just as the goad is movable, so are the words of Torah?! [Therefore] Scripture teaches, "like nails." If so, [we should conclude that just as] the nail is deficient and not abundant, so are the words of Torah deficient and not abundant?! [Therefore] the Torah teaches, "planted" — just as this plant is fruitful and multiplies so do the words of Torah.

"Masters of gatherings" — these are *talmidei chachamim* who sit in various groups and occupy themselves with the study of Torah. [There are] those scholars who declare a thing *tame;* others *tahor;* those who forbid, while others permit. Some invalidate; others validate. Perhaps a man will say, "How can I ever study Torah?" Scripture states [that all are] "given from one Shepherd." One G-d gave them; one leader proclaimed them, from the Mouth of the Master of all matters, Blessed is He, as it is written, "And Hashem spoke *all* these words, saying . . . "[19]

---

18. *Ecclesiastes* 12:11.19. *Chagigah* 3b.

19. *Chagigah* 3b.

This passage is revelatory about the role of the *Chachamim,* [20] and suggests the proper perspective from which to consider much of the criticism we discussed above. When *Chazal* interpret the Torah, they do not offer mere suggestions and opinions, subject to revision and override by thinkers of later generations. Rather, their interpretations — and indeed all their words! — are fixed, compelled, and unchanging, coming as they do from a far loftier plane of understanding than we are used to.

⋘ What Torah Does for Us

The Gemara analyzes a series of images about the nature of Torah. The first compares the words of the Sages to a cattle goad. It guides the animal to walk a straight line in plowing its furrows. The Torah as well marks out a straight and true path for us. On that path, we find life.

Some would stop here, finding this a useful and adequate summary of the Torah's meaning to us. But this sells Torah short. Civilizations have developed other systems that restrain its citizens, and keep people from swallowing up their neighbors. Perhaps we should accept Torah as just one of many possible ways to lend stability to society. Perhaps Torah can be exchanged for one of these other systems.[21]

This is why the Gemara challenges the first image. "Should we conclude that just as the goad is movable, so are the words of Torah?" Can the words of Torah move aside; can they be supplanted by updated versions?

---

20. Unlike the previous selections, Maharal does not introduce this passage with a list of objections that critics throw at it. He introduces it in order to develop and expand its thesis. His point seems to be that Torah functions in so many important ways that the correct interpretation of it could never have been left to an inexact process of human beings groping for the correct grasp of its meaning. The accuracy of the words of *Chazal* are vouchsafed by Hashem's interest in maintaining the integrity of Torah.

21. After all, times, conditions, and even fundamental attitudes of people change. Surely the recipe for achieving societal cohesion should be flexible and changeable, and no system should claim a monopoly over time. Many times in Jewish history there have been calls for "changing" the Torah to make it conform with changing times. Maharal was acutely aware of the winds of modernity sweeping across parts of Jewish Europe from the more "enlightened" Italian city-states.

~§ Why Torah is Fixed and Unchangeable

The next image addresses this possibility. The words of the *Chachamim* are compared to nails. Nails are unmoving, fixed, strong, and permanent. Torah goes beyond providing guidance for life. While the Torah is pragmatic, it does more than suggest solutions to the timely problems of life. The words of Torah grow out of Reason. Reason comprehends the unbending, unyielding principles that are the foundation of all reality. Torah provides access to truths that do not change.

There is yet another dimension to the difference between the roles of the goad and the nail. Nails attach objects to each other. Torah binds a person to the upper worlds of Hashem's spiritual universe.[22] "But his desire is in the Torah of Hashem, and in His Torah he meditates day and night. He will be like a tree deeply rooted alongside brooks of water."[23] Such a tree develops deep, strong roots. No storm will unseat it. Torah makes a person un-shakable and immovable — able to withstand any force that life will send his way — by anchoring him to Something that trans-cends this world. Torah is not just the best policy for living, for navigating the straits and shoals of life. It promises us spiritual transcendence.

---

22. Torah is the common language shared by Hashem and Man. It originates in the *Olamos Ha'Ein Sof* (*Nefesh HaChaim* 4:10), the most profound "part" of G-d. Comprehending Torah is a miracle of sorts. Since Hashem's knowledge is iden-tical with Himself (*Rambam, Yad, Yesodei Torah* 2:10), understanding Torah is equivalent to understanding the nature of G-d. This would be beyond the grasp of mortal Man were it not for the miracle inherent in our receiving the Torah. This might be part of what Maharal means in his discussion of whether the sixth or seventh of Sivan is the more appropriate date to mark what happened at Sinai (*Tiferes Yisrael,* Ch. 27). Shavuos, he explains, encompasses two separate events, each of which is noteworthy and deserving commemoration in its own right. That G-d would give us the Torah is extraordinary; that we could success-fully receive it is a wonder of a different sort. The original Shavuos fell on Sha-bbos, since Shabbos had been designated in the first days of Creation as the time to bond Hashem's supernal blessings with the lower worlds. This, says Maharal, made Shabbos the perfect time to bring Torah "from the upper [worlds] to the lower [ones]."

23. *Psalms* 1:2-3.

≈§ Torah Means Spiritual Vitality

There is still more. Nails are inanimate, lifeless. The next image in the *pasuk* refers to these nails as "planted." These are vital nails, reproducing and growing. Through Torah, through anchoring us to a higher place, we benefit from Divine blessing. Hashem is the source of all *berachah,* all that is good. The tree analogy cited above from *Psalms* alludes to this: ". . . whose fruit it will bear in the proper time, and whatever he does will be successful." The closer one is to Hashem, the more he can draw on the storehouse of goodness that is innately part of Him. Connection with G-d, therefore, means not only rootedness, but enrichment. *Chazal* put it succinctly: "Whoever involves himself in Torah study, his property prospers."

To sum up so far, *Chazal* describe here what effect Torah has on us. Firstly, it guides a person both to fulfilled life in this world, and on to gaining the next. But Torah's benefits move far beyond this. Torah connects us with the spiritual worlds above ours. Here, a person finds incredible strength, and the *berachah* that is the by-product of connection to a giving G-d.

There are further levels of depth of the Torah experience. The next image from the Gemara sees Torah as studied by "masters of gatherings." Torah study is a group process, more than the province of individual savants. The reason for this is complex and profound, and turns on the interconnection between physical and spiritual realities, and their common essential nature.

≈§ The Evasiveness of Simplicity

There are no "simple" substances in our world. Everything we see can be divided and further divided, into smaller and smaller building blocks.[24]

---

24. To the Maharal, the basic blocks were the four essences that were seen from antiquity as the components from which all is assembled. Modern science continues to search for its version of the smallest packets of mass and energy. From what used to be a fairly simple set of sub-atomic particles like the neutron, proton, and electron, modern physics has amassed a dizzying collection of hadrons, leptons, and others. As

This should not surprise us. As Jews, we appreciate that the Oneness of G-d is unlike the oneness of anything else.[25] We understand that there is only one One, one truly monolithic entity. That is *HaKadosh Boruch Hu* Himself. It is precisely a lack of oneness that differentiates everything else from G-d. Outside of the unique simplicity of G-d, there is only diversity and plurality. So wherever we turn, we find complexes of things — even the cooperative merging of polar opposites — rather than simple essences.

Although we think of them as diametrically opposed, physical and spiritual realities have more than a passing resemblance. Everything physical is rooted in some spiritual analogue, which is its source. It follows that the physical universe neatly mirrors the spiritual one that nourishes it. The opposite is also true. Physical reality is merely a refraction of spiritual essence. The way something takes physical shape speaks eloquently about its "form" (as it were) in the spiritual worlds.

We now understand that the *composite* nature of all we observe must derive from complexes and composites within the spiritual realms. Torah is sometimes described as "Hashem's Wisdom"; it is, however, still the part of that Wisdom to which we mortals can relate. While rooted in the most profound part of Hashem, Torah is part of our world as well. It, too, will obey the same laws as all other phenomena in our corner of the universe.

---

the list grows larger, so does the conviction that eventually we will find a still more elementary set of subatomic "Lego" pieces. From the joining of these bits and pieces, we get atoms and molecules, and all of chemistry and biology! So the search goes on for the most basic components among exotic entities called quarks, which never exist unbound, but come in a variety of "flavors." Their aggregates (together with super-strings, if you want to find a smooth way to incorporate gravity as well) explain the structure of everything.

Curiously, the number four still has an important role in the search for simplicity down to our own day. The number of basic forces continues to hover around four (i.e. electro-magnetic, strong, weak, gravitational). Every now and then, science discovers a link between two, and the list shrinks, only to be followed by the discovery of a new basic force. (E.g., the electric and magnetic forces in the last century were shown to be more properly understood as a single electro-magnetic force. Shortly thereafter, the weak nuclear force was elucidated.) In the arena of biology, all the diversity of life owes to a code based on the sequence of the four nucleotide bases of the DNA molecule.

25. See the second of *Rambam's* Thirteen Principles in *Peirush HaMishnah* to *Perek Chelek* of *Sanhedrin*: "There is no Oneness like it."

Torah, then, is never simple, but complex. There are no completely simple, completely one-sided entities within Torah. Nothing in the Torah is completely — that is, simply and essentially — *tamei*. Nor is anything entirely *tahor*. Aspects of *taharah* live symbiotically with those of *tumah;* what is *asur* has some aspect of *heter* associated with it.

✑ The Whole is With the Many

Not all people — not even all scholars — think alike. When they examine a particular area within Torah, they are likely to discover different aspects and facets. No one person will be able to see the entire picture. Proper Torah study is a mass phenomenon, a group effort. Only the "masters of gatherings," the product of the minds of many, can succeed in exploring and uncovering all the nooks and crannies of a Torah subject.

At times, one authentic halachic decisor may conclude, "*Mutar!* Permissible!" A colleague may be equally passionate about the opposite conclusion. They are both correct. Each one identifies a different item among the complex of reasons that makes up the Torah issue; each one sees a different part of the whole Truth.

This is why the Gemara asserted that "One G-d gave them." The source of all legitimate Torah argumentation is Hashem Himself, even when conclusions seem to conflict with each other! We might be puzzled by this disparity of views coming from the Mind of the One G-d. The absolute Unity of G-d should generate nothing but unequivocal, singularly perfect lines of Divine thought.

But is this reasonable? Could we not apply the same argument to the physical world? From the Unity of G-d should come nothing but — complete Unity! But this bears no resemblance to what we observe. We live in a world of astounding diversity, of tension between polar opposites. For this reason the Gemara continues to describe G-d as "the Master of all things." Our Creator is One — but He is a Master of many different kinds of things, at least from our imperfect perspective. This mastery of the many allows Torah thoughts as well to be molecular, rather than atomic.

Does this relativism turn halachah into a free-for-all? Not a bit. There is no question that some lines of reasoning are more important than other equally "true" ones. These are fixed as halachah. The parallel to the physical world is complete. Different and opposing forces seethe beneath the surface of much of the physical soup that we look at. But some of these forces contribute more importantly to the way the mixture hangs together. Similarly, some of the elements of a Torah argument predominate, and they determine how we should act.

⋙ These and Those

At times, the sides are completely balanced. Neither camp exposes more elements (or more important elements) than the other. "These and those are the words of the Living G-d"[26] is the Gemara's description of such stalemates, such as the disputes between Hillel and Shammai.[27] When Shammai said "*tamei*" and Hillel countered with "*tahor*" — both of these words were the words of *HaKadosh Boruch Hu*, because He endowed the focus of their dispute with both *tumah* and *taharah*.

Why is halachah consistent with the school of Hillel? The same Gemara provides the reason. They were easygoing and patient. A certain simplicity (in the positive sense) shaped the main elements of their temperament. Their thinking gravitated towards the simple, the straight and true.[28] The thinking of Beis Shammai was no less accurate. If anything, the Gemara says that they were sharper and more incisive. But their arguments tended towards more unusual, elaborate, and out of the ordinary constructions. The halachic bottom line, the

---

26. *Eruvin* 13b.

27. Maharal himself later explains this phenomenon. Before the time of Hillel and Shammai, there were no protracted disputes in the world of halachah. Questions that arose were resolved by submission to a highest court, to *Sanhedrin HaGadol.* In time, this came to an end. Questions and disputes would become part of halachic living. *Klal Yisrael,* though, could not shift to the paradigm of constant, ongoing disputes without some sort of transition. Hillel and Shammai provided that bridge; there were disputes, but both sides were balanced and matched. Both sides, in a sense, were the victors.

28. For more on the interrelationship between *middos* (personality traits) and grasp of Torah, see *Pardes Rimonim,* cited by *Shelah, Beis Chochmah.* R. Chaim Vital sees Shammai relating to *gevurah* (strength and judgment), and Hillel to *chesed* (selfless giving). These *middos* link to different *sefiros,* which in turn determine which parts of Torah their followers could comprehend.

perspective that finds a tried and true path for the many to walk on (for this is the very nature of halachah), must relate to the less complicated, the middle of the road, the approach that the many can encompass.[29] Hillel and his students were well suited to this.

---

29. Halachah is the "Great Unifier." As the common denominator of expectation of everyone, it must reflect a grasp of the underlying Torah principles that is common to the most people. Intellectual tours-de-force can be exhilarating, but they leave too many gasping to keep up. The "simple" halachic approaches are those that the most can relate to.

THE SECOND WELL

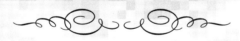

Beyond

the

Obvious

The Sages seem to endorse and embrace improper activities.

On the balance of things, this objection should never be voiced. The thorough righteousness and justice of so much of what *Chazal* write speaks persuasively. When we encounter a small number of difficult passages, we ought to realize that we cannot take them at face value. We understand that the fault must lie in our own limited comprehension, not in their deep thought. We ought to exert ourselves to uncover what is initially hidden, and discover the full, rich significance of their instruction.

Portions of *Chazal's* wisdom seem strange or incomprehensible to us because of differences in the way we comprehend things. *Chazal's* methods are based upon a tradition of wisdom received from G-d Himself. These approaches can remain opaque to those of us who must rely on natural means and make do with human reasoning.

I. False Witnesses, the Power of Thought, and the Limitation of Justice

> If [the witnesses who testified falsely] have not [yet] killed [their victim with their false testimony], they are executed [when they are proven to be *zomemim*]; once they have killed [i.e. the court has executed the accused on the basis of their testimony], they are not executed.[1]

---

1. *Makkos* 5b.

This irritates the skeptics. Why should we deal more harshly with those who only planned evil than with those who have carried it out?

It would be appropriate not to bother with this criticism. The rules of the Torah do not have to conform with our sense of "reasonableness" or "propriety." The Torah's mitzvos are Divine, and grow out of a G-dly perspective, radically different from our own. We have these laws because of an unbroken tradition from Sinai, not because of some growth and seasoning of Man's reasoning. The law that we here consider is no different from any other mitzvah of the Torah, whose ultimate reason and purpose is essentially hidden from Man! Nonetheless, I will not hide the truth. I will provide a bit of insight into their thinking, so that all will know how much greater are the thoughts of our early Sages than the ruminations of ordinary people.

Ramban already provided a defense of this law in his commentary to the Torah;[2] I will add some other important points. The truth of the Torah will become apparent and clear!

◄§ The Torah Only Punishes Some Murderers

First you must know how strict the Torah is in capital cases. Halachah stipulates that we question witnesses with seven types of inquiry and investigation. Individual judges, each according to his own wisdom, can pose additional questions to test the credibility of the testimony.[3] This demonstrates the exceptional gravity that the Torah attaches to taking a human life.

---

2. *Deuteronomy* 19:19. *Ramban* explains that once the accused is executed, he can be presumed to have been deserving of death. Hashem would not have allowed an innocent person to die through the activity of the Court. G-d retains the ultimate responsibility for meting out justice. When we assume some of the burden, Divine Providence rushes to our side to assist us. If the death penalty were inappropriate, Hashem would have guided the judges to a different conclusion.

3. *Sanhedrin* 40a; *Rambam, Eidus,* 1:4-6. Seven basic questions must be answered satisfactorily by the two witnesses, who are examined separately, each outside the presence of the other. These concern the place and time of the alleged crime. The reports of the witnesses must coincide as well regarding the main parameters of the criminal act. The court also questions them about details of lesser import, in an

You might object that these strict procedures, and many others like them, actually encourage the spilling of blood, as murderers take advantage of legal loopholes to avoid justice. It is important that you realize that this is not true. The strict, technical requirements for a conviction are only used when our nation, for the most part, acts righteously, and an isolated murder does not invite imitators. In times of loose moral standards, when a murderer who evades punishment might encourage sinners, a different standard is used. The Gemara provides the license for this: "The court may punish and put to death, beyond the letter of the law,"[4] according to the exigencies of the time and the situation.

At times, however, society is strong enough that unpunished murder will not necessarily lead to a cheapening of human life. In such a generation, we can safely make use of the pure righteousness and fairness of Torah law.

Surely, you will object, it is righteous and just that the guilty pay for their crimes! While this reaction is justified, it disregards other features of human jurisprudence. Is this the only insufficiency of justice that you observe? Who will punish the murderer who went unobserved? What about the perpetrator of an act of immorality or theft, who succeeds in concealing his evil? What recourse does any court have when it cannot muster the basic evidence or testimony it needs to proceed? Where is justice then?

All our attempts in dispensing justice are miserably incomplete without sharing the labor with a Partner. The One Who knows all, to Whom the hidden is all revealed — He is Witness and Judge! Righting the wrongs of this world is ultimately not our responsibility, but His!

Moreover, we usually confuse the identities of the greater and lesser partners in the quest for justice. We tend to see ourselves in the more prominent role, invoking Hashem merely to fill in certain gaps. The truth is precisely the opposite. Only G-d is the Guarantor of justice. At

attempt to get the witnesses to contradict each other. If the court discovers contra-dictions or inconsistencies in the two reports, it invalidates their testimony. (However, simple inability to answer a question of this type — i.e. the witness claims he simply does not remember — does not compromise the testimony.) The court is urged to put as many of these questions to the witnesses as possible.

4. *Yevamos* 90b.

times, He asks us to participate in the process. Effectively, He deputizes us to act as His surrogates, only where He has seen fit.

He calls for our intervention in a limited subset of all issues that arise. It is only upon much rarer occasions, however, that He assigns mortal, fallible humans a critical role in capital cases. Infrequently we rise to His standard of Justice to the point that He instructs our own hands to take the life of the accused.

☙ Thought Becomes the Equivalent of Deed

We will now consider why the paradigm of the plotting witnesses is such an anomaly, even within the limited sphere of human involvement with justice. You will quickly realize that plotting witnesses are not punished for anything they "do." In the halachic sense, they never "do" anything.[5] Any unhappy deed that follows from their testimony is actually carried out by the court itself. If the only parameter that we valued or examined were action, they would escape legal consequences, claiming that they were inactive causes for the action of the court.

But the mandate of the Jewish court is not to punish *evildoers*. Rather, the Torah instructs: "You shall destroy the *evil* from your

---

5. In many different ways, Jewish thought puts a premium on direct action. Halachah differentiates between activity, speech and thought, often (but not always) regarding activity as the most serious. Mere thoughts of crimes, for example, are rarely punishable, even by G-d Himself. (A rare exception is accepting the divinity of some idolatrous being. *Kiddushin* 40a teaches that in this arena, G-d exacts retribution for what is really a crime of thought, not deed or speech.) Damage to another party inflicted by speech will rarely lead to a court judgment. (Defaming a woman by claiming her promiscuity — *Deuteronomy* 22:13-19 — is an exception.)

Furthermore, halachah makes distinctions within the realm of activity itself. Consequential damage is rarely treated as seriously as direct damage. This is true even where there is no question that a particular action set into motion a cascade of consequences, without which the final consequence never would have occurred. Halachah still differentiates between "doing" and "causing." Although the false witnesses can be said to have *caused* the death of the victim, halachah rarely treats causation with the same severity as deed. (See *Sanhedrin* 77a, regarding murderers who are not subject to execution by the court, because their method of killing was not sufficiently direct.) Causing (without directly doing) does carry moral responsibility, however, including the need to make amends. See *Bava Kamma* 55b.

midst."[6] Arguably, there is evil in the plotting and planning of a malevolent heart as surely as there is in the transgression itself.

Typically, the evil of a crime endures beyond its commission. An act of murder changes the world. The killer leaves tracks; the impression of his misdeed is not washed away by time. There should be no statute of limitation. The ugly act remains a festering sore, and it is appropriate for the court to address it at any time.

The plotting witnesses, however, are never punished for an actual deed. It is the court itself that actually takes the life of the hapless victim, and they, of course, are completely innocent of any malicious intent or negligence. So the "crime," in the conventional sense of an offensive activity, cannot be punished. Those who committed it are innocent for lack of intention; those who brought it about should escape punishment, it would seem, for not having acted directly enough.

Instead, the Torah obligates us to execute them for a parallel evil — the evil of their *thought.* Thoughts themselves do not usually leave impressions and marks. Once the thought is translated into testimony and the case closed no blatant evil remains. In order to execute the witness for an evil thought (for reasons that we shall soon explain), that thought must be fresh, potent and functional. Thought occupies the main ring of judicial focus only when captured in full blossom, in flagrant display of its diabolical potential. This is so only while the witnesses are caught in the midst of their plotting, but never later.

⋙ The Power of Thought

You must know that *Chazal* here reveal to us the startling power inherent in human thought. Even if we were to accept our explanation above, it still strikes us as strange that the plotting witnesses should be punished for a crime of thought alone. The very unusual punishment of *zomemim* owes to the unseen potency of the human mind. When we ponder how crucial thought is to human experience, and just how wonderful a gift it is, we will

---

6. *Deuteronomy* 17:7.

perhaps begin to understand why Hashem endowed it with so much power.[7]

If Man is important (and we are taught that he is the ultimate purpose for Creation), thought trumps all competitors for his choicest asset. Inventory all the props available to him, and you will find nothing as important. As long as body and soul are united in this world, nothing in Man's experience is as personal and profound as the fruit of his conscious mind. His thoughts define him, and they mediate how he responds to the challenges that G-d throws at him In a sense, then, the entire "success" of Hashem's Man-centered plan for Creation rests on the quality of Man's thought. If a bit more Divine empowerment attaches itself to thought than we would have imagined, we should not be surprised.

Thoughts, we are taught here, have a life of their own.[8] They seek completion and resolution through action. When they are not translated into activity, they turn back against those who crafted them. Think of throwing a ball at some surface. If the target is suitable, say something soft and cushiony, it absorbs and dissipates the ball's energy. The potential energy in the projectile seems to disappear as the ball stops in its tracks.[9] When this cannot happen, when the ball strikes something firm and unyielding like a wall, it rebounds in the direction of the thrower. Its energy is redirected back at its source!

The evil plotting of the witnesses must be understood in the same way. When their plans to take a human life bear bitter fruit, and the victim is executed, the potency of their thoughts expires. They are not punished with death (at least by the hands of the human court), because they did not kill directly. If their plot is uncovered before the execution, however, the energy that they create with their plotting must be resolved. Their thoughts generate a homicidal force that will be satisfied and completed only when someone is actually killed. The Torah teaches us that the natural targets of this force are those who

---

7. Maharal offers no explanation here of just why human thought is more potent and powerful than we would have imagined. He merely states the point. I have supplied my own conjecture.

8. For more on this theme, see *Michtav MeEliyahu*, vol. 3 pp. 96-97.

9. Actually, the energy is converted to the mechanical energy of the vibration of several surfaces, and to heat energy.

unleashed it. Thus, they are executed; in effect, they are killed by the power of their own evil design.

You will find mirror images of this principle expressed elsewhere. Achashverosh ordered the execution of the figure who merely plotted the destruction of the Jewish people, but who failed to translate his evil thought into action. "[Haman's] wicked scheme, which he had *thought* about the Jews, should *recoil on his own head*."[10]

In another example, *Chazal* caution: "Whoever [unjustly] suspects innocent people [of misdeed] will be afflicted bodily.[11]

Simply alleging a wrongdoing carries consequences. When those consequences find no home with the innocent accused, their force is redirected to the accuser. The person who energized the spurious accusations, who created this pool of negativity, must absorb their fury.

⇜ Two Systems of Justice

You may still find our law unsettling. It seems unfair that the plotting witnesses who are not exposed until after the execution literally seem to "get away with murder." I have already told you, though, that there are two different systems of justice. Law, as it is given to human hands, oversees one of these. It is crucial, according to the Torah, that the human contribution to law abides by a clear standard, defensible through reason. Only a person whose hands directly take the life of another fully deserves to die. The Torah accepts nothing less as grounds for execution. Complicity never suffices: not through false testimony (where it is the court that actually kills the victim), nor through contracting the services of a hired killer.

Where the guilt of the criminal falls short of law's requirement — even a bit — the court has no option. No one has yet invented a partial execution. At this point, law must give way to the other available system of justice — the judgment of Hashem. G-d and only G-d can respond to wrongdoing with hairbreadth precision. He can choose from an infinite array of methods and strategies; He can punish as appropriate, neither too much nor too little.

---

10. *Esther* 9:25.
11. *Shabbos* 97a.

The sinner therefore "gets away" with nothing, although G-d is often in no hurry to settle all scores. The human observer may not be able to detect the link between the evildoer and G-d's response to him. At times, human society cannot adjust to G-d's timetable. When people are unworthy, and acts of murder and near murder can precipitate further erosion in the value of human life, *Beis Din* can execute whomever they think necessary, as we explained earlier. Operating not under the cloak of the law but beyond its margins, they can invoke emergency, extralegal powers to protect the community.

Sometimes, though, they never have to make use of these powers. When a particular generation is righteous enough, Hashem's Presence dwells close to His people, and He solves the problem for us.

Chazal illustrate this:[12] Two people kill, one intentionally, and one unintentionally. No one witnessed either act, so each criminal escapes his prescribed punishment. What does Hashem do? He "arranges" that the two killers should meet in one place. The unintentional killer climbs a ladder, and falls off, killing the intentional killer who just "happens" to be sitting below. This time, there are witnesses, and so the one who killed without premeditation is sent to one of the Torah-mandated cities of refuge,[13] where he deserved to be exiled for his previous crime.

Where human justice remains hopelessly incomplete, G-d's Providence completes the job. He efficiently removes sinners from the midst of the nation, and restores the sin-tarnished luster to His people's moral stature.

---

12. *Makkos* 10b.
13. *Numbers* 35:11.

II. The Unanimous Verdict

> Rav Kahana said: "If all [the judges] of the Sanhedrin saw [fit] to convict [a defendant], he is acquitted. What is the reason? For we have learned [that where the vote is to convict,] an overnight delay of the court proceedings [is required in order to give the judges an opportunity to find a basis on which [to acquit the defendant], and these [judges, having voted unanimously to convict] will no longer consider any basis for acquittal."[14]

This appears quite bizarre to our tastes. Can it really be that if all the judges believe the accused to be guilty, they must proclaim the opposite?

Our comments to the preceding passage lay the foundation for the explication of this one. We established there that true justice can come only from the scrutiny of the Higher Court of Hashem, and the subsequent intervention of the Divine Presence, operating among the people. The *Beis Din*, the human court, freed from acting as the final recourse to justice, has a far more limited role. Our judges are not expected to address every legal issue that arises. They do not need to, since they do not share the urgency that non-Jewish judges might. Our jurists know that they cannot deliver genuine justice, and that at the same time, G-d Himself can be depended on to provide it.

Torah judges act only when they can exhibit Law at its best, not at its most desperate. It is almost an act of arrogance to try to fill G-d's judicial shoes, as it were. We give it our best only when we can showcase the Law in its most brilliant form. The court intervenes only when it can show how the Law is wedded to a higher, objective, Divine Truth, rather than a makeshift, ersatz human approximation of it. It is crucial, therefore, that the members of the court perform their duty without bending the optimum rules in the slightest.

---

14. *Sanhedrin* 17a.

⊷§ The Limitations of Human Justice

Torah law[15] demands a laying-over of the court's decision in capital cases. After hearing all the evidence, the judges take as long as they need to analyze and debate the merits of the case. When they reach a verdict, the law enjoins them from announcing it the same day. They are forced to wait, and return the following day.

Do not think that this practice is just a pragmatic device, simply to afford them a final time to reconsider their conclusion. Rather, it illuminates the Torah's evaluation of our efforts at justice.

We could try to define the process of human justice as the seeking of truth. This definition quickly makes us uneasy. Man's grasp of ultimate Truth is necessarily limited. Man is a physical being. All physical things are limited and bound. Man is therefore a poor instrument to grasp the full sweep of supreme Truth and Reason. These inhere within G-d Himself, Who is the very opposite of limitation and restriction. Man's access to Truth, then, can never be instantaneous and intuitive. He can peek at it from the distance and admire it, but he is not instantly at home within its precincts. He can comprehend bits of it, but only after much work and Divine assistance.

If the human court is to remain a reflection of a higher Law, the deliberations of the court themselves must reflect Man's distance from that Law. It must display for all to see that Man is unable to grasp without struggle. The Torah prescribes a laying-over, a waiting period, before pronouncing judgment. (This is particularly needed in capital cases, where any mistake cannot be undone. The Torah establishes no such requirement in monetary cases, where errors can be remedied by ordering payment to the proper persons.) Injecting time into the deliberations broadcasts to the world that the members of the court understand the frailty and fallibility of their comprehension. Without that statement, their actions are a trespass. Having made it, they have done all they could to place their contribution to justice in the proper context.

---

15. Ibid. 40a; *Ramban, Sanhedrin* 12:3.

When all judges find the accused guilty, the process of deliberation had to have been marred. If two distinct positions, two opposing camps do not emerge — if a counterargument cannot be championed by even a single member of the panel — then something is amiss. We must regard their legal process as too ambitious for our taste. We see them as somewhat deficient in the dynamic of struggle and tension. When judges recognize that they seek a higher, absolute Truth, they will probe and analyze. We expect that some argument for the accused will fall into place, as a dividend of their search, no matter how obvious the outcome initially seemed. Once they prematurely withdraw from this process, they can no longer "find any merit," in the words of the Gemara, for the accused. They give the dangerous impression that human justice and Divine justice are equivalent, or that people can effortlessly grasp Hashem's deeper wisdom. We cannot allow this to happen.

❧ Tilting the Scales of Justice

A different way of circumscribing the limited role of the human court gives us yet another perspective on this passage. Righteousness is a property closely related to justice. We expect that the court should be saturated with a sense of propriety and righteousness.

From what is thoroughly and completely right and proper, no evil will ever flow. A court fixated on these ideals will generate only good. We have already shown that the mission of the court *cannot* be the seeking of truth and justice. We leave this to Hashem Himself. Rather, our preoccupation with righteousness forces us into a one-sided role: seeking merit for each accused! The image before our eyes is not that of blind justice. This is beyond us mortals.

Instead, our efforts are deliberately skewed and unbalanced. We do not seek justice as much as righteousness, recognizing the subtle difference between them.

Every person accused of a crime suffers damage to the good standing under the law that he previously enjoyed. The modest goal of the halachic criminal justice system is the restoration of good standing. We may not be able to right every wrong; we cannot always discover the facts as they actually occurred. We can, however, remove the cloud of guilt that hovers over the accused. Through our verdict, we can restore his good name and position in the community. In a word our job is to find *innocence,* not to discover the Truth!

This is the primary task, the goal we approach. In working towards it, we sometimes begrudgingly discover that we cannot find sufficient grounds to acquit. Having come so far, we cannot either disregard what we have learned. We understand that there is tributary value in finding for conviction as well. The Torah instructs us to eradicate the evil from our midst.[16] Such an outcome, though, must always be arrived at as an almost accidental by-product of our chief interest, which is moving towards acquittal, and removing the stain of suspicion from the accused.

✑§ Righteousness Cannot Be Sacrificed

Once we delimit the function of judges this way, we better understand the importance of laying over their decision. When judges unanimously concur about the guilt of an accused, they may quite well have reached a reasoned and defensible conclusion. They will, however, have sacrificed their chief function! If the facts seem so apparent and so foreboding, then they cannot adequately search for merit for the accused. Our reaction to this is unequivocal. If they, the members of the court, cannot do what they are supposed to do — if they cannot be a court of *righteousness* — we must dismiss them altogether!

A related halachah supports this approach. The court may wish to reopen a case after an initial ruling. New evidence may have surfaced; some judges may have reconsidered their opinions or developed new lines of argument. The Gemara rules that capital cases may be retried only to win acquittal, but not to make a new attempt at conviction.[17] Why the inequity? Why is courtroom procedure tilted and weighted on the side of acquittal, rather than perfectly balanced?

Our remarks above explain this strange law as well. Finding innocence is the primary function of the court; finding guilt is a secondary

---

16. *Deuteronomy* 17:7.

17. *Sanhedrin* 32a. The Mishnah there lists quite a few of these anomalies that skew courtroom procedure in favor of a not-guilty decision.

by-product, an occasional unplanned consequence. The secondary must give way to the primary; the primary and essential never yields to the secondary and accidental. A court that duly follows all prescribed procedures, and obtains an acquittal, has done just what it was meant to do. It has traveled the straight and narrow in pursuit of its mission and objective. Trading in that acquittal, even for the "truth," amounts to abandoning the key journey for a private excursion.

Even the individual judge may not change course in the midst of deliberations. If he first opines for innocence, he cannot later take up the argument for guilt. The reverse is not true. A judge initially disposed towards a guilty verdict is permitted to reverse himself and champion the cause of innocence.

The stricture against switching over to the camp leaning towards conviction has its limits. It applies only to the back-and-forth between the judges, as they attempt to wade through the evidence. One who openly identified with the "good" side must stick with it wherever possible. After all, his chief function on the bench is to uncover the good, to advance the cause of righteousness, and we assume that some factors favorable to the accused are present in all cases. Even if he develops some misgivings about his previous arguments, he should not abandon his accomplishment of embracing the pursuit of innocence! Let him rather remain silent — it is quite likely that justice will emerge nonetheless, through the efforts of his 22 colleagues At the time of the actual vote, though, once all the facets of the case have been thoroughly explored, any judge may cross over and cast his final vote for conviction.[18] Our preference for righteousness is built into legal procedure, but not at the expense of mangling the truth, and forcing someone to vote against his conscience!

Again, the focus and direction of *Beis Din* are more important to us than determining "factual" innocence or guilt. When we compromise the very foundation of human jurisprudence, we lose far more than a single case. We cannot afford to pay such a price; we must remain true to our basic principles. The court must remain an instrument of righteousness.

---

18. Ibid. 34a.

III. Magic and Manipulating the Divine

Abaye said, "The laws about sorcery parallel the laws of [forbidden labor on] Shabbos. Some of them [i.e., some acts, are punishable] by stoning; some of them [leave the perpetrator] exempt [from stoning,] but [are nonetheless] forbidden; and some of them [are] permissible in the first place. One who [actually] performs an act [through sorcery] is punished [by stoning]. One who [merely] creates an illusion [actions] is exempt [from stoning] but [his action is nonetheless] forbidden. [Actions that are] permissible in the first place [are those that are] like [the actions] of Rav Chanina and Rav Oshaya, who would delve into the laws of Creation every *Erev Shabbos*, and a calf which was at one-third of its maturity would be created for them, and they would eat it.[19]

This passage appears to condone some varieties of magic. After all, it claims that there are three forms of magic, and that one of them is permitted!

G-d forbid that *Chazal* should have intended such a conclusion. What they permit is not a form of "magic" as we generally use the term. Nonetheless, the permissible activities of R' Chanina and R' Oshaya share a strong common element with impermissible magic. *Chazal* group them together because of this shared aspect.

Both permissible and impermissible theurgy have a very real impact on the ordinary world.[20] In the words of *Chazal*, magic is able to "contravene the Heavenly Court." G-d Himself gave us the ability to overturn some of the fixed laws of the "apparent" reality that we call Nature. In this sense, using one of the holy Names of G-d is "magic," since it, too, can accomplish the unusual and unexpected. But *Chazal*

---

19. *Sanhedrin* 67b.
20. *Exodus* 14:19-21.

certainly do not imply here that all three types of activity listed are cut of the same cloth. Since two of the three, in fact, do fall within the boundaries of the halachic definition of magic, they use the term for all three. (The fact that they call the last type permissible should be all the evidence needed to prove that it has no relationship with prohibited magic.) What R' Chanina and R' Oshaya did resembles magic only in producing the extraordinary. There the resemblance ends.

⋹§ Spiritual Roots

In a sense, what they did was quite the opposite of the magic forbidden by the Torah. Prohibited magic somehow sets into motion phenomena that run against the usual grain of Nature. Using the wisdom of a holy work like *Sefer Yetzirah* cannot be seen as inconsistent with G-d's plan. If anything, it is consistent with a deeper nature of the world He fashioned. Does not G-d constantly override the edicts of His Heavenly Court? G-d created spiritual "laws" as surely as He created physical ones. These laws dictate how the spiritual roots of things translate into the physical phenomena that we observe. These laws, authored by G-d Himself, are full of His Wisdom and planning. Hashem's love for us is so profound, however, that He often chooses to intervene against these laws, and act in a different manner.[21] This happens so regularly that disregarding the "expected" is quite "natural" and ordinary! (One of the Names of Hashem is "Sha-dai," because He destroys — *shoded* — the array of Heavenly Hosts that are the symbol of the fixed system of laws and justice that He often banishes.)

⋹§ A Parallel in Prayer

G-d Himself taught Man about the connection between His Names and the general, everyday laws of physical existence. Thus, he gave man access to the tools with which to accomplish unusual results. If you think about it, you will realize that this is no different from our everyday prayer. Do we not ask G-d to tear up Heavenly decrees? Do we not implore Him to act behind the scenes,

---

21. See *Derech Hashem* 2:5:6 and 2:8:1 for elaboration of these points.

and change what we might otherwise consider predictable and determined? Is not prayer itself a tool in our hands to countermand the "authority" of the Heavenly Courts and their Divinely inscribed set of laws? If we were to ban the use of *Sefer Yetzirah*, we would have to ban all petitionary prayer as well! Yet Hashem encourages us to pray. He expects us to utilize the efficacy of our entreaties to Him to reshape our world. He just suggests that we should often take up a spiritual hammer, rather than just a physical one, to bang the nails into the new structure.

We must regard the use of the Names of Hashem as working, in a broader sense, with the laws of Nature, rather than against them. Here we have arrived at the essence of forbidden magic. It is in the goal that is achieved, not in the means used. It is in the thwarting of what "should" be, not in making use of the "unnatural."

We can demonstrate that this idea was commonplace to *Chazal*. They held that Moses split the Red Sea with the 72-letter Divine Name. (Three verses precede the description of the Jews passing through the Sea.[22] Each is composed of precisely 72 letters.[23]) When Elisha cursed the young men who mocked him,[24] the result was the death of exactly 42 people. This is because he made use of the Name of 42 letters.[25]

⊷§ Sefer Yetzirah

*S*efer Yetzirah is no different. It, too, makes use of combinations of Names of Hashem. It was with these Names that G-d brought the universe into existence. The system of laws that they spawned represent the *Ur*-plan, the primal scheme of Creation. How could making use of it possibly be considered subverting G-d's design?[26]

---

22. *Exodus* 14:19-21.

23. See *Rashi, Succah* 45a s.v., *ani.*

24. *Judges* 22:24. See *Sotah* 46b for why Elisha acted this way.

25. See *Rabbeinu Bachya, Exodus* 2:12, who cites the same argument.

26. Maharal stresses that the Names of G-d patterned the original plan of Creation, rather than some temporary arrangement in which we may find ourselves at the moment. If we obeyed some makeshift, provisional laws that took effect later, we might still be seen as violating "natural" law.

Our thesis here is borne out by the illustration used in our passage. Why compare the prohibitions of magic specifically to those of Shabbos? The threefold division of activities (prohibited by Torah law; prohibited rabbinically; permissible[27]) is fairly common in halachah.

⁕ Connection to Shabbos

We realize that there is conceptual overlap between Shabbos and magic. Hashem orders that we refrain from creative acts on Shabbos, because it is a day of worldly completion and perfection. The process of Creation did not go on forever. By ceasing to labor, G-d created a sense of fulfillment, peace and tranquility that we know as Shabbos. Activity need not go on forever. Where G-d has satisfied Himself with the goodness of His Creation, there is no place for our insolent tinkering! Why change a good thing?

This is precisely the yardstick we apply to the prohibition of magic. Laws, consequences, reactions that are hard-wired into natural law should not be changed by artifice. On the other hand, some of our interventions are not really changes at all. Without our being aware of it, Names of G-d constantly combine and recombine, and the quanta of spiritual potential associated with them take shape in myriad observable phenomena. This is the reality behind our perceived reality. When we make use of *Sefer Yetzirah*, we do nothing different than what happens all the time: we translate the potency of the Names of Hashem

---

Maharal draws an even smaller circle in the next selection, making a distinction within the "original" laws themselves. He differentiates between using the primary forces of Creation, as opposed to other powers. The latter, he will argue, are not truly part of the fabric of Creation. Using them confounds the Master Plan.

A somewhat different distinction is drawn by the *Shach, Yoreh Deah* 179:18. He sees the use of *Sefer Yetzirah* and its attendant manipulation of Divine Names as acceptable, because it places all the focus on Hashem Himself. Using G-d's Names in wondrous manner only magnifies our appreciation of Him, rather than deflects attention from Him. Nonetheless, the *Shach* warns that using the Names is proper only for the greatest people, and to accomplish extraordinary mitzvos. He strongly advises against ordinary people getting involved with such activity.

27. In our passage, forms of work that are prohibited by Torah law subject the violator to stoning; those that are rabbinically proscribed are exempt from capital punishment, but are nonetheless forbidden; others are not really "work" by the standards of halachah, and are entirely permissible.

into physical form. We utilize the true plan for the universe, not change or overthrow it. If we seem to accomplish the unexpected and unpredicted, it is only because some paragraphs in G-d's Book of Natural Law generally go unread. Until we study them, their promise remains dormant and untapped. When we access them, we simply actualize a potential that is fully part of Hashem's blueprint for the world.

IV. *Zugos* and Demons

The Gemara in *Pesachim* 110a-b discusses drinking in *zugos*, or "pairs" — certain combinations of even numbers of cups. It sees this as problematic; drinking an odd number of cups is preferred. The even-numbered combinations make one susceptible to the advances of various demons.

Here too, our detractors find evidence that the Sages, while prohibiting certain forms of magic, fully endorsed others.

Their criticism is misplaced. The Sages eschew any involvement with magic and the occult. On the other hand, it is honorable and necessary to teach people how to protect themselves from its undisputed power. Would we prefer if they hide from several passages in the Bible itself[28] that deal with unsavory spiritual forces? Should we deny the apparent meaning of *Tehillim* 91?[29] Didn't Nebuchadnezzar call Daniel "*Rav chartumaya,*"[30] meaning "greatest of magicians"? Earlier,[31] Daniel and his friends are praised as " ten times better [in their reasoning] than all the necromancers and astrologers that were in his entire kingdom."

---

28. Maharal understands that these skeptics would never attack the Written Torah, and aim their barbs only at rabbinic contributions.

29. with its references to "the [demonic (*Targum, Metzudos*)] destroyer who lays waste at noon," and the "thousand [demons who] encamp at your side (*Rashi*), and a myriad at your right hand."

30. *Daniel* 4:6.

31. *Ibid.* 1:20.

Our Sages, like Daniel, mastered the knowledge of these disciplines. Because of this training, *Chazal* were able to point out dangers to others, as they do here in warning against eating or drinking in "pairs." It will be worthwhile for us to explore why they understood this practice to be problematic.

৵ Filling in the Gaps

Previously,[32] we distinguished between organs and the protective structures that are associated with them. We understood that the former were the immediate product of G-d's creativity; the others are forced by Nature to come along for the ride. We are now ready to appreciate that this differentiation spills out across the entire cosmos, physical and spiritual.

Explore any part of our world and you will find key building blocks and constructs that determine basic character and function. You will also find the mortar between the bricks: the many elements that fill in the gaps, that support, facilitate, and coordinate. These latter elements are hardly as purposeful (in the sense of immediately serving Hashem's purpose for Creation) as members of the first category.

In a sense, all things fall into one of two groups: things that were created and things that sustain creation. G-d hardly created the world for the sake of lowly burrowing insects. Without them, however, our world could not exist as we know it.[33]

The spiritual world created by G-d mirrors this duality perfectly. There are primary beings and forces created to implement G-d's Will, and there are other entities which merely fill in the spaces, in a manner of speaking, between them.[34] Among these are the unsavory beings called spirits and demons.

---

32. See First Well, page 6.

33. Insects provide necessary maintenance service to the soil. Their activities soften it for plant growth, and provide needed nutrients. And without them, of course, we would lack a host of species, including fruit, which rely on insects for pollination and reproduction.

34. See *Derech Hashem* by R' Moshe Chaim Luzzatto 1:5:1, who observes that the Gemara's attribution to *sheidim* of both physical and spiritual properties essentially describes them as *intermediate* between the two realms, in effect filling up the "space" between them.

The distinction that we have drawn between primary and secondary is purely a function of our human nature. The world as we experience it requires precursors and cofactors and facilitators and energizers.[35] Living in a world of limitations, of cause-and-effect laws, phenomena do not "just happen" without complex interactions between many factors.

All of the physical, chemical, and biological agents scurrying about to do their appointed tasks are completely foreign, in a sense, to the nature of G-d. From His perspective, as best we can understand, all of them are irrelevant. There is His Will, and nothing more. His Will can translate itself into any reality He desires, and it does so instantaneously. The options available to Him, the different configurations with which He could design a world are inexhaustible. *Teva*, the world of law and Nature that we observe, is a contrivance, an invention to suit the needs of flesh-and-blood. It is not *a priori*. To a Being Who does not need to build from the ground up, nothing is crucial; everything is expendable. His Will is primary, and there is no room for anything else.

To leave room for, and ultimately necessitate, secondary phenomena, you have to move away from the Absolute Oneness of G-d. In the transition between "one" and "two," or between "one" and "more-than-one," a niche develops for phenomena that mediate other phenomena, for sluggish movement between design and implementation. Here enter all the underlings of the corporate effort, rather than the single efficient stroke of the Master Engineer.

In the number "two," then, we have found the turf for all that is secondary. "Twoness," or plurality, creates the stage for a drama requiring a large cast. Two is thus the magic number for demons/*sheidim*, and their ilk. They cling to its expression. More accurately, perhaps, they avoid any reminder of the number "one," the antithesis of their being. They do not belong in a world in which the Will of Hashem could be accomplished openly and directly.

---

35. Physiological activities that we take for granted depend on complex metabolic pathways, and utilize scores of designer-made molecules that most of us don't concern ourselves with. They operate efficiently in the background, frenetically shuttling back and forth reliably and efficiently without our taking notice — at least until something goes wrong!

In this we find the most effective antidote to their power.

> Whoever recites the *Shema* at his bedside is [considered] as if he held a double-edged sword in his hand [to protect him against demons while he sleeps], for it is stated,[36] "The lofty praises of G-d are in their throats, and a double-edged sword is in their hand."[37]

In reciting the *Shema*, one clings to the Oneness of G-d. Within His Oneness, there is room for the direct objects of His Will, but not for the secondary. Attachment to the One nullifies any power of the *sheidim*, for whom Oneness is anathema.

The sense of Oneness that a person must cleave to is sophisticated. G-d's Oneness is unlike any other known to Man, and completely removed from his direct experience. A king, for example, may rule with awesome and complete control. Concerning power and authority figures in his kingdom, he is indeed singular, unique, and alone. In so many other regards, however, he is commonplace. When seen as a human being, he shares a plethora of phenomena with every other person on the planet. He is "one" only in a single facet of his being.

Hashem is the only true Oneness. This is why the sword of reciting *Shema* is described as double-edged. What makes a sword important is its sharpness. A single edge shows that sharpness in only area. A double-edged instrument displays this characteristic every place physically possible. This is akin to the unique Oneness of G-d, which is true in every possible regard. This is the Oneness that negates the very existence of demons and spirits.

---

36. *Psalms* 149:6.
37. *Berachos* 5a.

V. Lost Property and the Value of Money

> Once owners give up hope of ever retrieving an object they have lost, halachah rules that the object need not be returned, even if the finder determines the identity of the loser with certainty.[38]

M any are affronted by this law. How can our Sages permit us to keep what we did not toil for, what we did not earn, and indulge our desire for the property of others? Our common civic sense dictates that this is improper — and Torah is usually far more demanding than our common sense!

Civilized societies base many of their laws on commonly held assumptions of propriety and impropriety. Dig beneath the surface, and you will find that the animating idea behind this system of beliefs is practicality. We accept — and expect from others — behavior that will efficiently keep the cogs of society turning with the least amount of friction between parts. We reject behavior that stymies the smooth flow of commerce and social intercourse.

The Torah's rules are based on *sechel* — Absolute Reason,[39] rather than on what is neat and efficient. There are decided conflicts between the two systems. At times, our sense of societal propriety will demand what *sechel* does not. Sometimes, though, the positions are reversed.

---

38. *Bava Metzia* 21b.

39. Maharal means by this consistency with an absolute Truth, which is related to the unequaled understanding of Hashem Himself, the Originator of all truth. It implies not only accuracy, but full grasp of all elements as they really are, and harmony with all other arguments that are true. *Sechel* cannot obligate something that seems just and fair and practical under the circumstances, but grates on the internal logic of some other precept or ethic.

Sechel should not be confused with what we consider "reasonable" or "logical." In fact, Maharal uses these terms within this section itself to contrast with *Sechel*. *Sechel* emantes from an Intelligence that, in its fullness, is beyond Man's grasp. We grasp what we do of it, because Hashem created within our souls a limited capacity to do so. We access it through the method and content that Hashem bundled together in the Torah.

Returning lost objects is a case in point. Our accepted norms of civility call for their return, regardless of the owner's losing all hope of reuniting with them. We support this intuitively, because all of us wish to have every possible chance to retrieve the property that we ourselves often lose or misplace. We don't want to see strangers claiming our possessions for themselves.

On the other hand, our civic codes are liberal concerning identifiable property[40] that has gone unclaimed for long periods of time, especially after several attempts to locate the owner. Society is no longer served by endless waiting. Let the finder keep the object, and put it to some good use, we argue.

The Torah pointedly disagrees. Even after many public announcements that he has found lost (but theoretically identifiable) property, the finder may never keep the object for himself. Instead, he holds it in perpetuity, or until Eliyahu the Prophet[41] arrives and unravels the mystery of ownership.

✑§ We Are Not Our Money

What separates the viewpoints of Torah/*sechel* from our civic instinct? Our fundamental relationship towards money and property divides the two. Our secular laws take pains to safeguard money and possessions, because we recognize how important property is to people, and how property rights are essential to the orderly function of society. *Sechel*, however, views the value of property at its essence and root, not through pragmatic lenses alone.

Money should never be regarded as "the bone of his bones and flesh of his flesh."[42] Possessions extend our reach. They are part of our personal universes, but always as peripherals. They should never be confused with our essential selves. We truly own things only when we possess them. Absent the control of possession, and they are no longer fully ours. We should never see or experience them as enlargements of the borders of our personal definition.

---

40. Where identifying markings or characteristics make it possible to eventually locate the owner, we cannot always assume his despair, even after long periods of time.

41. According to tradition, he will be the harbinger of *Mashiach*.

42. A paraphrase of *Genesis* 2:23.

The Torah, therefore, sees possessions as legally connected to us only as long as a case can be made for meaningful connection. The Torah recognizes two forms of association: physical possession and psychological attachment. When you lose an object, you lose the utility that comes from your ability to control it. On the other hand, you remain psychologically connected to it. You haven't let go. The proof of this is that you still seek its return (or don't even realize that it has been lost, in which case it is very much included in your inventory of personally significant objects).

As long as one of these two indicia is alive and well, the Torah recognizes legal title. Someone can leave property in his own house, believing it to be lost, in no way hoping for its return. Legally, he retains title, because he never lost physical possession.[43]

The inverse is also true. When we lose physical control, but we remain psychologically bonded because we have not yet given up hope, we remain legal owners.

❧ You Can Take it With You

Strip away both of these aspects of possession, however, and *sechel* cannot allow us to keep title. If we were to do otherwise, we would create the impression that money is far more important than its actual worth. It would imply an essential link between physical objects and our very selves.

We all realize that we do not take our property to the grave. In fact, we do believe that we take a different kind of "possession" with us. The Torah we have studied and the mitzvos we have performed are the more important accomplishments of our days on this earth. Like our material possessions, we have picked them up along the way, and added them to our inventory of personal holdings. These possessions, however, become part of our essential selves, and we do take them beyond the limitations of our physical existence. We cannot treat monetary possessions the same way. We dare not put money and property on the same plane with acquisitions of eternal worth and significance. If we do, we cheapen what really matters in life.

---

43. See *Tosafos* to *Bava Metzia* 26a, s.v., *venezal.*

Someone pays a price for this moral subtlety. By turning this ethic into a working legal statute, the person who gave up hope (but whose identity is well known to the finder) fails to recover his lost object. But is there an alternative? The Torah is a system of truth, and man was created to live by Truth alone, as rooted in genuine *sechel*. The Torah's definition of title to material things is a true one, even if we inconvenience some people. It reflects an enlightened understanding of the difference between our material and spiritual acquisitions.

On the other hand, this same understanding of legal title yields a stringency in halachah relative to secular systems of law. As long as title remains intact through our "true" definition, no other person has the right to make use of that property. Where the owner has likely not despaired of return, no one else may keep or use property that still bears the name of another, even if a hundred years elapse. How likely or unlikely it is that the owner will still arrive to reclaim his object is largely irrelevant to us. We may not make use of the property of another without permission. Let it remain dormant and unused, until the arrival of Eliyahu!

You will still object that this law makes you uneasy. Isn't it proper to return the object in order to spare the hapless owner his unfortunate loss? Isn't this also a Torah ethic? You are right, of course, and halachah[44] strongly encourages us to return identifiable objects even where the owner has despaired of their return. The *Gemara* derives this from the verse, "You shall make known to them the path in which they should go, and the deeds that they should do."[45] We understand the sense of this verse as a charge to go beyond the letter of the law, and to maximize acts of *chesed,* lovingkindness. It remains clear, though, that the law itself cannot demand of us to return property to an "owner" who really isn't. The law must determine the bottom line of property title, even as it urges us to perform acts of *chesed*.

---

44. See *Choshen Mishpat* 259:5,7.
45. *Exodus* 18:20.

VI. The Three Shabbos Meals

Whoever fulfills [the precept of eating] three meals on Shabbos is spared from three misfortunes: from the travail of [the coming of] *Mashiach*, from the judgment of *Gehinnom*, and from the war of *Gog* and *Magog*. [46]

I found this passage as well listed among those to which the critics object. I am not quite sure what their objection might be. Perhaps they find it unseemly that our Sages should encourage people to increase mundane activities, like eating and drinking. Wise, holy people should guide people away from the physical and towards the spiritual, our opponents think. Certainly, they should not elevate baser drives to the level of religious service.

If this is their argument, then these skeptics have missed a prominent feature of Torah thought. Our faith encourages joy and rejoicing on many occasions, such as the holidays. We are told, " You shall rejoice with all the goodness that Hashem, your God, has given you."[47] Isaiah encouraged us to observe Shabbos properly. "Proclaim Shabbos a delight,"[48] he ordered. There are many more examples.

⊷§ Quality, Not Quantity

Their criticism is doubly inappropriate, when you consider the reason behind this encouragement. Shabbos does not just mark the fact of Creation; it celebrates the quality of that Creation. G-d ceased the processes of physical creation on that first Shabbos, because He had created a complete world.

We could imagine G-d designing a wonderful world for us, but withholding some finishing touches. We might not even realize what they were, or what we were missing. We experience this regularly in the

---

46. *Shabbos* 118a.

47. *Deuteronomy* 26:11.

48. *Isaiah* 58:13.

workplace. Even when we are satisfied with our efforts, when we please our employers or clients or customers, we know that if we wanted, we could have done better yet.

Shabbos tells us that Hashem applied a different standard to Creation. G-d did not stop because the world was good, or very good, or good enough. He stopped because there was nothing more that remained to be done. He had created a world of unstinting perfection,[49] of wholeness and harmonious completion. Nothing is missing.

We could conceive of Shabbos without special meals. By refraining from *melachah*, we could acknowledge and thank Hashem for bringing the world into existence, and renewing that existence every day. We travel well beyond this point, though. We prepare lavish Shabbos repasts; we pamper ourselves with unaccustomed delicacies served with our choicest finery — all to make a statement. Hashem doesn't just sustain and maintain us. Our well-set tables eloquently proclaim that we lack nothing at all! We announce ourselves as the beneficiaries of a world that is complete in every manner.

►§ Oneg Shabbos is a Statement

Our *oneg Shabbos* — our Shabbos delight — shows our exuberance over the quality of earthly life. We make all parts of the day redolent with this theme. Wherever we might otherwise find ourselves empty, hungry, or flagging energy, we move swiftly to fill the void with delight.

Shabbos begins with an evening phase. If we allowed it to pass unremarkably, it would leave room for deficiency and incomplete-

---

49. ... relative to the needs of Man. This is not to say that imperfection cannot be found in our world, both from the perspective of our limited comprehension, and from that of Hashem's world, in which anything that is limited and not eternal has no real place. The imperfection of our world is a frequent theme of Maharal. See, for example, his treatment of the "disobedience" of the trees in Creation (*Gur Aryeh, Genesis* 1:11); the existence of physical mechanisms built into Nature that produce earthquakes (see Fourth Well, p. 124) ; the role of circumcision in teaching Man that it is his job, not G-d's, to further improve and perfect the world (*Tiferes Yisrael*, p. 11. See on, note 56).

The point here is that there were no errors of omission during Creation, no holding back of Hashem's beneficence. What we regard as imperfections in this world are precisely engineered for the ultimate good of Man.

ness. Halachah therefore mandates an evening meal during the opening hours of the day.

We direct more of our energies and our focus on the relatively more active phase of Shabbos, the daytime period. A single meal cannot carry a period of this length with a sense of contentment and fulfillment. So we are sure to add an additional meal. This brings the total to three, precisely as described in the passage we are studying.

We return to our critics. Perhaps what perplexes them is the link between the three meals and the calamities of the travail of *Mashiach*, the judgment of *Gehinnom,* and the war of *Gog* and *Magog*. Because they have not grasped the words of our Sages properly, they have much about which to be perplexed.

·≈§ Learning to Notice Perfection

Nothing perplexes the one who comprehends. When we vocally proclaim that Hashem's Creation is perfect, we acquire the tools to detect perfection where we were previously blind. We become newly enabled to relate differently to fixtures of our existence that we might initially regard as quite imperfect and flawed. We come to understand their true roles and functions, and recognize them as tools of perfection.

What we see depends on our perspective. Helped along by Divine prisms, we can see flawless brilliance where we once saw only deficiency. By relating differently, we become impervious to limitation, because we have removed imperfection from our working vocabulary. We know only of perfection, and limitation passes us by without notice.

We can imagine all sorts of calamities. Our passage promises immunity from only three specific ones. To understand why, we must first survey these tragedies and their causes.

Many tragedies are manmade. Some of these we deliberately visit upon ourselves; others we bear responsibility for, because sins introduce imperfection to our world. This imperfection warps the progress of history and natural law, producing all sorts of undesirable consequences. There is no fixed number attached to these unwanted phenomena. These, however, are not the subject of our passage.

◄§ Calamaties of a Different Order

The three that are mentioned are different, because they are not consequences of the failings of man, but were written into G-d's script for Creation.

Initially, *Gehinnom* would appear to violate this rule, earmarked as it is for human sinners. In fact, however, *Gehinnom's* manufacture was not a result of sin, but preceded the rest of Creation![50]

As the place reserved solely for punishment of evil, *Gehinnom* seems to be the antipodal point to perfection. Destruction and darkness are here elevated to dominant themes; it is the ultimate Night. Our first meal — that of the night of Shabbos — is the perfect antidote to *Gehinnom.* We proclaim that the perfection of G-d's Creation extends even to places where our limited grasp can detect no light, no purpose. We begin to understand that a *Gehinnom* is a necessary component of a perfect world. Without it, there would be no final balancing of the books. G-d gives man the free will to chose between good and evil, and does not immediately intervene against the evildoer. *Gehinnom* makes sure that there is a pay-back, that inequities are ultimately righted. Because of *Gehinnom,* freewill does not have to mean freedom to wreak unjust havoc. The evil are dealt with there; fear of retribution, such an important rein on human conduct, is nourished by the horrifying specter of *Gehinnom*. The world, simply put, could not last without it.

By attaching ourselves to G-d's perfection (as we do at a meal proclaiming the perfection of His Creation), we become a bit more perfect ourselves. *Gehinnom,* the destiny of the imperfect, becomes irrelevant to us, and loses its hold. Thus we are saved from its judgment.

Darkness can obscure the perfection of the world from the untrained eye. Light, at times, presents its own mysteries. The prophet Zechariah says, "It will be a unique day; it will be known as Hashem's [day], neither day nor night, but it will happen towards evening time that there will be light."[51]

---

50. See *Nedarim* 39b, which counts *Gehinnom* among the seven items that Hashem created before the rest of the world. See *Gevuros Hashem* by Maharal, Ch. 70, for an explanation.

51. *Zechariah* 14:7.

✧§ Evil's Last Stand

Zechariah associates an unexpected late afternoon light with the terrifying and tumultuous events associated with the setting of the sun on the old world order. Before the world can receive *Mashiach* and his radical agenda, many of mankind's entrenched ideas must disappear, to make room for the new ones that must replace them. But old ideas die hard. It may take a period of complete societal upheaval to shake the world of institutions that survived for millennia. Revolutions have a nasty habit of discarding the good along with the bad. The period before the arrival of *Mashiach* — the time known as "the travail of *Mashiach*" — performs general housecleaning on the collected ideological debris of human history. The chaos that it brings, however, makes it a difficult time to live through.

It signifies the actual arrival of *Mashiach,* or the dawning of a new day for the Jewish people. Fierce resistance meets it, in the form of the uprising of *Gog* and *Magog*. [52] It is as if parts of the world cannot begrudge it its move towards completion and perfection, and feel threatened enough to make a last, desperate stand against it.

We link a meal of celebration to the morning period. We do not allow the anticipation of *Gog* and *Magog* to dampen our enthusiasm. With the third meal we complete our visit of personal and historical cataclysms. It is our tribute to the perfection of the world even as the sun sets on history. We do not flinch, even as we behold in our mind's eye the confusion and disorder that erupts violently in the decline of the world order. Within apparent tragedy, we find a Divine Plan that leads to the redemption of the entire world. We discern the distant goal, and realize that unpleasant events must sometimes occur to bring a greater good. Once again, deeper understanding triumphs over any sense of imperfection or fault.

Our three meals, in a sense, are a grand tour of important epochs in history. We examine them in the course of a Shabbos, and find all of them — periods of early and late light, and of full darkness — consistent with our celebration of the perfection of Creation. We find the

---

52. Described in the contiguous verses in *Zechariah,* and in *Ezekiel* 38:18 — 39:15.

world complete, not only in its initial outfitting, but even in the rules that G-d employed to guide the march of history to its inevitable and elevated end.

VII. Scientific Knowledge: Unlocking the Secrets of Creation

R' Yose says, "Two things entered the thoughts [of G-d] to be created on *erev* Shabbos, but were not created until the departure of Shabbos. At the departure of Shabbos, He placed in Adam understanding reflective of the Divine model. And [as a result] Adam brought two stones and ground them together, and flame shot out from them. He brought two animals [a horse and a donkey] and crossbred them, and a mule issued from them."[53]

I am not sure why they object to this passage. Perhaps they take exception to the idea that G-d first thought of creating something, and then apparently reversed Himself, at least until a later point in time. We may not attribute such indecision to G-d, as we find written, "For He is not a person . . . that He should change His Mind."[54]

Alternatively, perhaps they are disturbed by the discussion of the invention of crossbreeding. They see this practice as unseemly and repugnant,[55] akin to forbidden sexual practices. Why should *Chazal* endorse it so warmly?

The real message of this passage eluded our critics. *Chazal* here compare Nature to the activities of Man — and find the latter superior![56]

---

53. *Pesachim* 54a.

54. *Numbers* 23:19.

55. *Leviticus* 19:19 prohibits us to crossbreed animals. See *Yoreh Deah* 297. One opinion forbids this practice even to non-Jews. See *Sanhedrin* 56b; *Rambam, Melachim* 10:6. However, see *Shach, Yoreh Deah,* 297:3, who disputes this ruling.

56. In *Tiferes Yisrael,* Ch. 2, Maharal enlarges on this theme. He sees the mitzvah of circumcision as a mandate to Man to improve and elevate the world, and understand

❧ A Composite World

The world that we touch, examine, and manipulate is a composite one. All things that we encounter are fragile, in the sense that they can be split into yet smaller pieces. With the proper instruments, we can continue to divide and subdivide. We can analyze and tear apart things chemically as well, reducing them to their essential building blocks. Like nested dolls, though, the process continues. There are always ways of splitting these simpler substances as well. In theory, if we continue the process we should ultimately discover the most basic, indivisible strings of our universe, from which all else is intricately and wonderfully woven together, in a dizzying variety of shapes and forms.

In the days of Creation, Hashem formed the primary materials of this world. He also nudged many combinations of these materials into existence, creating a rich assortment of composites. When He finished, the potential remained that substances would continue to combine, just as they had during the creative period.

On the macro level, animal reproduction is one example. The combination of male and female gametes spawns the production of new offspring. Here is a kind of "creation" that was really set in motion by G-d's original Creation. This is all natural to us.

There is, however, another kind of combination that was made possible by the work of Creation, albeit a good deal less natural. Some combinations may not occur on their own, but are still imaginable and effective. They are not *necessary* continuations of the processes of Creation, but *possible* ones. They were not made to be firm fixtures of the six days of Creation, but their potential was spring-loaded, ready to explode with force. This is what our Sages mean when they speak

---

that he must finish the task that Nature only began. For this reason, *milah* is performed on the eighth day. The number six, corresponding to the six days of Creation, aptly symbolizes physical creation. Seven adds the spiritual powers that were invested in Creation, and to which we are drawn each Shabbos. Eight must signify an improvement upon what precedes it! Man is instructed to create more *kedushah,* more holiness, than that which is hard-wired into existence. He cannot content himself with responding to the spiritual potential that is already there, but must generate new and fresh *kedushah.* In doing so, he leaves behind a better world than the one Nature provided him at birth.

of G-d *thinking* to create and then not following through. These objects were not quite part of the fabric of Creation, nor were they strangers to it. His thought created their potential; it remained for Man to actualize the potential, and put the pieces together.

The gift of human intelligence would carry Man in a different direction as well. Besides creating new complexes from the raw stuff of this world, he would also do the opposite. He would explore, probe, and rip apart the natural complexes he observed. By doing so, he would liberate simpler and more basic substances that do not ordinarily exist in the free state.

A good example of this is the discovery of fire. In our direct experience, fire is not a "substance."[57] Its heat and light, potent that they may be, are ethereal intangibles. They hail from the hidden underworld of physical law. Man took a quantum leap forward when he took the coarse graininess of two common stones and transformed it into sublime luminosity!

⊸§ The Light of *Havdalah*

It was a step so significant that we mark it each week in our *Havdalah*. Interestingly, we do not use the moment to praise Hashem for any of the other myriad blessings that He bestowed upon the world we reenter. We choose the gift of illumination, because it makes a powerful point about the overall quality of creation. By granting us a new dimension of light through artificial illumination, G-d shows us that He crowned our lives with more than necessities. Light is more refined, less "physical" than the other props on the stage of life. Through it, He

---

57. I have tried here to transpose Maharal's argument to a more modern idiom. In the original, the reasoning is more straightforward. Maharal accepted the classical system of four essences that form the basis of all physical existence. In a sense, these four essences were seen as the indivisible "atoms" of which all else was formed. (The word "atom" is not a modern term. It was used by the ancient Greeks.) This view remained in vogue in the times of the *Rishonim* and beyond. My point is that even if the reader finds that this reasoning and vocabulary clash with contemporary scientific understanding, the thought expressed here by *Chazal* and Maharal remains as cogent as ever. As Maharal himself stresses often, *Chazal* employ the science and imagery available to their audience as a communications tool. The kernel idea they wish to express is far more important than the vehicle they use to convey it, and it may change from generation to generation.

added stature and prominence to our lives. We recognize a level of extraordinary completeness of our world, of elevation beyond the purely natural. The light of *Havdalah* elevates it to a higher level, by increasing our consciousness of what we owe G-d.

Having arrived at this point, artificial light is crucial in one other regard. If it takes Man to complete the development of the potential of this world, it requires a complete man to do so. Vision is arguably an important tool in applying human talent and ingenuity. As important as it is, vision is frustrated each day by the "natural" onset of darkness. Providing Man with the wherewithal to extend his vision completes Man in the same way that he completes the world. It actualizes a potential that would otherwise have to remain dormant for much of the time. Standing in the warm afterglow of Shabbos, the day of completion, we are better attuned to the true character of human completion. We do not marvel at how all the pieces of our existence fit together, as much as how we can make better use of the richness within.

Ultimately, all of this is a commentary on the stature of Man himself. Man's intelligence does not really fit with the rest of his earthly surroundings, but transcends its raw limitations. Indeed, Man does not properly function as fully human until he actualizes this gift of transcendence.[58] Man, thus, represents potential — potential that is fulfilled only when he uses the Divinely given gifts of comprehension and

---

58. Maharal parenthetically adds that there is no reason to be uneasy with the example *Chazal* used here: the hybridizing of the mule. While it is true that the Torah forbids this kind of activity to us, that does not preclude its importance in the natural world. There are many animals, for instance, that are prohibited to us. Does this mean that they have no role to play in the natural order of things?

Torah, he continues, has its desiderata that can conflict with what seems good for the natural world. The mule truly belongs in that world — but we are forbidden to be the agents who create it. *Adam HaRishon,* living before the giving of the Torah, did not live under this halachic constraint. For him, the launching of a new kind of animal was laudatory.

The critics erred in assuming that crossbreeding animals was intrinsically unseemly, that it contains some distant relative of sexual impropriety. This is simply not so, says Maharal. The Torah even forbids plowing with different species at the same time, although this practice clearly is not related to any impermissible sexual act. Rather, the Torah objects to the joining of many things that were created separate and distinct. "The way of the Torah is on the one hand, the completion of the world on the other."

understanding. By applying these gifts, Man similarly enhances the rest of his world. He actualizes potential that G-d built into the universe, but left for Man to develop. He can do this synthetically, by building up, or analytically, by probing for simpler components. They are two sides of a single coin. The mule and the fire turn out to be a matched set.

Maharal gives no clue as to why the Torah should have different requirements than the fleshing out of the order of Creation. We can only speculate. One possibility comes from R' Shamshon Raphael Hirsch, who expands upon what he calls the "great law" of "after their kind" (*Genesis* 1:25):

"You must, by respecting the boundaries of that [natural] order, guard yourself against allowing the free use and transformation of this world, which He has granted to you, to degenerate into a G-d-forgotten, world-destructive presumption" (Horeb, p. 283)

While Mankind as a whole may have a mandate to develop the hidden potential of the world, the Jewish people must sensitize that world to the ethic that change and transformation can run away with themselves. We must find ways to responsibly limit the damage we can do by promoting change for its own sake. We must be conscious of what happens when we destroy boundaries.

Another possibility is that the Torah wishes to underscore that the completion and development of the world, while admirable, is not the end-all of human experience. See *Pachad Yitzchak,* Chanukah, section 9, which beautifully demonstrates that the above distinction may separate the Jewish and non-Jewish spheres of influence. Non-Jews are expected to understand the world around them, and find ways to preserve and improve it. Jews are expected by the Torah to build a *different* world, through the strength of the spirituality that they can produce.

VIII. Well-placed and Misplaced Love

> He who loves his neighbors, and draws his relatives close, and who marries his sister's daughter, and who lends money to a poor person in the time of his need — regarding him the *pasuk*[59] says, "Then you will call, and Hashem will respond; you will cry out, and He will say 'Here I am.' "[60]

This passage as well appears among their complaints. They cannot fathom that *Chazal* would urge people to marry their relatives, finding this near-incestuous.

They overlook the obvious, of course. Amram married his Aunt Yocheved. The illustrious children of this marriage were Moses, Aaron, and Miriam. An inappropriate union would not have been so extraordinarily blessed by Hashem.

Prohibitions of incest and consanguinity apply only where the Torah specifies — and nowhere else. They are akin to *chukim* — other statutes of the Torah whose reasoning we do not readily understand.[61] We do not and cannot detect some compelling principle of forbidden unions which would move us to forbid all relatives simply because of their familial ties.

We are much more confident of a different Torah principle, however. The Torah places much stress upon an ethical consideration governing our general relationships with others. We are instructed to strengthen our connection to those with whom we are already attached or affiliated. Wherever the Torah does not ban a relationship with a relative, the Torah deliberately encourages it!

As usual, the critics missed the entire point of the passage. *Chazal* urge us here to strengthen bonds that already exist between people.

---

59. *Isaiah* 58:9

60. *Yevamos* 62b.

61. Maharal's assumption here is similar to that of *Ramban, Leviticus* 18:6, who also cannot easily detect a compelling reason to ban marriage with blood relatives, and accepts the prohibition as a Divine mandate whose reason must remain obscure.

The passage discusses four situations; each is an example of this principle. Three of them are fairly obvious.

You are "close" to your neighbors, because geography joins you. The Torah encourages us to build on this connection. (As *Proverbs* puts it, "A close neighbor is better than a distant brother."[62])

Relatives, on the other hand, do not need any prodding to feel a kinship, since they are each other's flesh and blood.

On a deeper level, we are also connected to our people. This is the relationship that the passage urges us to enhance when it asks us to lend money to those in need. It alludes to the verse, "When you lend money to *My people*, to the poor person who is with you . . ."[63] The Torah stresses the bond of peoplehood as the reason to lend to him.

~§ Reach Out And Touch Someone

This leaves us one final illustration to explain — the encouragement to marry a niece. If you look carefully, you will see that the passage orders its examples carefully, deliberately and hierarchically. Starting with neighbors, the passage urges us to "love" them. It speaks of nothing more than an internal orientation. We are urged to develop a loving, caring attitude to those close at hand. We move to a more active role regarding our relatives, as we are told to "draw them close." Bringing them closer demands performance, involving ourselves with their daily concerns in order to assist them. We progress far beyond the attitudes and smiles we offer our neighbors.

The reaching out deepens in the next stage. The ultimate connection with a relative is marriage. Husband and wife become, in the words of *Genesis*, "one flesh."[64] A man's wife is like his own self; they join to become a single person. Marrying a niece would seem to be the most far-reaching way of bringing a relative into one's life. The third example, we would think, should be the final one.

Not quite. *Chazal* saw room for a fuller and richer form of extending oneself towards another. Marriage, after all, offers ample rewards to those who invest in it. Lending money to someone down and out

---

62. *Proverbs* 27:10.

63. *Exodus* 22:24.

64. *Genesis* 2:24.

yields no gain, and runs the risk of ending in disaster. It is possible, if not probable at times, that the debtor will not be able to repay the loan. To reach out to someone under these conditions is the most perfect form of connection. You cannot really give selflessly without making the recipient part of yourself. Doing so without indulging or enhancing your own ego is the most elevated way to do this.

The reward promised in this passage is a guarantee that Hashem will answer when called upon. A *pasuk* in *Deuteronomy* illuminates the link between the verse in Isaiah and the behavior we are asked to embrace. "For which is a great nation that has a G-d Who is close to it, as is Hashem, our G-d, whenever we call to Him?"[65] The Torah equates successful petitioning of Hashem with a sense of *closeness*[66] to Him. Because we are near to Him, because we are called His children, Hashem brings Himself close to us in listening to and answering our prayers and requests. In other words, when Hashem responds to our prayers, He shows that He values His connection *with us,* and acts to sustain and fulfill it. When we imitate this characteristic of Hashem, we can expect to see more of it applied to ourselves.

---

65. *Deuteronomy* 4:7.

66. The word *karov,* which means close, is also the root for the word "relative."

THE THIRD WELL

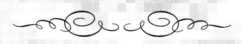

Words'

Deeper

Meaning

The challenge:

Many of the *derashos* of *Chazal* seem farfetched. Some of them seem actually erroneous, based on faulty grasp of Hebrew grammar and language.

This could be catastrophic to our belief. So much of the Oral Law is built upon the Sages' explanations to verses of the Torah.

The response:

If you probe beyond the exterior of those "implausible" explanations, you will discover the deeper, core meaning of the texts they address.

Chazal's mission was to ferret out the essential teaching of every Torah passage. They wrote, however, in a way that makes it easy to miss their point — unless the student will apply himself diligently to plumb the depths of their instruction. All their comments, down to the smallest details, require explication and wise consideration.

We will choose the passages that people regard as the most difficult and extreme. Through them, we will demonstrate our point. Rather than clever word games, the comments of *Chazal* offer the richest approach to the words of the Torah.

I. Ears, Fingertips, and Self-censorship

Bar Kappara expounded, "What is meant by 'A peg should be among *azeinecha*'?[1] Do not read this as *azeinecha* — your weapons — but rather as *aznecha* — your ears. If one should hear something inappropriate, he should place his finger in his ear." This is similar to what R' Elazar said: "Why are man's fingers tapered like staves? . . . So that if one hears something inappropriate, he should place his finger in his ear." A member of R' Yishmael's academy taught, "Why is the entire ear hard, except for the lobe? If a person hears something inappropriate, he should bend the lobe inside it."[2]

Many are troubled by this passage, which takes up a position so remote from the plain meaning of the text. If this is what the Torah meant, how are we supposed to make sense of the verses that follow?[3] It is not any more palatable to suppose that *Chazal* condone looking at a verse in isolation, while ignoring its context.

The greatest difficulty, of course, is their far-fetched approach to the shape of fingers and the constitution of the outer ear. These are words which do not enter the ear of the listener!

Look further, however, and you will discover the wisdom of *Chazal.* A peg or stave is meant to be driven into a hole. With it, you fill some space or void. Now, if the Torah were interested only in telling us that soldiers should carry one of these pegs to use as a makeshift trowel, it should have stated its case more simply. "You

---

1. *Deuteronomy* 23:14.

2. *Kesubos* 8a.

3. The plain meaning of the text is that a soldier must carry with him an implement with which he can loosen soil to cover up after relieving himself. In the verses that follow, the Torah refers directly to the covering of wastes, which has nothing to do with refusing to listen to inappropriate speech.

should carry a peg with you ..." Why add "... *al azeinecha*"? The Torah alludes to a connection between the function of the stave, and the ear.

⪧ Banishing the Unseemly

There can be no question that *azeinecha* in its context means "weapons,"[4] and not "ears." But it is part of the Torah's style to chose words that associate with similar sounding words.[5] Consider what the Torah conveys here on the literal level, and you will better appreciate the allusion. The soldier in Hashem's army is commanded to maintain his elevated sense of human dignity, even under trying field conditions. He is ordered to dig a hole before relieving himself, rather than do what is most convenient. He is then told to take the same implement he used to scratch out this field latrine, and discreetly cover his tracks. Even under the pressures of military engagement, the soldier cannot dare to forget that some kinds of human behavior should be emphasized while others must be downplayed and even hidden. We must cover up what is unseemly.

⪧ The Greater Battlefield

Couple this theme with the fact that the word *azeinecha* (which, as demonstrated above, could have been deleted altogether without altering the meaning of the text) naturally alludes to the word for ear. What emerges is at least a strong hint that there is a constant battle against the offensive and unrefined, not only in times of war. We must be prepared to banish from the "front lines" what does not belong, whether we find ourselves on the battlefield or off. We must never allow the external world to overwhelm our inner refinement, whether by the primitivizing effects of the armed camp, or the ca-

---

4. Or belt. See *HaKesav Ve-HaKabbalah* to *Deuteronomy* 23:14.

5. See the introduction of *Netziv* to his *Ha'amek Davar*, section 3. The Torah describes itself as "*shirah,*" or poetry. In contradistinction to prose, poetry is an evocative language, not just a descriptive medium. Thoughts are framed so that words unleash a torrent of links and associations. Poetry cannot be read once, simply and quickly, but must be explored for its layers of meaning.

cophony of sounds that enter our ears uninvited. We are able to seal up the channels to our profound selves. We can, and therefore must, fully control these portals, stopping them up when need be. The literal sense of the Torah passage may refer to weapons, but the idea that it advances clearly applies (as the key word also alludes) to our instruments of hearing as well.

One could argue that blocking out what we should not hear is so important that the human body itself ought to provide some assistance. Indeed, this is R' Elazar's point. While some apparently have difficulty with his contention that man's fingers are tapered in order to stop up the ear, they miss an essential point about the creation of Man.

◄§ Physical Man and "the Image of G-d"

Man was formed in "the image of G-d."[6] To deserve this description, even the physical form of Man must reflect the perfection of Hashem, and must show no obvious flaw. Now many openings and orifices communicate between the body and the external world. They do the most good when they operate in both open and closed positions, allowing us to take in what we need and exclude what we don't. Virtually all the openings that come to mind have gateways and closures. Eyelids and lips are good examples.

The ear, however, is an obvious counter-example. It lacks any structure to shut out what does not belong. This would seem to be an obvious deficiency. It is a gap, though, that can be plugged up by Man's fingertips. They can neatly and effectively shield our hearing apparatus from what we do not need to hear.

◄§ Why the Ear is Different

Other bodily orifices and sensory input channels come equipped with structures that are structurally related to the organs they protect. They therefore seem more suited to their apparent function than do fingers as makeshift ear-stoppers.

---

6. *Genesis* 1:27.

There is good reason for this. Scientific authorities will offer you cogent reasons for why the ear lacks a structure similar to the eye's lid, but do not listen to them. They can only deal with arguments of cause and effect, and have no grasp of the inner wisdom of Creation. The underlying reason for the anomalous architecture of the outer ear relates to its special character. Only the ear functions unceasingly as a gatherer of information. It is available to receive new data at all times.[7] As much as we want and need a way to stop the ear at certain times from performing its task, Hashem did not design it with its own closure. That would be inconsistent with its clear and apparent function: to always remain open and ready!

Constricting the flow of information is incompatible with its function. On the other hand, allowing no built-in control at all is at variance with our fuller needs as spiritual beings. Hashem created the perfect compromise. He provided the seals, without cutting back on the flow. A pot is a good analogy. We want the largest opening in order to place and remove things. Oftentimes, though, we need to close it up. The pot, therefore, is made with a wide opening. We fit it with a cover, which stands apart from the pot itself, but can be snugly moved into place when the need arises. Such a role is suggested by the shape of the fingertips. They are not connected to the ear, but were shaped by Hashem so that we should use them to shut out what doesn't belong.

⧉ Equipment That Isn't Optional

This does not sit well with R' Yishmael. It simply cannot be, he argues, that Hashem would not have cast the ear's mold without a device to lessen the roar. Besides, he reasons, Hashem would just not utilize the fingertips for this purpose. Placing them in the ears soils them, and G-d would never rely on something this indelicate. Rather, it is the earlobe that fills the gap. It covers the ear's opening quite nicely, but refuses to stay in position without some assistance. So the ear never really *remains* closed on its own, but comes equipped with an

---

7. Perhaps Maharal means that all other sensory modalities have on-off periods. They are never used constantly. Most have mechanisms for focusing and tuning in. One modality stands ready to alert Man of any important changes in the surrounding world, even as he sleeps. Around the clock, the ears act as information-collectors, effectively allowing the other parts of man to refresh and renew themselves.

attachment that can be pressed into its service. The fingers are still needed, much as many doors will not stay shut without some bar holding them in place. (The door analogy is a well-established one. Precisely because the door and the ear are so similar, the Torah mandates that a servant who wishes to stay with his master beyond his required term must have his ear pierced through[8] — on a doorpost!)

❧ Two Kinds of Perfection

Thus, what the unlearned critics take to be a silly and trite play on words is actually quite the opposite. *Chazal's* probing eye detected an element of perfection in Man — physical Man — that evaded the grasp of others. They teach us here that Hashem combined different dimensions of performance, each perfect in its own way. The figure of Man announces two messages simultaneously and harmoniously. On the one hand, it speaks of efficient function. It houses organs, parts, and systems perfectly appointed to their assigned tasks. On the other, aspects of its design suggests a higher, moral plane, beyond mere "functionality." These suggest that Man needs to rein in his physical capabilities from time to time, in order for him to arrive at a much higher place.

---

8. *Exodus* 21:6.

II. Yisrael the Unforgettable

"But Tzion said, 'Hashem has forsaken me, and Hashem has forgotten me.' "[9] . . . Reish Lakish said, "*Knesses Yisrael*[10] said before *HaKadosh Baruch Hu*, 'When a man takes a second wife after a first, he still remembers his first wife's deeds. But You have both forsaken me, and forgotten me [as well]!'

"*HaKadosh Baruch Hu* answered her, 'My daughter — I created 12 constellations. For each I created 30 hosts; for each host 30 legions . . . . and I created all of them only for your sake. And you say, "You have forsaken and forgotten me"! Can a woman forget *ula* — her young child; [can she fail to] *merachem* — have compassion for — the product of her womb. . .?' " *HaKadosh Baruch Hu* said to her, 'Could I forget *olah* — the burnt offerings — and the *pitrei rechem* — the firstborn offerings — that you offered Me in the wilderness?'

"*Knesses Yisrael* said before Him, 'Master of the Universe! Since there is no forgetting before the Throne of Your honor, perhaps You will also not forget the incident of the Golden Calf?'

"He said to her, '. . . Even these may forget . . .'[11]

"She said before Him, 'Master of the Universe! Since there is forgetting before the Throne of Your honor, perhaps You will forget my activities at Sinai?'

"He said to her, '. . . But I will not forget you.' "[12],[13]

---

9. *Isaiah* 49:14.

10. Literally, the Congregation of Israel, a collective figure encompassing the souls of the entire Jewish people.

11. *Isaiah* 49:15.

12. Ibid. v.16.

13. *Berachos* 32b.

At first, this *derashah* seems exceedingly remote. It is built on the substitution of *olah* for *ula,* and of *rachem* for *rechem.* What sense is there in ignoring the plain meaning of these lines, surgically removing some words and replacing them with others, which just happen to sound similar?

As I said earlier, the *derashos* of *Chazal* respond to textual clues, to problems with the way the plain meaning is expressed. The two lines in *Isaiah* upon which our passage is based are replete with textual oddities. One phrase begins by rhetorically questioning whether a mother (singular) can ever forget the baby she bore. The phrase that follows moves to the plural, when it states, "Even these [women, plural] may forget, but I will not forget you." (Although *Radak* observes that the plain meaning of "these" refers to all women in such a position, this does fully answer the difficulty. Why should the text shift abruptly from singular to plural?) The sense of the line as a whole is that even if a mother could do something as improbable as dismissing her child from memory, it is entirely impossible that Hashem will abandon His people. Then why not simply state this as a declarative sentence? Why first ask a rhetorical question (i.e. can a mother really forget her young?), whose answer should be a resounding "No!," only to follow it with a bit of hedging. "Well, not really, but even if you could imagine something of this nature, Hashem is never going to do it to us!"

Finally, a few of the phrases are too verbose. Forgetting and abandoning could have been telescoped into one phrase: "But Tzion said, 'Hashem has *forsaken and forgotten* me.' " The analogy to the mother could have been sculpted more economically, by simply asking whether she could abandon her young. The phrase that follows (i.e. can she fail to have compassion for the opening of her womb?) seems to be gratuitously repetitious.

Through all this obscurity, *Chazal* saw more in these lines than a plaintive cry of the Jewish people. They are saying much more than, "How could You have left us?" G-d's response, in turn, goes far beyond a vigorous denial, "No, I really haven't." These modest two lines encapsulate a sophisticated round of claim and counterclaim, tugging at the sleeve of Hashem, and imploring Him to justify His remoteness from us in exile.

We do not just cry out against what looks like being forsaken and forgotten. There are two distinct stages to our claim, and this is why each deserves its own phrase. First, we observe that for Hashem to forget us seems not only painful to us, but simply unnatural. In our world, we consistently observe a special relationship with anything that first fills a void. A first wife can die, and another woman can take her place. The first will never be forgotten, erased entirely from consciousness. The first successful attempt by a man to forge a full sharing relationship with another person can never be purged from memory. The freshness, the originality, the full energy, unreserved commitment, and zealous motivation that accompany a first marriage create a bond and connection that is not duplicated later on.

Whatever we may have done to disappoint G-d later, we were the first people to pledge ourselves to Him fully and without reservation. Whatever the aftermath, it is hard for us to comprehend that a bond so close and so meaningful could dissipate and vanish, as if it had never been there.

There are two distinct parts to our argument; hence the *pasuk* dedicates two phrases to our opening of the dialogue. First, we question whether a husband can ever forget his first wife. We cannot comprehend how Hashem could make our relationship vanish without a trace. There is nothing in our experience that allows us to grasp this! The nearest analogy we have to our relationship with G-d is the closeness to a first wife. We cannot imagine a husband forgetting a first spouse; we therefore cannot *imagine* being forgotten! We then continue. But the unimaginable has indeed occurred! And it was Hashem Himself who visited this rejection upon us! How could this be?

⋙ Forgetting the Nonexistent

The answer comes in no uncertain terms. Forgetting us indeed is impossible. We can only forget[14] what ceases to exist, either in reality or in its psychological impact upon us. When the hold that something has over us gradually wanes, when its importance to us

---

14. As in so many other areas, the language we use concerning Hashem is limited to our own grasp and experience. G-d, of course, quite literally *cannot* forget anything! His knowledge is part and parcel of the reality of His very Existence. (Nor, for that matter, does He actually "remember" in the sense that we do.)

When we use any human language in reference to Hashem, we recognize the

recedes from the horizon of our scrutiny, then it can be forgotten. Another way of looking at this is that the more peripheral, or nonessential, to us something becomes, the easier it is for the bonds of memory to slip loose.

It follows that only bits and pieces can ever be forgotten, but not something which is *everything*. Different elements, details can cease to exist, and can lose their importance, relative to what remains. Therefore, they can be forgotten. Something that is so basic that if you remove it, everything else crashes into nonexistence — that cannot be "forgotten," because its value can never be diminished.

Klal Yisrael occupies just such a role. We are not just another option, a different possibility, another candidate for the job of G-d's people. We are everything. We are the *raison d'etre* of the universe, the *sine qua non,* the quintessential, keystone component of existence. When *Chazal* paraphrase the words Hashem used in the verse, they point to the vast, limitless reaches of the universe. The Torah's position that He created all for the good of Man, provides us with a powerful measure of our importance.

⊷§ Wives and Children

We likened ourselves to a first wife, and marveled that she could be forgotten. Hashem responds with an analogy to a mother forgetting her young child. The difference is not stylistic. Nor does it mean that we love our children more deeply than our spouses, and therefore we can be assured that we have not been abandoned by G-d. The point is simply that we are Hashem's *children.* We argued that we are *special;* Hashem responds that we are *essential.*

Children issue from their parents. Parents do not choose them, or

---

inherent imprecision of using notions common to the human sphere and thrusting them upon a place they do not belong.

Yet, the Torah clearly encourages us in many places to relate to G-d through human experience and language. We understand that we are not speaking of the essence or inner reality of G-d, which we cannot begin to grasp. Instead, we speak of the very real way in which G-d's actions relate to us. If a passage in *Isaiah* complains that G-d has "forgotten" or "forsaken" us, defining the term — in decidedly human usage — is crucial. It will help us understand not only the complaint, but Hashem's response as well.

voluntarily associate with them. They produce them. The relationship between them is essential and organic.

Precisely in this manner are we the children of G-d. In contradistinction to all other things, Hashem created us directly. All other things are adjuncts to creation, coming into existence to meet the needs of something else. We are thus connected to Hashem in a more fundamental and essential relationship than anything else in the universe.

This is what the Torah means when it states, "You are children to Hashem,"[15] and, "Yisrael is My firstborn son."[16] (The latter verse goes beyond the former, since one can have more than one child. It establishes *Klal Yisrael* as unique and unparalleled.) This last *pasuk* introduces a demand to Pharaoh that he "send out My son so that he should serve Me."[17] As the context shows, Hashem asks specifically for service through *korbanos* — offerings. The notions of "son" and "service" are not arbitrarily linked. The purpose of all *korbanos*[18] is to bring us closer to G-d, to bring ourselves as near as humanly possibly to Him. Precisely because we are *children* of Hashem, because we are already close by our nature, the institution of *korbanos* can help us traverse the final mile of our journey towards Him.

◆§ Yisrael the Unforgettable

The related images of "son" and "firstborn" are preserved in our passage. "Could I forget *olah* — the burnt offerings — and the *pitrei rechem* — the firstborn offerings?" More than any other offering, the *olah* is a potent symbol of maximum proximity to G-d. The *olah* is offered up in its entirety on the altar. Nothing is held back. It expresses the strivings of those who already understand strong affiliation to Hashem, and yearn to remove any remaining barriers or distance.

The passage underscores the offerings of "the wilderness," rather

---

15. *Deuteronomy* 14:1.

16. *Exodus* 4:22.

17. Ibid. v. 23.

18. The word *korban* is often unfortunately translated as "sacrifice." This usually masks and perverts the significance of the concept, since it naturally invites inaccurate comparison with the practices of other religions. *Korban* is actually derived from the Hebrew root that means "close."

than the sum of all Jewish service over time. So often, the defining elements of anything are present from the very beginning. All that occurs later is a sprouting of the initial kernel of potential. It was in the wilderness that the Jewish people first strove to build bridges to Heaven through their offerings. This first chapter in our service to Hashem exposed the basic, initial conditions of our approach to G-d. Our first service, the wilderness offerings, manifested an essential truth about ourselves. *Essential* truths, as we showed before, cannot be forgotten or dismissed.

Next, Hashem points to *pitrei rechem* — the firstborn offerings. These grow out of the special responsibility to consecrate every "first" in our lives. It is our way of reciprocating Hashem's choosing us as His firstborn, and His intervention against the firstborn Egyptians. Together, the two images spell out our relationship with Hashem: an organic togetherness so fundamental that we cannot be forgotten.

We are aware that the term "forget" cannot be properly applied to G-d, Who cannot literally forget anything. Like so many other terms, we simply mean to describe a set of behaviors with a handy verb from our own experience. In relation to G-d, "forgetting" means acting as if the forgotten object was no longer close and attached. It means removing from His immediate Presence, ridding and rejecting.

No sooner do we contemplate this than a dark cloud obscures the bright image of the preceding paragraphs. Does our penchant for drawing close to Hashem, as shown by our early offerings, really show that we are inseparable from Him? Could we have built the Golden Calf if we were as essentially bonded to Him as we would like to believe? As surely as we drew close, we quickly proved that our foundation of closeness was more jelly-like than granite-tough! If we could so easily abandon G-d, then it is not impossible that He should "abandon" us. Our connection could not have been one of defining essence, if we were able to break it so quickly.

"Even these may forget" is Hashem's terse response. The Hebrew *eleh* — these — is pregnant with allusion. The Gemara[19] relates the word to "harshness" and "strength," seeing it as sharing a common

_____

19. *Yevamos* 21a remarks that the punishment for transgressing the laws of forbidden relations is especially severe, since the Torah includes a verse of warning: "Whoever does *eleh* — these — is abominable to Hashem" (*Deuteronomy* 22:5).

ancestry with "and he took *elei ha'aretz* — the *powerful* of the land.[20]

Hashem, as it were, concedes the point. The model of first wife proves to be incomplete. So does the model of child. Children are difficult to abandon, because they are outgrowths and extensions of ourselves. But parent and child are two different people. Their identities do not coincide; they are not clones of each other. Wedges can be driven between any two individuals, even parent and child. Complete psychological disengagement is unlikely, but not out of the question.

The parent/child model thus offers us only an approximation of the truth. It is still not quite a statement of definition of our essence.

Some things are just so, shaped by their definition. All other things are the products of possibilities that could take many forms, like a child's building toy.

Klal Yisrael showed their fundamental attraction to the service of Hashem when they served Him in the wilderness, but they could have chosen not to. No overarching natural law predetermined the outcome of their choice. Since the making of the relationship was only on the order of the possible, the breaking of it is also possible!

The same reasoning, though, allows Hashem to downplay the importance of the Golden Calf. *Klal Yisrael* was not compelled to build it by some irresistible inner quality and force. They *could* have chosen not to build it. They did build it, and it was a great failing. It does not reveal a final severing of a relationship with Hashem, because it, too, was not an *essential* leave-taking. It, too, can be forgotten.

Are we stalemated, hanging in limbo, conscious of our spotty performance showing us to be neither essentially close to nor removed from Hashem? Not unexpectedly, G-d has the final argument, the winning combination. Responding to our query about forgetting our standing before Him at Sinai, Hashem thunders back, "I will not forget you!" It is not up to you! I will be your G-d, declares Hashem, regardless of your choices and possibilities. "With a mighty hand, and an outstretched arm, and with poured-out anger I will be King over you!"[21] What is true of Me knows of no change or fickleness. I am only

---

20. *Ezekiel* 17:13.
21. *Ibid.* 20:33.

Essence. Once again, the bond between *Klal Yisrael* is restored in full glory — not through our actions, but by an act of G-d.

◄§ The Mountain Over our Heads

HaKadosh Baruch Hu made sure that we understood this from the beginning of our relationship. As we stood at Sinai, Hashem held the mountain over our heads,[22] forcing us in essence to accept the Torah on pain of death. Hashem wanted us to realize that the relationship between us is an essential one, in the sense that the association between us grows out of the very essence of what we are.

Although we seemed to be given the choice of accepting or rejecting the Torah (and in fact rose to our finest moment with our *naaseh v'nishmah,* pledging to accept first and attempt to understand later), it was important for us to realize that there really was no choice.[23] There could be no world without Torah, and there could be no Torah without a *Klal Yisrael.*

Furthermore, *HaKadosh Baruch Hu* left no loose ends in Creation. Every creature possesses some outstanding feature or quality. This feature is always available to it as part of its basic design. It is not something that is acquired externally, or casually picked up in the creature's life cycle when it is in the mood. The seeming exception is Man, whose salient characteristic is his rational faculty. For Man to be a rational creature by nature rather than by choice, he must be subjected to the rule of Reason — by nature, and not by choice! Torah provides this rule of *sechel.* To take its place among all the other rules of nature, however, it cannot hinge on a vote, or a mood or a whim. It must be written into the fundamental rules of reality. Thus, Torah is not an option but a necessity. Without it, Man's most important characteristics grate on the pattern of all other existence.

One final argument is the most important in terms of our passage. The Sinai encounter created a covenant between ourselves and Hashem. Like any contract, a covenant entered into unilaterally is

---

22. *Shabbos* 88a.

23. Maharal points to a longer development in Chapter 32 of *Tiferes Yisrael.* The arguments cited here are taken from there.

invalid. Indeed, G-d made a point of sending Moses to speak to the people and encourage them to accept the Torah, while, as it were, He waited for Moses to return with a formal answer.

All this is well and good, but Hashem changed the script at the last moment. Precisely when the "deal" could have taken effect, *HaKadosh Baruch Hu* forced the issue, compelling *Klal Yisrael* to accept the Torah. The preliminaries to, the trappings of, a bilateral covenant were all there, but Hashem changed the agreement. He turned it into an imposed, dictated arrangement. He didn't merely facilitate a covenant. He created the bond between us. Once again, we see that the relationship between the Jewish people was not of human manufacture, but an exercise of Divine Will. Since we did not make it, we cannot break it.

Indeed, history bears out this subtlety. Hashem is our G-d because He ordered it that way, not because we accepted Him. Nothing ever changed that relationship. The Golden Calf came and went, as did various other deities that *Klal Yisrael* flirted with. Despite such egregious behavior, *the Jewish people never rejected the substance of the First Commandment!* It was phrased as a stated fact ("I am Hashem your G-d"[24]), because it would forever remain a fact. It is Hashem Himself who insures that we are His people. The nine commandments that followed were phrased as demands upon a population. Those who heard them would have the ability to obey or disobey. Obedience remained a contingency. The sin of the Golden Calf proved that they might even disregard the prohibition against idolatry of the Second Commandment.

Contingencies, in the final analysis, are not essentials. What comes and goes can be "forgotten," can in time be forgiven by Hashem. By no means does this imply that everything is up for grabs, that all can change in the course of time. The special relationship between Hashem and His people will endure to the end of time. Nothing we do will ever jeopardize it, because its sanctity does not depend upon us.

We have exhausted all elements of the verse that served as the basis of our passage. We have accounted for all its elements, and solved all the difficulties we initially encountered.

You will understand that we have explained only a small amount

---

24. *Exodus* 20:2.

of the depth of this passage. Much of it simply shouldn't be committed to writing. But you will certainly stand back and reflect on it with awe, marveling at how *Chazal* exposed the depth and true sense of the verse in *Isaiah*, doing so with great precision and exactitude.

III. *Derashos* and the Plain Meaning of Text

If the match between *pshat* — the plain, manifest sense of the verse — and *Chazal*'s explication is so perfect, why do our critics have such a hard time with it? The explanation could not be simpler. *Chazal*'s approach to the verse is attractive only if their message resonates within a comprehending listener. Some people are in a position to listen to their profound instruction, while others are not. Those who appreciate and recognize true wisdom will see the wonderful merger of careful *pshat* with profound understanding, and the commentary rings true. Those distant from wisdom will complain that *Chazal*'s comments do not match the plain meaning of the text, and will reject the latent message as well.

What we have here is really a model for the rest of our tradition. Objections abound to rabbinic teaching surrounding the entire *Tanach*. Where the kernel message and teaching of *Chazal* is not appreciated, their comments inevitably seem forced and distant.[25] The discerning student knows that if a passage seems hollow, then he has simply not broken through yet to the font of wisdom that is always there.

---

25. R' Samson Raphael Hirsch (*Exodus* 21:2) amplified on this idea with an analogy. Students often use class notes to study for exams. These notes can be terse and compact. Sometimes a scratch mark, or a cryptic half-phrase will allude to a complex chain of arguments. If a student attended the lectures himself, grasped what they were about, and now simply needs his memory jogged, his notes will be effective. Someone who never attended the course lectures but now wishes to master their content by borrowing someone else's notes will probably fail. Looking at the notes, he will likely see them as devoid of meaning or sense. Similarly, the *derashos* of *Chazal* are the notes that remained after involved, protracted discussions in the study halls of long ago. Those who were there were reminded by them of hours of work that had accompanied their writing. Maharal here adds that those who can relate to the points of *Chazal's* instruction can often be successful in reconstructing parts of the original teaching.

⇜§ Derashos

Our approach here holds true for the entirety of *Chazal's* exegesis. Every *derashah* of theirs, whether major or minor, whether in the Talmud or in the other collections of *midrash* — every *derashah* exposes the actual intended fullness of the verse.[26] The word *derashah* — literally, inquiry — itself points to this. It means an inquiry, a probing and plumbing of the depth of a verse or concept, and brings to light its true intent.

Do not object that their *derashos* often contradict each other, with different authorities coming to very different conclusions regarding the same text. Despite the apparent differences, the varying approaches actually share a common appreciation of the core sense of the verse. From one such teaching, however, many different conclusions can be drawn, and many applications made. The different opinions in *Chazal* only vary in some of the conclusions that can be drawn from the kernel teaching.

This is consistent with much of our life experience. Many things seem ordinary and simple at first sight, and others would describe them in much the same way. Only after more careful scrutiny do we learn that there is "more than meets the eye," that multiple layers lurk beneath the surface, all different, and all true.

⇜§ Empty Sermons

I offer these thoughts in rebuke to a number of speakers and authors. Rabbis announce that they will give a *"derashah"* upon the words of *Chazal,* and proceed to offer the polar opposite of a proper *derashah.* These rabbis are really interested only in their own words and insights, and need a platform from which to launch them. They care precious little whether their words coincide with *Chazal's* intended meaning in the passage they expand upon. They capitalize

---

26. Centuries later, the *Malbim* would pen his famous line in his introduction to *Leviticus*: *Hadarush hu hapshat hapashut hamuchrach vehamutba b'omek halashon* — the *derashos* of *Chazal* amount to the actual plain sense of Scripture, compelled by deeper semantic consideration of the text.

on the fact that so many of *Chazal*'s *derashos* seem (before proper study) to be so remote from plain text. Because of this, their own fanciful adventures can also be sold as a form of *derashah*. The stranger they seem, the more pleased these rabbis are.

This is nothing less than perversion. As we have shown, the *derashos* of *Chazal* draw the reader closer to the author's intention, not further away. They are serious inquiries into words and images, not flights of the imagination. No one should ever treat the words of *Chazal* any differently. They are not playthings, to be invoked as support for every unsupportable notion that pops into the head of every would-be orator.

IV. Sichon's Accounting and Scriptural Allusions

R' Shmuel bar Nachman said in the name of R' Yochanan, "What is the meaning of the verse, 'Therefore the *moshelim* [those that speak in parables] say. . .'? *Moshelim* means those who rule their evil inclinations. *Come Cheshbon* means come, let us reckon [from *cheshbon,* a reckoning] the account of the world: the loss incurred by the fulfillment of a precept against the reward secured by its observance, and the gain gotten by a transgression against the loss it involves. *You shall be built and established* : If you do so, you will be built in this world and established in the World to Come. *Ir Sichon* : if a man makes himself like a young donkey [from similarity of *ir* and *ayyar*] that follows the gentle talk [the seductive talk of sin; from similarity of *Sichon* and *sichah,* talk]. What comes next? *For a fire goes out of Cheshbon* : A fire will go out from those who calculate [the account of the world] and consume those who do not calculate. *And a flame from the city of Sichon* : From the city of the righteous who are called trees [*sichin,* similar to *Sichon*]. *It has devoured Ir Moav* : This refers to one who follows his evil inclination like a young donkey that follows gentle talk. *The high places of Arnon:* This refers to the arrogant [as in haughty and high], as it is said, 'Whoever is arrogant falls into *gehinom.'* *Vani-ram* — the wicked one says, 'There is no High One' [similarity to *ain ram*]. *Cheshbon has died* — the accounting of the world has perished. *Till Divon* - *HaKadosh Baruch Hu* said, 'Wait until judgment comes' [similar to *yavo din*]. *And we destroyed till Nophah* — until there comes a fire which requires no fanning [fanning is *naphah*]. *Till Medvah* — until it will melt their souls [from *daav,* to grieve].''[27]

O ur critics find this passage bizarre for two reasons. Firstly, *Chazal* took the entire sequence of verses completely out of their Scriptural context. The *pesukim* really deal with *Sichon's* military success against the city of *Cheshbon.* Furthermore, the *derashos* themselves are too far-fetched to be taken seriously. Supposedly, *Chazal* want us to believe that many words of the original text allude to different, related words. All coming together, they tell a story of our need to take stock of our actions. In fact, though, there is little in the original to suggest the supposed allusions. No reasonable person would see any connection between them.

◄§ Themes and Allusions

O ur response presupposes that you have understood the point of our last piece. The passage at hand teaches us an important corollary to the principles we established there. Here we discover just how confident *Chazal* were in the precise, reasoned methodology they employed to ferret out the deeper meaning of Biblical texts. Simply put, once they felt certain that the kernel message of some sequence of *pesukim* concerned a given topic, they were equally confident that they would find multiple allusions in adjoining verses. They would accept such allusions even if these hints and connections would ordinarily be seen as improbable, since they recognized the unmistakable

---

27. *Bava Basra* 78b.

signpost of the Author[28] pointing to this thematic interpretation.

Before considering any deeper meaning of the verses in question, *Chazal* understood that the *pshat* — the simple meaning — could not refer to the historical fact of the conquest of the city of Cheshbon by King Sichon, stripping it from the Moabite empire. The term *moshlim* — those who compose *meshalim,* or allegories and parables — makes this approach impossible. Recounting the outcome of a battle doesn't require *moshlim,* or anyone else of great literary accomplishment. Anyone can report where the cease-fire lines were drawn.

The subtlety of the *moshlim* was in the double entendre of the word Cheshbon, referring at once to the city by that name, as well as the idea of "plan" and "accounting." Keeping in mind this latter meaning of the word *cheshbon* gives the verses a different drift. Make an exacting accounting, they urge, and you will understand why the city fell to Sichon and his people. Add up all the factors, perform a more complete reckoning, and you will realize that it was appropriate and fit for Cheshbon to fall to a new master.

৺§ Generals and Accountants

A familiar rabbinic idiom is *din u'cheshbon.* What is right and just — *din* — goes hand in hand with *cheshbon,* or subjecting claims to the scrutiny of a legal accounting. The "fire" that goes out from *Cheshbon* is the fiery determination of legal rectitude, the outcome of *din.*

---

28. Maharal points to a similar assumption, phrased far more cryptically, in the closing line of *Tosafos* to *Bechoros* 20b.

An analogy might work. Poetry at its core is a language that communicates on multiple levels. Every reader of poetry expects to find a rich assortment of allusions. If you are completely unfamiliar with the background, style, and interests of the poet, it will take more compelling evidence to convince you that the author intended the allusion, than if you know something about his agenda. When you approach the poem with an expectation of finding some particular set of allusions, you will find some that you would ordinarily have passed by without another thought.

Chazal react the same way. If they find strong internal evidence that "anchors" the fuller meaning of a text in a certain topic, they feel confident that they will find a host of related allusions to that topic in the surrounding text. The uninformed observer would find these allusions weak. This weakness, to *Chazal,* is offset by the exceptionally strong hint the Author included, which amount to an invitation to seek out further allusions. (See above, note 5, for the *Netziv's* observation that the Torah calls itself poetry, inviting the search for allusions.)

When all the arguments were collected and weighed, Moab was found wanting in her entitlement to a territory that included *Divon,* and *Nofach,* and *Medvah.* Once she lost the justification for holding onto this area, it was inevitable that she should let it slip from her grasp.[29]

Having arrived at a better understanding of the *pshat* in these *pesukim,* we can easily understand why *Chazal* insisted on finding a deeper meaning. It is inconceivable that the Torah would lavish precious space on a bit of ancient military history. The territorial takeover didn't have any lasting effects, since *Klal Yisrael* later conquered the entire region anyway! A more profound and momentous message must be included in this passage.

Here again, the deeper message is an outgrowth and extension of the plain meaning. As we have shown, the simple *pshat* deals with *cheshbon,* with a strict examination and accounting. While it might not have been apparent to the rulers of Moab, their reasons to hold onto Cheshbon no longer added up. Had they done the accounting themselves, they might have changed history, or saved themselves a costly battle.

This essential idea continues to call to us across the gulf of time. Sichon's victory is an allegory. It illustrates the value of proper accounting, of absolute awareness of all the important factors in our lives. It is an object lesson in the larger battle that looms before each of us. Life is too important to leap before looking. We must be sure that there is a *cheshbon* — a roadmap of where we want to go, and a deliberate and well-designed plan for the execution of all the moves we need to get there.

Once *Chazal* assured themselves that they grasped the latent lesson, they understood that the associated verses of this passage must also support the theme. *Chazal's* tradition included a firm grasp of Hashem's use of style in crafting the Torah. It left them fully confident that the Author incorporated strings of allusions to accompany the central one. They made it their business to bring them to our attention, not terribly concerned that some of them might seem forced. They were simply faithful to the Author's guidelines for understanding His own work.

---

29. This is a reversal of the familiar maxim, "Might makes right." The *moshlim* suggest that, at least in this case, right made might!

V. The Waning of G-d's Strength?

"Because Hashem lacked the ability [*mibilti yecholes*] to bring them to the land He had sworn to give them . . ."[30] It should have written *yachol*! R' Elazar said: "Moses said to *HaKadosh Baruch Hu, 'Ribono Shel Olam*! Now the nations of the world will say: He has become weak like a female and is not able to deliver them'."[31]

It appears that *Chazal* took the word *yecholes* as second person feminine address, as if to be read "You are not able." This would be a gross error. The word is a noun, and means "ability." Moses warned that the nations of the world would assume that Hashem lacked the ability to see His people through to their destination. Not only is there no need to comment on this rather straightforward verse, but their comment is inaccurate!

Chazal, of course, made no mistake. They did not confuse the meaning of the word *yecholes.* They did observe, however, that the verse might have been constructed differently. It could have read, "*mibli yachol* — You are not able.*"

⋙ Jumping for the Heavens

Chazal picked up on a subtle nuance that separates the two expressions. We would not tell someone, "You don't have the strength, power, and savvy to launch yourself bodily to the heavens." The issue isn't one of strength and power, but of complete unsuitability. What Man lacks in this regard is not ability, but *possibility.* The words *mibli yachol* do not indicate which sense is meant; they allow either reading.

Thus, had Moses used the direct phrase, "You are not able," his argument might have been construed as this:

---

30. *Numbers* 14:16.
31. *Berachos* 32a.

You must bring them into the land of Israel. If You don't, all the skeptics of the world will gloat. They will claim that You have shown that it is impossible to lead the Jews into the Promised Land. G-d would never contravene the natural forces of history, to snatch territory from seven mighty tenant nations, and award it to a weak, upstart people. G-d just doesn't work that way.

Now, such a mistaken conclusion is bad enough. But it isn't quite as objectionable as the conclusion that Moshe actually predicted. By using *mibilti yecholes,* which points directly to Hashem's strength and power, Moses' argument took quite a different turn.

You must see them into the Land. If You don't, all our enemies will smirk. They will be convinced that You have been diminished in stature. The mighty G-d Who performed all those wonders in Egypt must have lost some of His stature. He cannot perform as He did before.

Let's examine the difference between the two. The first argument reduces G-d by placing an upper limit on the kinds of things that He can or will do in this world. He cannot, or will not, override the natural laws that make it impossible for an inconsequential, fledgling nation to take on the great seven powers of Canaan. This assessment is a frontal attack on the Perfection and Ability of G-d. It leaves G-d, however, still far more powerful than anything in human experience.

The second argument destroys the entire notion of Divinity by attributing change and frailty to G-d. It implies that His powers can ebb and wane, G-d forbid. It finds a chink in the Heavenly armor. It offers hope to humans who wish to ignore Him. Perhaps they needn't be so concerned with His power. If matters go well for Man (and not so well for G-d), there is at least the possibility that they can escape the consequences of His reality and presence. His strength can be sapped; perhaps it can be drained altogether![32] Once again, *Chazal* saw in the text

---

32. Greek mythology provides a model for this. The Greek gods certainly inspired fear and awe. It paid to have them on your side. They weren't very Divine, however. They had their weaknesses, and many fell from power. You didn't really have to deal with all of them, as much as figure out which one was going to prevail under the circumstances you found yourself. And if you knew his weakness, you could try evading him later, if it became too costly to continue to serve him. The gods were essentially human, just bigger. They had super-strength, and super-flaws. In them

what the rest of us miss. They teach us that Moses used a far more potent line of reasoning than we would have realized.

There are other, albeit related, ways to understand why *Chazal* assigned a feminine dimension to G-d's power and strength. Seen from the male perspective, the female (especially the female spouse) moves from a point external to him to bond and join with her mate. However close their relationship, the fact remains that they are not entirely inseparable. They do not become a single organism, lacking any boundary between them. They can work to reduce the psychological chasm between them, but they do not become one by nature. Hard work can bring their identities closer to each other; hard work could reverse the process as well. The female remains an adjunct to the male — attached, connected, but not absolutely merged and integrated. Some externality must remain.

Moses argued that Hashem's "inability" to bring the Jewish people into Israel would become scandalous. The world would assume the worst. We understand that whatever Hashem is, He is by His essence. This is one of the reasons that it is so difficult, if not impossible, to speak accurately about the nature of G-d.[33] Any words we use about Him fail to encompass His nature. If we describe Him as wise, we really detract from His wisdom, because His wisdom surpasses anything that we can imagine.

Additionally, we can imagine ourselves as wise, or not so wise. Our being doesn't stand or fall on our degree of wisdom. In a sense, our wisdom is not us. We can be, without being wise. G-d's "wisdom" is radically different. It — and all other characteristics that we attribute to Him — are part of His very essence. He cannot be G-d without his wisdom, and strength, and mercy, etc. His attributes are part of His reality and definition. They are not add-ons, and they cannot be stripped away.

How would a theologically challenged world look at a G-d Who abandoned His charges in the desert? They would, claimed Moses, see Hashem in the most primitive way. They would completely misunder-

---

you therefore found the complete and utter debasement of the idea of an ultimate Higher Authority.

33. This issue (which is *not* developed here by Maharal, but by me in an attempt to clarify just a few of his cryptic words — YA) is an old and thorny one. For a fuller treatment, see *Moreh Nevuchim* 1:59-60.

stand the nature of Divinity. They would see G-d as a mysterious figure, who happened to have many interesting attributes, none of which are essential. For G-d's power to fail Him, it must be *outside* His actual self. Like the female to the male, it could not be part of His absolute nature. It must be an adjunct, an external that moved closer, something that came along for the ride. Hashem's image would sustain unthinkable damage, crippling the world's understanding of the true nature and Unity of G-d.

There is one more completely different — and very simple — argument for taking *mibilti yecholes* as "feminine" usage. The typical and expected expression is *mibli yachol.* It unequivocally is masculine. *Mibilti yecholes,* on the other hand, works equally well with a masculine or feminine object. By using it, any distinction between masculine and feminine is downplayed, since the Hebrew word for "ability" is the same for both genders.

Why would the Torah pass up an expression that preserved gender difference, and replace it with one that blurred it? *Chazal* saw the subtlety. The Torah suppressed any masculine imagery associated with His power, and diluted it. Relative to the "pure" masculine form of *mibli yachol,* the neutral form that the Torah used is a kind of emasculation of the expected expression, or a partial feminizing of it. This is what *Chazal* meant.

From all of the above it is clear that *Chazal* were not "soft" on grammar. To the contrary, they were sensitive to its every nuance. They paid much closer attention to faint shades of differences between words and phrases — certainly much closer than their critics did!

VI. Organic Torah

[Maharal cites several more passages in which *Chazal* seem to have misread verses because of a faulty grasp of grammar. In each case he argues, mostly on technical grounds, that a more precise look at the words demands further commentary, which *Chazal* provided. Having staved off a number of such charges by the critics, he concludes this chapter with a flourish.]

We have seen that *Chazal's* teachings are based on precision and insight. Their comments are called *midrash chachamim,* because they are the result of a careful, studied *inquiry* [34] into the full depth of Biblical text.

⌇ *Midrash* Growing On Trees

I do not mean to belittle the plain meaning of the text. The Gemara[35] cautions us not to remove a verse from its *pshat.* The relationship between *pshat* and *derash* is like a tree. From a single trunk and set of roots, a tree spreads out luxuriously in many directions, its branches producing leaves and fruit. From a verse's firmly rooted *pshat,* many tributary ideas branch out. Thus, the Gemara tells us,[36] "A single verse can yield many teachings."

We should not be surprised when we see a verse expounded in such different ways by different authorities. We note the same occurrence in the natural world: Many different things spring from the same source.

Do not suspect for a moment that this analogy might be trite. If it is true of a tree, it is certainly true of the words of the Living G-d! If a

---

34. The essential meaning of the Hebrew root *DRSH,* (דרש) which in turn is the root of the words *derash* and *midrash,* or the general area of rabbinic commentary and exegesis that the critics target.

35. *Yevamos* 24a.

36. *Sanhedrin* 34a.

small seed can eventually branch out in many directions, then every word of Hashem's Torah can diversify and divide into different words and different facets.

Words are not trees, you will object. Plants are organic and alive; they are meant to thrive and flower. Words are tools. They are effective, but they aren't alive. They contain nothing more than the will of those who give voice to them.

This might be true for the words we mortals use. But this is not so in regard to *HaKadosh Baruch Hu*. His words are not just vehicles to carry His Will from Him to us. His words are reflections of Divine *sechel* — wisdom. Wisdom is organic. From any part of it flows much more of it. And the words of the Torah are not just means to enable us to understand the wisdom behind them. They are part of that wisdom itself. Each word is precise, just-so, crafted by the Absolute with which it connects.

The tree analogy is a very effective description of the true nature of Torah. Rooted in pure *sechel,* the words of Torah bring forth more *sechel,* more wisdom. Like the branches of a tree, what grows can be closer to the trunk, or further removed. The insights and conclusions that grow from a *pasuk* can be closer to the *pshat,* or further removed. In either case, they are still organically related to the *pshat,* offshoots of the primary sense of the verse.[37]

---

37. Maharal steers a course between two other approaches to *midrash* which have present-day proponents. One view sees *midrash* as a wonderful enlargement of the text beyond its original meaning. *Chazal* were rich in imagination, inspired in content, and prolific in scope. They refused to be limited to the ordinary meaning of words, so they creatively linked some of the choicest fruit of their thought to sacred text. The link, of course, was not necessarily there. They had the courage to press on, though, since they were completely certain of the truth of their thought and mission, even if there was objectively little to recommend their conclusions. Some recent so-called authorities have called this a form of deconstruction, referring to the modern literary theory of valuing what a text means to a reader in a given historical milieu, regardless of the original intent of the author.

Another view takes the polar opposite position. The proponents of this view see *Chazal* as decoders of an original message that was built into the text. All they did was mechanically apply certain rules (which were always part of the tradition from Sinai), and the original message showed up clear as day.

Maharal rejects both of these positions — the first because it is blasphemous, the second because it isn't true.

To be meaningful to us, the thought of *Chazal* must represent the Divine Will, not

✦ Taking the Back Road

There is an entirely different way to deal with the objections of our critics. Truth be told, not everything that *Chazal* linked to different *pesukim* actually derived from those verses.[38] There are many truths that were well established to them without recourse to Biblical verse. They turned to the text afterwards, not so much for support, but because they understood that Torah is a complete and perfect work. Any truth must invariably be represented within the words of the text. An allusion might in fact be remote. But it must be there, someplace.

---

the insight of some very gifted human beings. Hashem's Torah is meant to give us the certainty of engaging the Divine and the Infinite, not to be a springboard for human imagination.

On the other hand, the conclusions *Chazal* sometimes derive from various texts simply seem too remote from the plain meaning to be integrally related to the text. And the sheer number of different conclusions, often at loggerheads with each other, make it difficult to believe that *Chazal* were only mechanically decoding the original. If they were, some of the attempts would have to be incorrect!

Maharal here preserves the sanctity and authority of the message, without stretching our credulity. *Chazal's* conclusions were not, G-d forbid, of their own manufacture. Every bit of their insight is contained within Hashem's Torah. But the ideas do not repose entirely in the text alone. The words teach us various messages and insights, on many different levels. Those ideas link to other ideas, but not only through the linkage of words and the associations they set off. Wisdom itself is organic. Small insights blossom into larger ones. Their illumination ripples through wider and wider circles.

This is inherent in the nature of true insight and wisdom. And there is no more reliable and pure wisdom to be found than the Divine *sechel* of Torah. The conclusions of *Chazal* occur after the fall of many intellectual dominoes that previously stood erect, one next to the other. It is always a Divine Hand, stretched out through an idea latent in the text, that knocks over the first one.

38. Maharal here, while likely dealing primarily with *aggadah,* echoes the arguments of both sides of a long-standing dispute about *midrash halachah.* Which came first? Was it the halachah, the legal conclusion, or was it the *derashah?*

According to the former, *Chazal* always knew the halachic conclusion through the *mesorah* tradition. They used the *derashos* only to demonstrate that these assumptions of the Oral Law were well anchored within the Written as well, if only by implication.

The latter sees the *derashos* as actually spawning and producing new halachah. As new problems emerged that had not been addressed in previous generations, the

Our few words on this complex topic can hardly suffice to explain the *derashos* of *Chazal.* After all, they amount to the very backbone of the Oral Law; they are what the Talmud is all about. Nonetheless, we have succeeded once more in defusing the arguments of our critics. Once again, we have demonstrated what we have shown before. If you take the time to probe and analyze the depth and profundity of *Chazal* from within, you will find no deficiency.

Sages approached the text anew. They sought to extrapolate new information through the methods of *derash* that had been traditionally preserved. What they found, seen this way, was wholly a product of the *derashah,* which "came first."

At least concerning *aggadah,* Maharal admits to the existence of both varieties.

THE
FOURTH WELL

Relating

to

G-d

The
response:

I. G-d's Prayer

R' Yochanan said in the name of R' Yosi ben Zimra: "How do we know that *HaKadosh Baruch Hu* prays? Because it says: 'I will bring them to My holy mountain, and I will gladden them in My house of prayer [literally: in the house of My prayer].'[1] It does does not say 'the house of their prayer,' but 'the house of my prayer.' This teaches that *HaKadosh Baruch Hu* prays. What does He pray? 'May it be My Will before Me that my *rachamim* will suppress my anger, and that My compassion will prevail over My [other] attributes, and that I will deal with My children with compassion, and that I may treat them beyond the strict interpretation of *din*.' "[2]

Some people level trenchant criticism against this passage. To whom does G-d address His prayers? Hashem transcends everything, and lacks nothing!

This criticism is foolish and myopic. Who was it, after all, who taught us about the unique Oneness of G-d? Who, if not *Chazal*, drive home and refine that understanding day in and day out through the mes-

---

1. *Isaiah* 56:7.

2. *Chullin* 60b. A few lines above, the Gemara relates that the two great luminaries were originally created to be equal. The moon was puzzled that two "rulers could rule at once." G-d concurred, and instructed the moon to reduce itself.

sages they incorporated in the order of prayers and *berachos?* Are these skeptics unaware of the uncompromising position *Chazal* took regarding the Unity and perfection of G-d? Could they really think that *Chazal* meant what a superficial reading of this passage would seem to indicate?

⋖§ What the Word Means

The great gap between *Chazal's* understanding and our paltry comprehension causes the confusion. Our Sages understood the real meaning of prayer, and the root of the word "*tefillah.*" It is well known that the word derives from the word *pilel*, as in "Pinchas arose *vay'palel* — and executed judgment."[3] This word, in turn, relates to a similar usage in *Genesis*: "To see your face, I never *pilalti.*"[4] Rashi and Onkelos both render this as "I never *thought* I would see your face again." Judges are called *pelilim,* because they think through issues, and render judgment by considering arguments and weighing evidence.

Tefillin got their name by taking this route as well. They are called both "sign" and "reminder,"[5] reflecting the two different purposes they serve. The latter requires you to think, and places the *tefillah shel rosh* (head phylactery) at the seat of thought, fixing there a constant awareness of Hashem as G-d. The *tefillah shel yad* (arm phylactery) has a parallel function. It binds us to Hashem through the constant emotional attachment of our hearts. (Interestingly, the word *tzitzis* as well marries name to function. *Tzitzis* are also signs. The Torah ordered that their purpose, though, was to be seen.[6] It is related to "*metzitz min hacharakim,*"[7] peering out from the lattices, and thus stresses the visual nature of this mitzvah.)

Prayer demands thought. It is built upon intention, focus, and concentration. Prayer, simplified, is a recipe with only two ingredients: isolating what you think is significant, and understanding that you can

---

3. *Psalms* 106:30.

4. *Genesis* 48:11.

5. *Exodus* 13:9.

6. *Numbers* 15:38 — "And you will see them."

7. *Song of Songs* 2:9.

achieve it only by G-d giving it to you. In the order of prayer prescribed by the Sages, we clarify our essential wants and desires. When we realize how profoundly we want and need, how vulnerable and unprotected we are, and how dependent we are on the beneficence of Hashem — only then have we prayed effectively.[8]

Ironically, perhaps, some of this applies to *HaKadosh Baruch Hu* as well. Our prayer only makes sense when we turn our clarified needs towards Him. This part of prayer is obviously inapplicable to Him. On the other hand, we do share a sense of will. We deliberate about what we find crucial and vital in our lives. We will that we should have it.

✺§ Arriving at G-d's Will

Hashem, too, has a Will.[9] Arrival at this point of Will is precisely what *Chazal* mean when they attribute *tefillah* to G-d.[10] Taken this way, the passage could have simply stated: "It is the Will of G-d that His compassion should suppress His anger, and that His com-

---

8. The order of *Shacharis* (the morning prayer) greatly supports this. The central element of the standard, mandated prayer is *Shemoneh Esrei*. Long before we arrive at it, we work our way through *Pesukei DeZimrah*, a section that reminds us about the Power, Intelligence, and involvement of G-d in our world. In *Shemoneh Esrei* proper, the first three *berachos* make succinct statements about the role of G-d in history and everyday life — and His transcendent holiness, despite that involvement. In other words, we first remind ourselves about what we know of the nature of G-d, and His ability to grant us what we need. Only then do we enter into *bakashah* (petition), and unroll our wish-list of requests.

Once inside this section, we do not spontaneously let go with all things on our mind. The 12 specific requests (or 13 since Talmudic times) are highly structured and organized. They are divided equally between personal and communal needs, and again between spiritual and physical ones. *Chazal* who wrote these prayers obviously wished to introduce a careful sense of balance about our *davening*. They were as interested in teaching us what to *daven* for, as they were in providing us with the proper words to do it. (See R' Samson Raphael Hirsch, *Genesis* 48:11.) Seen in the light of these words of Maharal, they help us us clarify what is really important. They show us what remains when we think Jewishly and strip away competing value systems.

9. We understand that G-d's Will is something completely different from ours. We use the best approximations we have when we speak of G-d, recognizing that nothing in our experience can give us an accurate notion of what G-d is "really" like.

10. Hashem, of course, does not have to *arrive* at a sense of Will. It is always there, unchanging; shifting circumstances and conditions do not alter it. We are merely trying to describe elements of Hashem from our very limited human perspective, as prisoners of space and time. *Chazal* do this often.

passion should prevail over His other attributes, etc." There is no question that this is what the passage actually means. It remains for us to show why they did not simply state things this way, but instead chose the vocabulary of prayer.

First, we turn to other difficult parts of the passage. Why do they introduce Hashem's prayer with, "May it be My *Will* before Me?" Why do they not simply begin, "May My compassion suppress My anger"?

Know this. *Ratzon,* will, denotes wanting and desiring to the fullest extent possible. It is the strongest way to express the idea of wanting. Most of the petitions and requests we make of G-d use the word *ratzon* for this reason.

This is why *Chazal* insisted on the word *ratzon* in this passage. The *tefillah* of *HaKadosh Baruch Hu*, the focused and clarified central idea of His relationship with this world, is the *ratzon* to be compassionate. If that prayer would be depicted according to the expected script — that He should "deal with His children with compassion" — our understanding of His compassion would be flawed. We would picture Hashem wanting — and effecting — many acts of *chesed*. We would not see the forest for the trees. We might have an appreciation for disjointed incidents of *chesed*, but not see its pursuit as the fundamental, all-important fulcrum upon which all is balanced.

Rambam's solution to an important philosophical problem provides a different explanation for the use of *ratzon*. The word "Will" applied to G-d is a crude approximation.[11] His Will does not operate the way ours does.

---

11. Of all the "attributes" of Hashem, "Will" is the most difficult to deal with, says R' Yehuda HaLevi in *Kuzari* 2:2-6. We can explain virtually all the anthropomorphic representations of Hashem in the Torah as describing His actions, rather than His Essence. G-d cannot really get angry, because any emotion is a reaction to a changing condition, and G-d, as a perfect Being, neither learns anything new, nor is capable of any change. When the Torah speaks of the anger of G-d, it means that Hashem acts in a manner that would be associated with anger if the practitioner were a human being. *Ratzon*, though, is an internal state, not an action. How do we come to grips with it, as applied to *HaKadosh Baruch Hu*?

With great difficulty, says R' Yehuda HaLevi. But how else are we to understand where all the wonderful phenomena of this world originate? How did it come to be that things are the way they are? The place that all starts in our experience is in our will. We borrow the term from our world to describe what we cannot comprehend — "how" or "where" an idea originates within Hashem. Whatever it is that is "happening" — we label that unknown element *"ratzon."*

Rambam describes the difference in *Moreh Nevuchim.* [12] Our will is ephemeral. As situations change, so does our interest and resolve. We may need something today, and will it to be, and then decide tomorrow on a different course of action. We may learn that what we planned to do is too difficult, or that the materials we need are not available. Chameleon-like, our will sheds its old skin, and assumes a new identity. The observer who watches our change of conduct can correctly assume that we have changed our mind.

No such change applies to Hashem. Situational parameters do not mean anything to Him. There are no obstacles to overcome, no hurdles to leap. Nothing can interfere with the accomplishment of what He wants. Whatever it is that G-d wills — becomes! While G-d does not do all things at all times, this does not mean that He is influenced by changing conditions as we are. He does not make it rain one day and sunny the next because His attitude changed. Rather, the on-off nature of G-d's actions is itself part of His Will! Where there is Divine *Ratzon*, there is no gap between Will and its fulfillment, and no essential change.

If we employ *Rambam's* insight, we arrive at an alternate justification for the roundabout "May it be My *Ratzon* before Me."

Ratzon, imperfectly as we understand it, sums up the workings of some capacity of G-d's to constantly will something, although that objective does not become manifest at all times. *Chazal* chose this, the more accurate phraseology, rather than refer to Hashem "wanting" or "desiring." [13] Those terms would lead to the objection that G-d seems to change His mind. The notion of "will" transcends such change, and is far more accurate. (We offer this second line of reasoning tentatively. The first explanation we proposed — that *ratzon* expresses a more

---

12. 2:6.

13. In other words, in contradistinction to the critics who saw *Chazal* attributing human qualities to *HaKadosh Baruch Hu*, our sages took pains to underscore the infinite gap between Hashem and ourselves. We have always understood that, as mortal human beings, we really comprehend nothing of the Essence of G-d. Whatever we say about Him lessens what He really is. Yet our *mesorah* (tradition) calls for us to say much about Him, always with the understanding that whatever we say is impoverished allegory. Maharal's point is that *Chazal* were extremely careful and precise when they attempted the impossible! Even when they had to employ the language of the everyday man, they insisted upon preserving as much of the ineffable nature of G-d as possible.

complete and fundamental state of mind than "want" or even the activity linked to that desire — is certainly true.)

Why does Hashem need this "prayer"? Why must we picture Him actively asserting, as it were, that His fundamental *ratzon* is *rachamim.* Surely whatever it is that He does is part of the Divine Mindset!

The point, though, is that there is a profound difference in the expression of G-d's different *middos.* Some aspects of Hashem's relationship with the world flow from His sense of *mishpat* — of law and judgment. These aspects do not require any special "prayer." They are there because Hashem's justice determines that they are proper. *HaKadosh Baruch Hu* will certainly perform according to a standard of propriety that He Himself established. His prayer is needed where He operates beyond the limits of the law He Himself crafted.

How can He contravene the principles He embraces Himself? Only through His "prayer," i.e. by the fact that His *Ratzon* is *rachamim*. The tendencies towards *mishpat* and *rachamim* are not equal. One, as it were, is more fundamentally a part of what Hashem is. His most basic *ratzon* is to do *rachamim,* not *mishpat.* The *middos* (attributes) of *rachamim* and *mishpat* do not reign as equals. The prayer of Hashem is nothing more than the determination within the *middos* of G-d that the *middah* closest to His essence is *rachamim.* [14]

Once again we must ask: Why not just plainly say all of this? Why do *Chazal* force us to take a deep breath and plunge into their metaphor about G-d's "prayer" before surfacing with the true explanation in hand?

What drove them to this is the reference to "the house of His prayer." The *Beis HaMikdash* is the place, of course, for our prayers. Those prayers can be tied up neatly into one simple package. In all our

14. Maharal seems to allude here to the well-known bifurcation of the *middos* of Hashem into two chief categories: *chesed* (lovingkindness) and *din* (judgment). The different names of *HaKadosh Baruch Hu,* different *sefiros* (emanations and characteristics of Hashem through which G-d relates to the world according to the mystical system of *Kabbalah*), even the scope of human emotions — all are grouped according to this fundamental division. One look at the *ilan* (literally, the tree, or the hierarchical diagram of the ten *sefiros)* of the Ari *HaKadosh* should be enough to convince the reader of how traditional Maharal's claim here is. While the *sefiros* become separated into the two basic groups of *chesed* and *din,* they begin on the side of *chesed.* All *din* is initially an outgrowth of *chesed,* not an independent consideration.

What Maharal really conveys here is that in our feeble attempt to grasp a bit of what G-d is, we must see His leaning towards *chesed* as the all-important characteristic that spawns all other *middos* and activities.

petitionary prayer, we stand before our Creator, conscious of how little we deserve, and how much we ask. Were we to rely on the application of Hashem's judgment alone, we would often return empty-handed. Instead, we beg Hashem to treat us with *rachamim,* rather than *din*! The *Beis HaMikdash* is the house of *our* prayer, the place where, happily, our requests just happen to coincide with Hashem's most profound interest — crowning *rachamim* supreme!

But it is the house of His prayer as well. Hashem, as it were, waits for one thing before shattering the constraints of *din*. He waits for us to ask. Our asking allows the fulfillment of His *Ratzon*. [15] Our prayer precipitates the consummation of His ultimate Will. Our house of prayer is the house of His prayer.

◈ Against All Odds

The word "prayer," *tefillah*, is underscored. Asking and requesting are not enough. We understand that we are owed nothing, even if we were living our lives completely the way Hashem demands of us. And most of us are painfully aware of how inadequate our conduct has been, relative to G-d's expectation. If Divine justice determined that we were fully entitled to something, we would not have to ask for it! It

---

15. According to Maharal, when Hashem answers our *tefillos,* He does more than roll another item out of His Divine storehouse. He displays the *middah* closest to Him. By revealing more of His attribute of *rachamim,* He pushes aside the limitations of *din.* Prayer brings us closer to Hashem. We feel grateful and close to him when we reflect upon what He has given us, and upon how much more we need Him. When we are not aware of the gift, it is in a sense wasted on us. The Gemara (*Shabbos* 10b) instructs that even human gift-givers should never give anonymously. They should take advantage of the opportunity to build a deeper friendship, and let the recipient know that they have reached out to him, and enhanced his life.

The gift is also wasted if the recipient undervalues it. Drop off a Rembrandt with an unsophisticated friend, and he will thank you for an attractive wall decoration, not a priceless work of art. More valuable than any particular gift we ask of Him, is the revelation of some *middah* of Hashem. Insight into His nature will always draw us closer. If our eyes are not open, we are not candidates for revelation. To witness the triumph of Hashem's *middah* of *rachamim* over *din,* we must be watching for it. By asking for "things" alone, we stand a lesser chance of getting them, than if we focus on the deeper, potent meaning of our request. We get "things" when Hashem displays His *middah* of *rachamim,* as a way of proffering His love for us. This love is far more important than the "thing"; the object we desire is only a token of that love. When we are cold or unresponsive to G-d's embrace, we compromise, as it were, the relationship.

would be there! Since this is not the case, what we ask for does not come without resistance. We wish to unseat any counterforces to our supplications; we picture heavenly adversaries resisting our requests. We strain against *din!* Working against the rules, we are required to expend effort, to show more prodigious output. This is why the Gemara[16] lists *tefillah* among the four areas "requiring strengthening [ourselves]." Our wanting must be deep, not trivial. It must come from our most profound selves. We must take the time to clarify and express what is really within ourselves. This clarification, this thinking through is, as we said above, the real essence of *"tefillah."*

II. Rosh Chodesh and G-d's Atonement

Reish Lakish said, "Why is the he-goat of Rosh Chodesh different [from other *mussaf* he-goats], [in] that it is stated [regarding] it *'LaHashem'* [literally, a *chatas*, a sin-offering, for Hashem]? HaKadosh Baruch Hu said, 'This goat shall be a *kapparah* [atonement] for that which I diminished the moon.' "[17]

We use the term *chatas* in a very specific manner. It always refers to a Temple offering used to expiate some misdeed. How can this passage imply, G-d forbid, that Hashem is capable of some wrongdoing? And from whom would G-d ask forgiveness and atonement for His "sin"?[18]

The key to this passage is in the real meaning of *kapparah*. It does not really mean atonement. A more basic meaning of the word is "removal."[19] (Note this use in *Genesis*:[20] "I will appease him

---

16. *Berachos* 32b.

17. *Shevuos* 9a.

18. From what being could G-d possibly ask forgiveness, even if He were capable of some misdeed, which, of course, He is not?

19. When we use the term in regard to sin, we mean doing something that will remove the force and effect of some wrong that we have committed.

20. 32:21.

[*achaprah;* remove Esav's anger from me] through a gift."[21]) Hashem indeed does not require any atonement. The Rosh Chodesh offering does not atone for G-d. It does remove a "complaint" of sorts, an apparent inequity in His work of Creation.

Hashem gave the world two luminaries, the sun and moon. The sun illuminates and warms us each day, with only a cloud or two spoiling the constancy of its embrace. We could easily have expected the moon to do much the same, swathing us with a toned-down background glow each night, just enough to allow us to negotiate our way when we must be out and about at night. The sun and moon would each have been masters of their separate bailiwicks, sharing dominion over the diurnal cycle in separate but equal positions. The Torah alludes to this when it first describes the sun and the moon collectively as "the two great luminaries."[22]

Hashem had different plans. In one of the opening stages of Creation, He cut down the erstwhile *moshel*/co-ruler with the sun from its short-lived glory. The moon was shifted to a diminished role. It would wax and wane, regularly hiding in a decidedly unregal manner. It would be a fickle and undependable source of light, and a definite exception among the steady and reliable beacons in the perceived heavens.[23] The moon, thus, is a constant reminder of understated

---

21. The same point is made by the *Ritva* to *Shevuos* 9a. Note also that the covering of the *Aron* in the *Mishkan* was called the *Kapores,* from the same root as *kaparah* — atonement. R' Samson Raphael Hirsch claims that the word should simply be translated as "cover." This is the real function of what we call atonement. It covers up the crime, allowing life to go on as if the sin had never been committed.

22. *Genesis* 1:16.

23. The moon is a true anomaly. Its actual size is quite large relative to the many moons of other planets of our solar system. It shows us the same face at all times, which means that its period of rotation and period of orbit around the earth are in a 1:1 ratio. The periods of virtually all other bodies to the objects they orbit show no relationship at all, with the exception of Venus to the sun, which shows a ratio of 2:3.

Most interesting is the fact that the moon is a true nocturnal partner to the sun. The apparent sizes (the way they look to us in the sky) of the sun and moon are identical, about half a degree of arc. This is apparent to anyone who has ever seen the moon neatly obscure the disk of the sun in a solar eclipse. All of this makes sense according to the approach of *Chazal* that the moon initially was a true rival to the sun.

The Maharal apparently understands the diminution of the light of the moon not in terms of a reduction in size, or losing its own power of illumination to becoming a

presence, of the role of junior partner rather than the arrogance of prideful mastery.[24]

We know this about *HaKadosh Baruch Hu*: He has a preference for the small and insignificant. He chose Mt. Sinai upon which to give the Torah, not for its size, but for its lack of it. And He chose the scaled-down, more ignominious version of how the moon would look. Rosh Chodesh, when the moon begins to appear after its forced absence, is an anniversary, of sorts, of its abdication of its greater role, and a reminder of the diminutive one it assumed.

As such, it ties into *korbanos*. The word *korban* derives from the notion of drawing close, not from the idea of sacrifice. *Korbanos* are vehicles through which we move closer to our Creator.

The Rosh Chodesh *korban* makes a statement: "Small is beautiful." It is through smallness that we become great. By understanding our insignificance, we seek meaning beyond ourselves. We reach out to *HaKadosh Baruch Hu,* Who now finds room where our overweight egos used to crowd Him out.[25]

---

mere reflector of the sun's rays. Rather, he sees the moon as a body which might have provided lesser but constant illumination during the nighttime period. The only real reduction that the moon suffers is its monthly cycle of waxing and waning.

24. For a different approach, see R' Samson Raphael Hirsch, *Numbers* 28:14.

25. The way in which Hashem resized the moon may further explain how its example can bring us closer to Him. Hashem did not reduce the size of the moon, so much as introduce its periodic phases. Man has much to learn from this. We would like to imagine ourselves constantly and powerfully full of spiritual energy, just as the sun faithfully streams its beams at us without wavering, except for a rest period each night. Unfortunately, when we charge up the *Har Hashem,* the mountain of G-d, most of us trip along the way. We grow frustrated from failure, and one failure generates the next. The sun, as a model, is useless to many people.

Fortunately, there is another model. A month after the exhilaration of Yom Kippur, much of the magic is gone, replaced by the cynical question, "Did I really accomplish anything? I did not become a *tzaddik,* after all." The moon's example can restore some of the inspiration we felt at Yom Kippur — despite the failures shortly afterwards. The moon has its stronger days and its weaker ones. Each valley is always followed by a peak. After the peaks come valleys — but that does not preclude more peaks later on. We are reminded that very few people keep to an unflagging race up that mountain. The moon reminds us of the nature of many people, a nature that *HaKadosh Baruch Hu* understands well. We can learn to accept our failures if we are fully committed to undoing them, and convinced that there is never occasion to throw in the towel. We should strive for unrelenting vigor in our *avodas Hashem.* But if we do not have it, we must know that there is a great and important role for us nonetheless.

The scaled-back light of the moon, then, is an under-appreciated but powerful beacon, illuminating the way for shame-faced, inadequate human beings to return to Hashem. By the light of its message, we offer the *korban mussaf* of Rosh Chodesh. This brings some measure of atonement to us faulty mortals, restoring a quantity of lost wholeness.

In the process, it also makes good Hashem's record as Creator. Our monthly rapprochement with G-d justifies the rough treatment of the moon's fate. The wholeness of G-d's Creation is restored, as we remove an objection whose solution was obscured from our imperfect vision.

III. The Victory Over G-d and the Achinai Oven

R' Eliezer said to them [i.e., the *chachamim*, during his dispute with them regarding the Achinai oven], "If halachah accords with me, let Heaven prove it!" [Whereupon] a *bas kol* went forth and proclaimed, "What [argument] do you have with R' Eliezer, whom the halachah follows in all places?" R' Yehoshua stood on his feet and declared, "It [Torah] is not in Heaven!" R' Yirmiyah said, "[We do not pay attention in halachic matters to a voice from Heaven,] because the Torah was already given to man at Mount Sinai [to resolve disputes according to the majority]."[26]

R' Nassan found Eliyahu. He said to him, "What was Hashem doing at that time?"[27] Eliyahu replied, "Hashem laughed, and said, 'My children have been victorious over Me!' "[28]

---

26. I.e., the *chachamim*, who rejected the individual opinion of R' Eliezer.

27. I.e., what was Hashem's reaction upon hearing that the majority of *chachamim* "overruled" the Heavenly opinion that R' Eliezer was correct?

28. *Bava Metzia* 59a.

People find this passage puzzling for two reasons. Why should we reject the Heavenly voice? And how can *Chazal* describe a "victory" over Hashem? Can the commoner triumph over the Master in a halachic matter?

Listen carefully, and you will hear the words of the wise. Consider the precise phraseology of the Heavenly voice. Why did it emphasize that halachah was with R' Eliezer in all places? The phrase adds nothing to what the voice wished to convey — that the law regarding the disputed oven should follow R' Eliezer.

In fact, the voice did not referee this particular matter. The *bas kol* offered expert advice on the intellectual qualifications of R' Eliezer in general relative to his colleagues. In the race for Torah wisdom, all other contestants lagged far behind, maintained the *bas kol.* Do not be afraid of deciding like him, regardless of whom he should disagree with. If you must decide disputes based on intellectual strength, R' Eliezer is the intelligent choice.

₠ Majority Rules

The other *chachamim* did not challenge this assessment. They rejected the basic assumption! The evaluation of intellectual power by the Heavenly messenger might be accurate, but it could not be the final word. Torah is a reflection of the utter perfection and simplicity of the Wisdom of G-d. It transcends individual cognition and grasp. No one person, regardless of his gift and ability, could do justice to it. As universal truth, the Torah requires something universal to properly seize its essence. Only the embrace of another universal — that of the majority, representing an entire community — could come to a proper halachic determination.

The *chachamim* did not overrule the Heavenly voice. They possessed a deeper understanding of why the Torah instructs us to follow the majority. Conventionally, we understand this as increasing our probability of selecting the "correct" opinion. The more scholars who vote for a given argument, the more likely that it is correct. The *chachamim* knew that there was another dimension to the rule of following the many. The individual, no matter how gifted, cannot escape his own provincialism. As hard as he may try, he cannot jettison the personal nature of his own thoughts and experiences. He remains forever private and particular. If he is blessed with penetrating insight, it remains his insight. The different insight of a genius in the next generation would require that halachah would change according to his comprehension.

Torah transcends the particular. It is also aloof from the impermanence of change. The "superior" judgment of the intellectual titan moves aside to give way to a quality of Torah even more profound. There is a dimension to Torah that can be grasped by the many. Not an ersatz, imagined, diluted understanding, but a real one. Rejecting R' Eliezer is not a compromise of halachah, but a mark of distinction. Torah possesses a global nature that suits the collective, and is given stability and timelessness by a halachah dictated by the many. Only the many, the majority, the community can fix halachah.[29]

Nor did mortal men overule *HaKadosh Baruch Hu*. The authors of the Gemara wisely avoided having G-d say, "You chose well." That would invite the reader's mistaken impression that G-d changed His Mind, Heaven forbid! When a human father reports the victory of his sons over himself, he does not mean that they bested him in real conflict. Rather, it means that he has agreed to do things their way, rather than his own — and that this itself is fully his will!

In pondering the halachic dilemma of the oven in this passage, there are two distinct perspectives. From Hashem's point of view, R' Eliezer may have understood some points that his colleagues missed. They, however, rejected his insight in favor of a level of Torah more suitable to them from their vantage point: the global, all-encompassing one. The perspective of the recipients of Torah — the children — won out over that of the Giver. And that is precisely what G-d wanted them to do.

---

29. *Shelah HaKadosh* (*Beis Chachmah*, s.v., *va'ani*) offers a similar approach in more kabbalistic terminology. The ability of different people to grasp different parts of Torah truth is determined by their *shoresh neshamah* (soul's root.) Where (within the complexity of G-d's "geography" of characteristics, from the human standpoint) different souls are rooted determines how the Divine influence flows to them through the *sefirah* of *malchus*. A majority vote is a barometer, then, of "where" within Torah most *neshamos* are nourished, which Torah truths are appropriate to them, which Torah practices will affect them through the reciprocal reaction from Hashem.

This was R' Yehoshua's intent as well. By declaiming "Torah is not in Heaven," he was not asking G-d to stay away from their turf. Rather, he underscored that Hashem entrusted His precious Torah to an abode among men. There is an affinity that Torah has to us, just as we, the collective entity of *Klal Yisrael*, have a predilection to Torah. Receiving the Torah implies a Divine vote of confidence in us. It assures us that there is some overarching element within Torah that relates to the general *kedushah* (holiness) of the Jewish people. As individuals, we cannot hope to encompass the Torah's lofty magnificence. But we are guaranteed that as a community, we can bring it within range. Hashem made sure of that, when He created the Torah, and when He created us.

The Torah fixed this idea into legislation, through the rule of the majority. The right to relate to Torah in this way is a gift never to be rescinded. The *chachamim* insisted only on laying claim to the birthright of the Jewish people.[30]

IV. G-d vs. the Heavenly Academy

He [Rabbah] was sitting on the stump of a tree, and studying [Torah]. [At that moment,] they were disputing [the following mishnah] in the *Mesivta D'Rakia* (Heavenly Academy): "If the *baheres* preceded the white hair, [the person is] *tamei*. If the white hair comes first, he is *tahor*. [If there is] doubt, *HaKadosh Baruch Hu* says he is *tahor*, while the entire *Mesivta D'Rakia* say that he is *tamei*." They [the Heavenly Court] said, "Who will decide [this issue]?" Rabbah bar Nachmani said, "I am unique in [my knowledge of] *negaim*;[31] I

30. R' Yitzchak Hutner beautifully develops a similar point in *Pachad Yitzchak*, Chanukah §14. He shows two parallel methods of fixing halachah, including one that rests on the *tzibbur's* prescience of the appropriate way to act, even when unaccompanied by compelling reason.

31. The changes in appearance in skin, clothing, and walls described in *Leviticus* are understood to be Heaven-sent plagues, consequences of certain misdeeds. Rabbah meant that he attained unmatched competence in these extremely detailed and complex laws.

am unique in [my knowledge of] *ohelos*."[32]

They sent a messenger after him [to summon him to testify about the matter], [but] the Angel of Death could not approach him, because his mouth did not cease from its recitation [of Torah]. At that point, a wind blew, and made loud noises among the reeds. Rabbah thought that the noise came from a brigade of horsemen [who were coming to arrest him]. He said, "May the soul of that person [himself] pass on, so that he will not be given into the hands of the government!" As he was dying, he said, "*Tahor! Tahor!*" A *bas kol* issued forth and said, "Fortunate are you, Rabbah bar Nachmani, for your body is *tahor*, and your soul departed with [the word] '*tahor.*' "[33]

Two problems jar the reader. How can the members of the *Mesivta D'Rakia* take issue with their Creator? More importantly, how can a mortal human cast the decisive ballot to bolster G-d's position? Once again, I urge you to listen to my words. The proper intent of our Sages will shine through, and their wisdom will radiate like the sun in its full strength and power.

◄§ Divine Conflict Resolution

In this passage *Chazal* reveal to you how proper Hashem's ways are. Human kings order what they want, with little regard as to how those edicts suit their subjects. G-d rules differently. His decrees are scrupulously attentive to the needs of His subjects. Because our natures are so fundamentally different, humans and G-d will always have different ways of looking at the same thing. This passage teaches that when Hashem's view conflicts with ours, He will not impose His Will unless it is proper and suitable from our perspective as well. This is borne out by another enigmatic passage:

---

32. *According to Numbers* 19:14, people (and objects) that find themselves under the same covering as the dead become *tamei*. *Ohelos* refers to the area of law that describes which coverings (*ohelos*) convey the *tumah*.

33. *Bava Metzia* 86a.

R' Yochanan said, "Wherever the heretics have used [a verse in Scripture as support] for their heresies, the rebuttal [to their challenge] can be found in a [nearby] verse. 'Let us make man in our image'[34] [is followed by] 'G-d created Man in His [singular] image.' 'Let us descend and there confuse their speech'[35] [is preceded by two verses by] 'G-d descended [singular] to look at the city and tower.' "

[All] those [terms that the heretics use as a basis for their challenges,] what are they needed for? [Why did Scripture use a problematic plural, only to have to counter it with another verse?] R' Yochanan said, "*Hakadosh Baruch Hu* does not do anything unless He [first] consults the Heavenly Court."[36]

G-d does not need the advice and counsel of those whom He created. Whatever discernment, whatever comprehension they possess — all comes from Him. Consulting with them serves one goal: arriving at the complete harmony of Creation. Hashem sees to it that different components and elements get along with each another, without opposition or friction.

The creation of Man is a case in point. Keep in mind the difference between G-d's perspective and that of His creatures. G-d's purpose in creating Man — whatever it is — is advanced when Adam appears on the scene. From Hashem's point of view, nothing could be simpler.

Some rather interesting possibilities, however, spring into existence with Man's creation. Man might properly find his niche in his own backyard on planet Earth, but he is, by nature, a frequent trespasser on foreign territory. Not quite an angel, Man is often a good stand-in. He shares many of the characteristics of those occupants of higher places. Like the angels, he has discerning intelligence and comprehension. His soul has far more in common with these spiritual entities than with the assorted animal species with whom he shares terrestrial geography. Without becoming a permanent resident of the upper regions, Man often makes significant excursions to a world in which he does not fully belong.

---

34. *Genesis* 1:26.

35. Ibid. 11:7.

36. *Sanhedrin* 38b.

G-d could have created Man to be an anomaly. Leaping at times into more spiritual arenas, Man would have been a misfit. He could pass through the higher places, but without a sense of connection. The angels and he would grate on each other, making poor bed-fellows. They could share the same ship, but would insist on different cabins.

The system would have "worked" — especially from G-d's perspective. The goals of Man's creation would ultimately be achieved. But Hashem does not operate this way. His unity spills over to Creation, demanding that all the pieces fit together as one. It generates a seamless meshing of function and purpose, even when examined from other angles. He would create a world without conflicts of essential elements, even at their own levels. Man would connect with the angels, rather than step on their Heavenly toes.

₰ Trespassing Allowed

This is what *Chazal* mean by "consulting" with the Heavenly Cabinet. G-d created Man with the "approval" of the angels. When Man propels himself to celestial heights of spiritual accomplishment, he fits in, rather than intrudes. He belongs there too. Essentially.

₰ All's Well That Ends Well

We can find another reason for "consulting" with the angels specifically at the creation of Man, and not at the birth of any other creature. The Torah tells us that everything was created for the sake of Man. All depends on him. If Man is "accepted" by the angels on High, if the creation of physical man (and all that his existence implies) does not jar the spiritual worlds but fits smoothly with them, then everything else in Creation follows, carried along in his wake. By forging a connection between the angels and man, all other Creation is justified as well.

We have seen thus far that referencing our perspective can bring harmony and unity to the world. We can now return to our first enigmatic passage. *Negaim* and *ohelos* are distinguished for their difficulty. When a cloud of doubt hovers over a suspected *nega,* the difficulty escalates. In general, we follow the stricter contingency[37] whenever doubt arises about a halachah originating within the Torah itself, rather than in rabbinic enactment. Since we cannot eliminate the worst-case scenario, prudence — and the severity of Torah law — dictate that we must take its possibility seriously. If we do not know whether the piece of meat on our plate is kosher or not, we dare not eat it. The possibility of it being non-kosher looms too large. If we eat a full meal, and don't quite remember if we said *Birkas Hamazon,* [38] we must take into account the possibility that we did not yet fulfill our obligation, and recite the required formula. A doubtful or suspected *nega* should then be treated with the same severity as a certain and definite *nega.* This was precisely the position of the *Mesivta D'Rakia.*

If this seems well and good, it is only because we do not look at things the way G-d does. Hashem's existence is unlike anything we know. There is nothing in the universe — including the universe it- self, or space, or time, or our particular set of natural laws — that simply must be. Everything we observe is contingent on precursors and preconditions. Those elements themselves are contingent on other preexisting conditions or assumptions. G-d's existence simply must be.[39] It is impossible to conceive of His non-existence. It is essential, rather than accidental.[40]

When we think of Hashem contemplating our existence, we might imagine Him to be (using our very human and inexact words) amused! Should our short, tenuous, and "accidental" existence be dignified with the same term that relates to the reality of G-d?

Our existence is no joke to us. It is all we have, and we try to take it seriously. Yet even we shrink and shrivel when we think how insignificant our being is, when measured up to the Being of Hashem.

---

37. See, e.g., *Nedarim* 53a.

38. The Grace After Meals.

39. *Rambam* emphasizes this in the first of his Thirteen Principles, in his *Commentary* to the Mishnah, *Sanhedrin.* If Hashem would not exist, than everything else would cease to exist. On the other hand, if everything else ceased to exist, it would not minimize His existence, or diminish Him in any way.

40. These terms overlap with those used by the classical philosophers, and Maharal uses them frequently. "Accidental" is used in the sense of the confluence of different conditions that need not necessarily occur by the basic nature of things. If a passing bear had not embedded a seed in soil softened by rain, the tree would never have grown. The world would continue to exist anyway.

Even from Hashem's point of view, there are levels of pseudo-existence. There are things that at least belong integrally to this impermanent world of ours. They fit well with the beautifully engineered master scheme that keeps the world running. They work synergistically with the myriad of other cogs of the machine, in intricate and complex interrelationships.

⋧ Going Off Autopilot

Then there are things that do not really belong. *Negaim,* for instance. There are no natural laws that dictate the production of these plagues. They represent a Divine override of the pathways by which He maintains the world. And they are a Divine reaction to something that certainly has no place in this world — sin! Hashem wants the sinner to get the message, so his body must comply. But the phenomenon of the *nega* stands outside the ordinary, remains alien to a world in which everything has its expected place and function. It is as remote from essential as can be. It does not exist in the same sense as other phenomena.

⋧ No Room for Questions

The status of a doubtful *nega* moves the discussion a full level down. Ask Hashem how to view it, and His reaction, as it were, is to see it as laughably distant from anything that remotely could be called "existence." There are no doubts in His view. The reality of His existence would assign the *safek negah* to the round file of non-entities.

On the other hand, we recognize certain relationships that are crucial to the function and even existence of the world. Even these, however, are somewhat similar to the bear-and-rain-assisted tree. If protons and electrons would not have opposite charges, all chemical activity that we know could not take place. If gravitational attraction would decrease inversely to the cube of distance, rather than its square, none of the planets, including earth, could maintain their orbits around the sun, but would hurtle out to nowhere. If it fell off inversely with distance (and not its square), we would be quickly sucked into the warm embrace of the overpowering gravity of the sun. But in all these cases, the planet earth would not pop up in protest and announce, "I simply must be!" We do not know why the gravitational constant, or any other constant of Nature, must be what it is. Even these most fundamental relationships of Nature are, in the terminology of Maharal — accidents.

The *Mesivta D'Rakia,* populated by angels who are also created, non-essential beings, see things very differently. If they regard their own existence with any seriousness, which they must, they cannot see the *nega* as all that different. Where there is some question about the *nega,* the possibility of its "existence" cannot be discarded. Their vote, then, is to call it *tamei,* as a reasonable precaution.

Hashem bothers to listen to their choice in the same manner as we described above. He does not impose His viewpoint on the world, but takes into account the perspective of His creation, the recipients of His law.

✎§ Unique Can Mean G-dly

There was a dissenting voice. Rabbah bar Nachmani fully mastered two abstruse topics of halachah, *negaim* and *ohelos.* His accomplishment was singular, or unique, if you will. The quality of uniqueness grows from the idea of being one, and is derived from the Oneness of G-d. Rabbah took on a bit of the singular quality of his Creator. His existence, therefore, catapulted him to a higher plane. It became fuller, more real, more intense. Beholding the *safek nega,* he too saw but a phantom, a trivial trace of nothing. Casting his vote with G-d, he too called it *tahor.*

Postscript: Despite the tie-breaking ballot of Rabbah bar Nachmani, human halachah takes full advantage of this right that G-d grants us to deal with halachic material through our flawed axiology. Thus, *Rambam* [41] codifies the law according to the *Mesivta D'Rakia* — and the first opinion in our earthly Mishnah that holds the same — against that of *HaKadosh Baruch Hu!*

---

41. *Tumas Tzaraas* 2:9.

V. G-d's *Tefillin*

R' Avin bar R' Adda said in the name of R' Yitzchak, "From where [is it derived] that *HaKadosh Baruch Hu* puts on *tefillin*? For it is stated, 'Hashem has sworn by His right hand, and by the arm of His strength.'[42] 'By His right hand' — this is [a reference to] the Torah, for it is stated, 'From His right hand [He presented] the fiery Torah to them.'[43] 'And by the arm of His strength' — this is the *tefillin*, as it is said, 'Hashem will give strength to His nation.'[44]

"Those *tefillin* of the Master of the Universe, what is written in them? 'Who is like Your people, Israel, one nation in the land.' Is G-d, then, praised with the praises of Israel? Yes! [Indeed!]'"[45]

Why should G-d require *tefillin*?

The matters discussed here are wondrous and profound. We will expose but a finger's-breadth[46] and cover up what we can.

It is axiomatic that everything that Hashem summoned from nothingness exists to enhance His Honor. One of the seven *berachos* we say for a newlywed couple makes this explicit: ". . . that all was created for His Honor." This is echoed by a passage in *Ethics of the Fathers*, [47] "All that G-d created in His world He created only for His Honor."

While it is true, though, that all of G-d's handiwork is a reflection of Himself, and thus brings honor to Him, the eminence of G-d is not to be found equally in all of Creation. The thrust of this passage is to explain how we Jews bring honor to G-d in a different manner than any other people.

---

42. *Isaiah* 62:8.
43. *Deuteronomy* 33:2.
44. *Psalms* 29:11.
45. *Berachos* 6a.
46. An allusion to *Nedarim* 20b: exposing a handbreadth, and covering a hand-breadth.
47. 6:11.

To understand the idea behind G-d's "*tefillin*," we first need to understand their connection to similar items that are worn. Generally, these include two categories: clothing and ornaments.

⟨§ Two Functions of Clothing

The former is the larger and more common group. We wear clothes primarily because they protect us from the elements and from prying eyes. It is clear from our habits, though, that we expect far more from our wardrobes than protection.

Our clothes tell a story. They say something about us. They express our individuality. Most of us hope that they say something positive about us, something that makes us proud.

Another way of saying all of this is that clothing brings us honor. Honor is different from other characteristics that we possess, because it ceases to exist without other people. Without others around to take notice, we cannot be honored. We might have honorable traits and accomplishments, but we cannot be honored unless someone outside of ourselves takes note. Since clothes serve to get others to see us in a different light, since they help to externalize parts of our internal selves, they are inextricably bound up with the notion of honor.

It should not surprise us, then, that we often speak of the *levush* — the garb — of G-d. As mortal, limited human beings, we relate not so much to the inscrutable Essence of G-d, as to the Divine phenomena that teach us something about Him. These cause outsiders — us — to honor Him. So that which brings honor to G-d from external observers is appropriately called His *levush*. Thus we say about Hashem, "You *wear* glory and majesty."[48] This conceptual identity holds up in the negative sense as well, as applied to dishonor. "May they wrap themselves in their shame, as in a cloak."[49] Here, people's shame is described as a garment that causes others to take note of their degradation.

We put clothes upon our bodies, but they never become part of ourselves. We can switch them or abandon them at will. Honor, com-

---

48. *Psalms* 104:1.
49. Ibid. 109:29.

ing from external beings, should also be seen as not identical to our real selves. Both the tools that we use to gain honor, to attract the attention of others, as well as the honor itself, are extrinsic to our essential beings.

We quickly understand that the same is true of G-d's Honor. What is grasped by others, as well as the others themselves, are external to and separate from Hashem Himself.

Besides clothing, a second group of objects find their way upon our bodies. Ornaments and adornments afford us no protection, but speak eloquently about who we are. Like clothes, they are not "us," but something external we place upon ourselves.

Even in the marketing of our personalities, clothes and ornaments conjure up different associations. Clothing that is too tight discomfits us. We almost never wear a single item of clothing for long periods without taking it off. There are ornaments, however, that we keep on for years at a time. We sometimes place them so tightly upon ourselves that we must struggle to remove them. We bind ornaments tightly to ourselves, in dimensions of both space and time.

We are now ready to return to the image of G-d's *tefillin.* The Torah's word for *tefillin* is *totafos,* which means ornaments. (When the Mishnah[50] forbids women from wearing a *totefes* in the public domain on Shabbos,[51] the Gemara[52] takes it to mean an ornament that covers the head from ear to ear. *Ramban* concurs with this approach.[53])

We established before that everything that G-d created brings honor to Himself, and that honor is a commodity that is external to Him. In a sense, then, all Creation is His garb. Now we learn that G-d also dons ornaments called *tefillin,* symbolizing an honor that is much closer to Himself than the rest of Creation. Within these *tefillin* are references only to *Klal Yisrael.* While all His creatures, all nations, bring honor to the Creator, the Jewish people succeed in bringing that honor on a higher plane.

---

50. *Shabbos* 57b.

51. *Chazal* were concerned that the woman might forget herself and show the ornament to a friend while they continue walking in the public domain, in violation of the prohibition against transporting there.

52. *Shabbos* 57b.

53. *Exodus* 13:16.

❧ They are the World; We are the Children

While all things flow from G-d, only *Klal Yisrael* flows directly and immediately. All of creation is connected in some sense to Hashem. The contours of that connection reveal something about the Being with Whom it connects. But we, the Jewish people, are the ornaments, while the other nations are the clothing.

Our attachment is closer and more fundamental.[54] It is our nature and purpose to be the chief vehicle for exposing the true Essence of G-d to the world. When we are at our spiritual peak, we are a much better refraction of the Light of G-d. This is what we mean when we claim that *Klal Yisrael* are the children of G-d. It is in this sense as well that we claim[55] that the world was created for us. We have the greatest capacity to increase the honor of Heaven, which is what this world is all about.

We learn about every designer from his design; the work of art bears the signature of the artist, both literally and figuratively. It is no different with the Divine Artist. We are the piece of Creation that fits most closely and immediately with the Hand of the Artisan. All other pieces also reflect His wisdom and ability. But they are steps removed, fitting into nooks and crannies that connect to other pieces. Through the teaching and example of *Klal Yisrael,* they sense the purpose of Creation, and contribute to it. Our template is Hashem Himself; their template is — us!

When Moses asked Hashem, "Show me, please, your Honor,"[56] he wished to fully understand the meaning of this concept. G-d told Moses that He would allow him to see His back, but not His face. The Gemara[57] tells us that this "back" was none other than the knot of His *tefillin*! G-d told Moses that He would show him how *Klal Yisrael* was bound closely to Him. Moshe could see why *Klal Yisrael* dove tails with

---

54. A fuller appreciation of the idea of a more fundamental, or primary, connection with Hashem can be gained by revisiting the First Well, p. 10 and the Second Well pp. 42-43. See also Fifth Well, note 15.

55. *Tanna D'Vei Eliyahu,* Ch. 25 (commenting on Mishnah *Sanhedrin* 4:5, which does not specify the Jewish people alone.)

56. *Exodus* 33:18.

57. *Berachos* 7a.

the nature of G-d, and why we are the best vehicle to expose His Majesty. He was not allowed to see the *tefillin* themselves, to fully comprehend the inner workings of that Majesty.

‫⳥ The Two *Tefillin*

We do know this about *tefillin:* They come in sets of two. We give honor to Hashem in two distinct ways. Firstly, we share as a people a unique, essential oneness. Other nations bring separate individuals together in useful associations. The individuals remain separate and distinct beings, though. We are united and one by our nature, and a reflection of Hashem's Oneness.

The "design" of *Klal Yisrael,* then, points to the greatness of the Designer. We exist, though, in the real world, not just within the creative genius of the Designer. Implementing the design points to other qualities. G-d utilizes a host of strengths and abilities to bring *Klal Yisrael* into existence, and to maintain them through the turbulent meanderings of history. Indeed, all the forces of the physical world have been used — or overturned! — to accomplish this. So our survival calls attention to a second dimension of honor, that of His capability. Between the two aspects, Hashem shows Himself through us to be a capable Master, both in how He designs, and in the way He executes those designs.

These two aspects are the two *tefillin.* Design is a conceptual activity, and corresponds to G-d's head *tefillin.* The arm is a good symbol of strong and effective action. The arm *tefillin* represent His full capability in moving design into reality.

‫⳥ *Tefillin* Divided and United

The *tefillin* that we wear differ in their architecture. The head *tefillin* have four compartments; the arm *tefillin* join its contents in one larger chamber. They represent the execution of the plan, or coming into existence itself. Existence is unitary; it either is there, or it isn't. There is no way to subdivide it. The head *tefillin,* on the other hand, are linked to design, planning, and concept. These are all finely nuanced ideas and processes. They represent the *quality* of existence.

A single object may have many characteristics and qualities, often unrelated to each other. These qualities can be independent and discontinuous. Thus, the head *tefillin* have four sections, while the arm *tefillin* have but one.

Broadening our understanding of our own *tefillin* will help us understand those of G-d. Hashem chose us alone as the nation to which He would attach His Name. The *tefillin* proclaim that our greatest tribute is this attachment and connection. *Proverbs*[58] tells us that, "The crown of elders is grandchildren, and the glory of children is their parents." As children of Hashem, this is certainly the way we feel. We wear our Father's stature as a precious ornament, as our honor and pride. The contents of the *tefillin* underscore two specific aspects of G-d's greatness. The first section, the *Shema,* proclaims His Oneness. The third section revisits the Exodus, where the incredible power of Divine intervention became a commonplace. In other words, it points to the ability of G-d.

We bind these notions to ourselves, reminding ourselves of how we are honored by our closeness to G-d. The pleasure we feel, though, is somewhat vicarious. We know all too well from where the honor derives. We are ecstatic because of what He is, not because of what we have done. We therefore wrap the *tefillin* upon our bodies. They rest on us, not in us. We bind G-d's Majesty tightly, but recognize that the honor we feel is unlike any honor we achieved through our own effort. This honor is external, a supplemental honor, if you will.

≈§ The Geography of *Tefillin*

Because this honor is an external addition, we wear the *tefillin* outside our personal boundaries, just outside the margins. Two parts of our bodies can be seen as appropriate "end" points. The head is the highest part of our physical selves, and easily serves as a border with what is beyond. It is an appropriate place to host the head *tefillin.*

We use the arm as an extensor, pushing our reach to the limit. (The grasp of the hand might seem a more obvious symbol, but the hand

---

58. 17:6.

spends most of its time manipulating things close by. It is the arm that takes our grasp to distant places.) It, too, speaks of our limits. The *tefillin* sit upon the head and the arm, speaking of our crowning honor, but it is a prominence that comes from without.

We might suggest a variation on this as well. The word *rosh* — head — also connotes "beginning." The arm brings us to our furthest extremity, or to the "end." Wearing *tefillin* at our beginning and our end ties in all points between. We feel the honor of our attachment to G-d, our pleasure in what He is, with every part of our beings. We do not celebrate Him with our spiritual side alone, or comprehend Him with a detached intellect, or cling to Him solely with our emotions. The honor of G-d suffuses all parts of our existence, without exception.

✙§ Reciprocity of Honor

The verse in *Proverbs* claims that the honor is reciprocal. The father takes pride in his progeny. Our Heavenly Father takes pride in us, and therefore "wears" His analogue to *tefillin.* But how could this be? How could a perfect Being, perfect beyond our very conception of perfection, take pride in something that He Himself created, and that falls infinitely short of His greatness?

Let us return to the verse. Are descendants the only honor of the old? Are they even the chief source of honor? Does an obituary never list more than the number of surviving grandchildren? Surely every person crafts his own accomplishments! We must explain as we did before. The verse looks only to the tribute that comes from "remote" sources, besides the achievements that reside within. It points out, quite consistent with our experience, that beyond all that a person achieves, the accomplishments of his offspring often bring him intense satisfaction and honor. Again, we deal with an honor that comes from without, with a supplemental honor beyond that which is proprietary to the self.

So it is with Hashem. His *tefillin* say nothing of His real honor, but the honor that exists in a different arena, the honor that comes from outside. In that place, *Klal Yisrael* is the only thing to brag about.

✥ The Purpose of Creation

When all is said and done, we may have an answer at hand to a question that has long plagued many people. Why did G-d create the world altogether? Some have argued that Hashem created the world to make known His power and strength. Others propose that a perfect being will, by his nature, tend to share his good with others. I have difficulty with both approaches.

Chazal here suggest a third avenue to explore. The question simply does not begin. The world is appropriate in and of itself.

We would not question why Hashem happens to be wise, or power-ful, or able. We understand very little of what G-d is, but our tradition allows us to use certain ideas to conceive of Him.

We are comfortable calling Him "perfect," and we see certain at-tributes as essential parts of that perfection.

And so they are — literally! Certain attributes are part of Him ac-cording to His inscrutable Essence. There are reflections of G-d that are not of His Essence, but extensions, as it were, of Himself. As we said earlier, "honor" requires the contemplation of something exter-nal, of others outside of the honored being. When we try to imagine what G-d is (hard and inaccurate as this must always be), we quickly sense that several characteristics must be involved. He is powerful, wise, all-knowing, strong, compassionate, etc.

If we now try to imagine an arena in which there is even room[59] for something partially "outside" of Himself, then His perfection demands one more quality: honor! Imagine ways in which it is possible for Hashem to be perfect, and your expanded list will include the notion of honor. Seen in this way, we now expect G-d to evidence this quality. Indeed He does — by creating a world that hosts a *Klal Yisrael,* which brings honor to Him. We are the evidence not of one of His "internal,"

---

59. In an absolute sense, of course, there isn't. Nothing is outside of G-d. From a human standpoint, though, we sense a clear distinction between "Him" and "us." We are not G-d, do not think of ourselves as G-d, and only pay lip service to the notion that G-d is also within us, and animates every particle of the universe. How G-d can be both within everything and yet separate and detached as well is one of the thorniest issues in Jewish philosophy. The kabbalistic notion of *tzimtzum* tackles the problem head-on, but it is beyond the scope of this book!

essential characteristics, but of Himself turned outward. The possibility of the existence of this quality demands its reality. At our best, we sit, poised not within Him, but close by, clinging like a precious ornament. We are His *tefillin*.

Our world is not simply a nice place to live. It is not merely a cleverly constructed stage for the unfolding of some interesting human drama. The world is a suitable outgrowth of the perfection of G-d, at least when you look for the most exalted part of earthly existence. And that, of course, is the Jewish people in their perfection!

VI. Earthquakes and the Fuzziness of Creation

What are *zeva'os*? R' Ketina said, "An earthquake." R' Ketina was walking along the road. When he came to the door of the house of a bone necromancer, [the earth] shuddered and quaked. He said, "Does the necromancer know how such an earthquake comes to be?" He shouted out to him, "Ketina, Ketina, why should I not know? When *HaKadosh Baruch Hu* remembers His children, who endure in misery among the nations of the world, He sheds two tears into the Great Sea, and its sound is heard from one end of the world to the other, and that is [what we perceive as] an earthquake!"

R' Ketina himself said, "G-d claps His hands, as it says, 'I, too, will pound My hand upon My hand, and I will put My wrath to rest [and the earth shakes from the resulting sound].' "[60] R' Nassan said, "G-d emits a sigh, as it says, 'I will put My wrath to rest through [punishing] them and so I will find consolation [and the sigh causes the tremor].' "[61] And the Rabbanan said, "He kicks the firmament, as it says, 'He shouts *Hedad*, like those who trample the grapes at the wine-

---

60. *Ezekiel* 21:22.
61. Ibid. 5:13.

122   BE'ER HAGOLAH

press, to all the inhabitants of the land.' ''[62] R' Acha bar Yaakov said, "He pushes His feet under the Throne of Glory, as it says,[63] 'Thus said Hashem: The heaven is My throne and the earth is My footstool.' ''[64]

How upset our critics become when reading this passage! Its theme is blasphemous, they think. We should attribute only joy and contentment to a perfect G-d. Sadness is a sign of deficiency, a word that simply may never be used in relation to Hashem. Moreover, Hashem can certainly not display raw emotion. All knowledge and information is within Him; He learns nothing new. Therefore, nothing new can move Him, as emotions move us.

Besides the erroneous theology these lines seem to express, the entire premise appears to be faulty. How could the treatment of the Jews be the cause of earthquakes? What caused tremors before the birth of the Jewish people?

⮜ Science Answers "How," Not "Why"

Chazal, of course, are correct. Their concern is not with what we commonly call "Nature." Within natural law there is abundant discussion regarding the causes of earthquakes. Chazal understood that G-d authored all the laws of Nature, and that finding "natural" causes never really answers our questions. We can always ask why Hashem created His laws to operate the way they do![65]

"Blaming" Nature just begs the question. And it is patently un-Jewish. Secular savants satisfy themselves with scientific models and explanations, seeing no need to go beyond. We do not. In the Shacharis prayer we praise G-d Who "illuminates the world and those who dwell in it." All of us realize that a well-known orb called the sun provides the illumination. We look, however, well past the sun, and attribute all light to Hashem.

---

62. *Jeremiah* 25:30.

63. *Isaiah* 66:1.

64. *Berachos* 59a.

65. Maharal's reasoning here is also put to use in the Sixth Well, in "The Four Causes of Eclipses."

Our Sages specified a *berachah* for us to recite upon hearing thunder or experiencing an earthquake. Our critics don't contest this — it is the accompanying explanation they object to. But why should we praise Hashem, "Whose power and strength fill the world," for natural phenomena? Why not simply realize that He set up complex natural laws to create and maintain a world, and that certain phenomena are merely consequences and artifacts of some of those ancient rules? These rules may say something about His creativity, but little about His power! It is the power of Nature that we stand before.

Clearly, this is not our tradition. Our system of *berachos* is very old, dating back to *Anshei Knesses HaGedolah,* which included several prophets! We demand specific and individual *berachos* for a very great number of things, including thunder and earthquakes. We pronounce a *berachah* before every different food item we eat, recognizing each morsel as a Divine gift. We do not make do with praising Him for His wisdom in creating a food cycle and then thank Him for being on the right end of it! Clearly, our tradition sees Hashem as directly responsible for all phenomena, and senses that each one that impacts upon us teaches us something important about Him. We do not reject the importance of Nature. Neither do we attribute too much importance to it. Nature is the handmaiden of G-d, but we must always remember that it is He Who constantly empowers it. In moving from the various potentials of Nature to their concrete realization, we see the Power of G-d.

With this introduction in place, we are ready to analyze our passage at hand. With just a bit of effort, we could inventory all regular worldly occurrences, and rate them for their importance to us. Intuitively, we would have little problem making *berachos* for items on the list that we judged to be crucial to the running of the world as we know it. We recognize that we cannot be without wind.[66] We therefore have no

---

66. The real source of our drinking water is the ocean, that incredibly large store of water that does us little immediate good because of its saltiness. The sun's energy unleashed upon this reservoir frees up potentially potable water through evaporation. Vast quantities of purified water are sucked up from the ocean each day, hovering above as clouds until they can yield their precious cargo. Without wind, however, only the fish would benefit from rain! It takes winds to move the life-giving elixir onto land masses, where the water can rain down and collect in brooks and steams and rivers and springs and wells.

objection to reciting the *berachah* "Whose power and strength fill the world" when we feel a strong wind.

We have assured ourselves, however, of the active, purposeful involvement of Hashem in earthly phenomena, including those we are indifferent to or dislike, such as thunder and tremors. We accept that G-d engineers and orchestrates them, but we strive to understand why. What good do earthquakes ever do mankind? Couldn't Hashem have come up with a more reasonable[67] geology?

---

67. The ancients talked about *terra firma.* Today we realize that the ground we tread upon is anything but firm, at least in a geological sense. We know it to be a series of shifting plates that grumble and groan as they slide by, under and over each other. What good has ever come to Man because of this? What would we have lost had G-d created a world without the seething forces closer to the earth's core, a world minus the upheaval miles beneath the surface? Our Gemara's passage seeks the answer to this question.

The reader might object that earthquakes are a small part of what we would see as deficient in our vision of a perfect world. Maharal offered wind as an example of what we easily accept as a key component of our world. Further reflection makes us question this. None of us would object terribly to a gentle breeze on a hot summer day. Tell us that this same breeze will dump thousands of truckloads of water 50 miles away, and that some of it will percolate out of the water table weeks later, and we are doubly pleased. But who needs hurricanes and tornadoes?

Maharal seems to be at peace with all winds, even the destructive kinds. Likely, this is because we could not even hope for a world in which all phenomena occur precisely the way we would like them to. Such a world would point to the Hand of G-d so clearly that there would be no room for our free will. We would be so overcome by His pre-sence that we could never choose to escape Him. Nothing is more important in this world than allowing people to grow through the exercise of their free choice. There must be obstacles and hurdles. There must be ways for people to turn their backs, to hide from the immediacy of G-d, in order to credit us for making the right choices.

At one time in history, our free will operated on a different plane. Before the first sin, we did live in a perfect world, where all surrounding phenomena dovetailed with Man's desires and expectations. At that point, our wants were synchronous with His wants. Our sin changed all that, and we were quickly ushered out of the Garden of Eden.

In our present state, we have the best chance of achieving our goals when G-d makes it somewhat of a challenge to seek Him out. He makes things neither too hard, nor too easy, but we must choose to find Him, or at least choose not to ignore Him. He displays Himself through myriad clues dispersed through the natural world and through history. But He hides at the same time. He masks His presence, yielding enough free rein for the deliberate disbeliever to hang himself. He covers up His actions just enough to allow the stubborn to hatch alternative explanations for Divine phenomena.

✌ Multiple Laws of Nature

We may realize after a while that we live in a deficient existence, and that deficiency breeds more deficiency. Not, mind you, that G-d created an incomplete world, but that He turned over responsibility, of sorts, to Man for its smooth maintenance. When Man acts inefficiently or irresponsibly, he wears down the entire cosmos. The cogs of the great machine of Nature can only be greased by Man. When Man slacks off in his productivity, the machinery gets sluggish and worn. It may continue to operate, but without the elegance and efficiency that Hashem engineered into it.[68]

Perhaps this is the reason why the laws of Nature are not always so beautiful to behold, and why we sometimes contemplate the horrific

---

It comes as little surprise, then, that one of the most important rules of G-d's world is the random distribution of many elements of this existence, the bell-shaped curve that describes how much goes to how many. It leaves room to accept a cosmogony of randomness, at least to those who can doggedly hide from ultimate questions. Convince yourself not to ask about the ultimate origin of everything, and you still have a way to reject a Deity. Focus on smaller things, and ignore the bigger picture of design and complexity that is never appeased by half-truths about biogenesis — and you might still be able to live with yourself.

So we expect that the distribution of winds will include some that we do not like at all. There will be days of no motion of the air at all, of dead calm, when sailors will curse their existence. And there will have to be times in which the wind will strike with rage and fury. After we pick up the pieces, we understand that if there is to be wind at all, then these extremes in either direction need exist as well.

After all of this, we will still not understand earthquakes, which are not part of a larger phenomenon that is of any use to us in our present daily lives. Why didn't G-d simply do without them?

68. This is a frequently offered explanation for the Torah's description of the world of the Flood. Everything, including animals, "corrupted their way upon the earth" (*Genesis* 6:12). This does not mean, necessarily, that animals directly mimicked Man's perverted behavior. Rather, as Man fell into wholesale degradation, the laws that determine expected animal behavior became soft around the edges. Man's positive actions elevate the world; his misdeeds corrupt it. The relationship is linear. Every *aveirah* we do, every sin we commit takes its toll on the global mechanism Hashem set up that keeps the world going. We are the ones who fuel it, and the only currency with which we can pay for the fuel is *mitzvos*.

Animals exhibited behavior never seen before, not because they exercised free will or learned from observing Man. Instead, mankind simply did not maintain the world in the moral fashion that G-d expected. As a direct consequence, all laws of Nature showed signs of strain, and started sprouting leaks here and there.

aftermath of an earthquake. The earth is generally stable and unmoving. But if we live deficiently, the laws and forces that keep the world rigid and dependable also become deficient. If Man's output were constant and unchanging, Nature would produce fewer surprises. When our actions are found wanting, so are Nature's rules. Sometimes, we virtually pull the rug from underneath ourselves, and the earth moves.

This explanation is a good beginning. To understand our passage, we must refine it a bit more. It is not enough to say that our actions impact upon the rules of Nature. We need a better yardstick with which to measure the success or deficiency of Man's activities. In our tradition, we see a bigger picture than the sum total of human achievements and errors on a given day. While all *aveiros* leave their mark, the shortcomings of Mankind are not the best indicator of essential success or failure.

◈ This is the Way the World Ends. . .

History is not aimless. It leads somewhere. G-d set the stage for the drama of human civilization intending that one day the curtain would fall for the final time. Eventually, when all the work is done, the process of human striving comes to an end. The story ends on a happy note, as Mankind opens its eyes to the reality of Hashem, firmly plants itself on an elevated plane of moral and ethical accomplishment, and actualizes its potential for spiritual responsiveness.

History is goal-oriented. The point of human society is to achieve redemption by elevating all the latent *kedushah* of this world. G-d does not expect that this will happen by simply leaving people to seek Him out for a few millennia, and seeing what they come up with. G-d gave the world avenues of approach and tools to use. These guarantee that we will finally achieve the objectives that He wants.

Essential deficiency can really only be measured by how close or distant we are to the goal of Creation. Without being able to clearly see the finish line, we can only judge the progress of the race by seeing how well the runners are performing.

In this race, there is only one runner. *Klal Yisrael* is the most important tool in bringing the teaching of G-d to the rest of the world. Through the sterling quality of the lives of our forefathers, and because of their descendants' acceptance of the Torah, the timetable for redemption is in our hands. Without us, the world cannot be crafted into the place G-d intended it to be. With us, the process continues till completion. The redemption of the world is inextricably linked to the success *of Klal Yisrael* in leading a Torah life-style.

We now have an operational definition of crucial deficiency. If something should interfere with the process that is meant to wisk the world to its destination, then it can be said to be essentially lacking and deficient. This is precisely what happens when *Klal Yisrael* is stymied and impeded from producing *kedushah* at fullcapacity.

This, then, is the allegorical meaning of G-d's "crying." We cry when something that has meaning is negated. We can live with "ordinary" deficiencies. We grow accustomed to things falling short of expectation. At some point, though, a mechanism can fall so short of its planned function, that for all intents and purposes, it has broken. Functionally, it has been negated.

When Hashem takes note of the horrible treatment of *Klal Yisrael* at the hands of the nations of the world, He "cries." Besides the love He feels for His people, He notices a world of essential deficiency. When *Klal Yisrael* cannot operate efficiently, the world has effectively "died" for a while, and G-d mourns for it.[69]

---

69. In a long aside, Maharal justifies *Chazal* depicting G-d crying. They do not mean, of course, to be taken literally. They are part of a long tradition that deals with G-d according to the human ability to grasp Him, rather than according to His essence. The first *pasuk* of the *Aseres HaDibros,* says Maharal, yields up an enlightening *midrash (Pesikta D'Rav Kahana* 12:24).

R' Chiya bar Abba said, "G-d appeared to them in a manner appropriate to each and every affair and incident. At the Red Sea, He appeared to them as a mighty warrior waging war; at Sinai, He showed Himself as a scribe teaching Torah; in the days of Solomon — corresponding to their actions — He appeared choice and stately; in Daniel's times, He was perceived as an elder, studying."

Quite explicitly, *Chazal* tell us that Hashem can be described in many ways, depending on who does the observation. All the more so that G-d acts according to the preparation and readiness of the object of His actions.

One of the first narratives of the Bible itself demonstrates this principle. Upon considering the generation of the Flood, Hashem "had heartfelt sadness" (*Genesis* 6: 6). Now, G-d cannot actually become depressed. But depression, from our perspective, is an appropriate response to observing impending destruction. The citizens of this evil generation, slated for death, could not relate to the full glory of Hashem, or attach themselves to His Will. In other words, the display of G-dliness to them was a muted, subdued, remote, inaccessible, depressed one! The Torah speaks of G-d Who is saddened, but what it really means is the image and figure of G-d available to the

He shows this mourning through two tears. Two in this context means "as much as possible," since humans have two eyes, each one capable of shedding tears. The Egyptian magicians begrudgingly conceded that they recognized Hashem as the active force in the plague of lice. "It is a finger of G-d,"[70] they exclaimed. They saw the presence of G-d, but they could also imagine much more powerful plagues. The Torah terms this only a finger, much as an individual digit is only a part of the larger set. At a later point, how- ever, when Hashem's plagues came in full force, the Torah says, "Israel saw the great hand that Hashem inflicted.[71]" When Hashem displayed as much as humans could behold, when there was nothing else held back, the Torah uses the word hand. Because we can cry through two eyes, describing G-d as losing two tears is another way of saying that His mourning is complete, or that He relates to a world of maximum deficiency and loss.

ఌ Fragile — Handle with Care

Tears are a sign of loss. They also are active agents of further loss. When they well up in our eyes, tears cloud our sight. They cause us to lose our good vision.

Hashem's "tears" must also cause some sort of loss, not just react to loss and deficiency. What can this mean?

The answer is potentially frightening. In our experience, the most finely sculpted, delicately constructed things can stand the least stress and abuse. Coarser objects can withstand much more. We have few compunctions about throwing heavy objects at a punching bag, but we would not do the same to a Ming vase.

---

people of that time.

Indeed, how could it be otherwise? Do we imagine that G-d "appears" the same to lofty Heavenly beings as He does to us? Is it not intuitive that He can be seen differently by different people as well? Should not those who live closer to His expressed Will and wishes merit a different, fuller relationship with Him? Does this not imply that He relates in a less revealing and fulfilling — or more "depressed" — manner with those who flout His commandments?

After all is said, employing allegorical language to depict G-d's crying tells us something very important about His relationship with the world and with history. Rather than detract from G-d's honor, this passage greatly enhances it!

70. *Exodus* 8:15.

71. Ibid. 14: 31.

We usually stand in awe at the wonderful detail and fine complexity of G-d's Creation. We have now come, however, to the edge of a conceptual abyss. We have learned that the actions of Man — more specifically, those of *Klal Yisrael* — affect the efficiency of the rules of Nature. Furthermore, we now understand the mechanism for this. When G-d finds the world deficient, He changes the way He interacts with it; He restricts the availability of His Greatness to it. He gives to it in a less perfect manner. But a finely designed object like His Creation should tolerate no stress or strain at all! Diminish what G-d gives to the world, and we should expect its complete and utter collapse!

G-d's "tears" of negation should smash existence into oblivion. The ocean, though, receives them. Happily for us, this gives us a new lease on life.

The ocean, of course, is the collection of water that spans the globe. Water's properties are the polar opposite of the precisely engineered structure that we have been talking about. Liquids take the shape of their container. They show no obvious structure, but slosh about, changing orientation without much prodding. Water is an appropriate symbol of formlessness, of substance shaped randomly rather than purposefully.

ده Room for Nature to Breathe

If all of Nature were as finely structured as we sometimes think, any perturbation of the system would destroy it. The treatment of *Klal Yisrael* by the nations, constantly blocking our Divine mission, causes Hashem to change His relationship with the world. This jarring of the system could easily be its death knell.

In His infinite wisdom, G-d provided a buffer. The laws of Nature are not always as elegant as they could be.[72] They incorporate elements that are random and fluid. To be sure, we are astounded each day by the beauty and complexity of so much of the natural world. But we

72. This argument seems incredibly ahead of its time. So much of the science of Maharal's day assumed the utter perfection of the laws of Nature, as mirrors of G-d's perfection. Aristotle's universe described lots of neat spheres, all surrounding the earth at the center. While geocentricity fell after Copernicus, the idea of the world's innate perfection persisted. Galileo, who championed the heliocentric theory, nonetheless was sure that celestial bodies stayed in circular orbits. Circles, after all, are neater, more perfect figures than others. Even Kepler,

should also remember that water covers more than half of the world's surface! Much of our world rests contentedly in a rather chaotic state, with molecules moving about with much less organization than they would in solids. We find ourselves — quite literally! — perched upon islands of precise design that float upon oceans of looser construction.

The world survives because it is not as finely crafted as we might think. Many natural processes may not work as neatly as we would like, but the world endures because of it! The system of Nature can handle a push and a shove without collapsing altogether. The tears of G-d have a suitable place to "land." The ocean, symbol of all the randomness and free-play G-d left in the laws of Nature, "absorbs" the impact of G-d's changed Face to the world when He beholds its insufficiency.

≈§ Planned Inelegance

The unstructure of the world is the perfect match to the moral inelegance of the way Mankind comports itself. Part of that inelegance is our geology, which leaves us standing on something that more resembles toothpaste than the Rock of Gibraltar. There are cracks, and fissures, and sliding plates, and they sometimes produce earthquakes. Only a perfect world would eliminate them. A perfect world would require a perfect humankind to continue. Mercifully, Hashem provided for the realities of history when He created the world with a bit of leeway.

Even before G-d fashioned a people to carry His mission forward, Hashem had anticipated the reaction of other nations to the Jewish people. He knew that the world would often times operate deficiently.

---

who discovered that the orbits were really elliptical, nonetheless believed G-d incorporated some perfect geometrical principles into Creation. Sir Isaac Newton may have done more than anyone to help later generations reject the existence of G-d by providing the framework for a purely mechanical universe that continued on its own power, and that was entirely predictable in its behavior. Yet he, too, saw the need for some sort of perfection, writing that G-d occupies Himself with conserving the order He created against chaos.

Moral chaos, not the physical kind, was more important to Maharal. Man continues to sit at the center of the universe, by virtue of the impact his actions have on the quality of existence itself. Our spatial position in the physical universe is largely irrelevant.

So He wrote the planned inelegance of Nature into the rule books from the beginning of Creation. Earthquakes, then, did occur from time to time before we answered G-d's call.

Four opinions follow the necromancer's. They form a progression. All of them attribute G-d's reaction to His relationship with the world, and not to His essence, as we stressed before. Each opinion tries to underscore this, by referring G-d's action ever closer to the human scene, to the address of its recipient.

The necromancer portrayed Hashem's reaction in His "eyes." While we do not, G-d forbid, take physical depictions of Hashem literally, we understand that the meaning of symbols is consistent with typical usage of the words. Eyes are located in the head, atop the body. R' Ketina attempts to narrow the gap between G-d in this depiction, and the world that He relates to. He therefore moves Hashem's reaction to His "hands," the tools that translate into action the information that the eyes gather.

The Rabbanan push the action even closer to the earthly arena. They have G-d sigh. The focus has switched to the "heart," which meets the world's deficiency with a deep sigh. Finally, R' Acha bar Yaakov goes the rest of the distance, by switching to the "feet," or the nethermost part (and part closest to Man below) of G-d.

The earth, then, can absorb the "tears" of G-d, and has always been prepared to do so. That is not to say that they are not felt. Hashem's consternation with the negation of His plans has profound impact upon us. The earth is not shattered, but shock waves are produced that resonate from one end of the world to the other. Sometimes, the earth rumbles and shakes. G-d displays His great power, and we stand trans-figured. A *berachah* is in order. We have witnessed not an artifact of Nature, but a sensible and wise mechanism that allows the world's continuity.

VII. G-d's Daily Schedule and the Leviathan

> R' Yehuda said in the name of Rav, "The day is 12 hours [long]. The first three hours, Hashem sits and occupies Himself with Torah. The second [set of three], He sits and judges the entire world. If He sees that it is worthy of destruction, He arises from the Seat of Judgment and sits in the Seat of Mercy. [During] the third [set], Hashem sits and provides for the entire world, from the *karnei re'emim* [large animals] to the *beitzei kinim* [small animals]. [In] the fourth, G-d sits and sports with *Leviathan,* as it says,[73] 'This *Leviathan* You fashioned to sport within.' "[74]

The whole premise seems preposterous! Does G-d need to study Torah? Can G-d be reduced to "sporting" with *Leviathan*? This passage as well, however, will prove the profundity of *Chazal's* thought.

Chazal do battle here with a notion advanced by many non-Jewish philosophers. They see G-d as so exalted and aloof that He can have nothing to do with the petty events of this insignificant world. While G-d was responsible for Creation, any initial involvement with the world, they suppose, gave way to His withdrawing from and abandoning His earthly labor.

⋰ Torah is the Blueprint

We maintain, however, that G-d never abandoned His world. His Will is intimately and substantively bound up with it and with the creatures who dwell within. The first level of this association is conveyed in our passage by the image of Hashem studying Torah.

---

73. *Psalms* 104:26.
74. *Avodah Zarah* 36.

Torah is the order of all Creation. It describes how everything should operate. A well-known saying of *Chazal* tells us that Hashem looked into the Torah to create the world.[75] Another relates the first word of *Chumash*[76] to the *"reshis"*[77] of Torah, again asserting that it was with and through Torah itself that the world was fashioned into being. This means that it is the Torah's content that gives form and structure and proper conduct to all created phenomena.

We understand intuitively that the Torah describes how Man should act. Man is quite unexceptional in this. Torah shapes and molds the quality of man's actions because it does precisely the same for all things. This is part of what *Chazal* mean when they urge, "Turn it every which way, for all is in it."[78] The description is all incorporated within Torah, even if Man cannot always read the instructions seared in by its fiery truth. Man's limited comprehension obscures his vision. He can see the Torah addressing the revealed, obvious nature of things with revealed, open directives. Beyond the horizon of his gaze, he often fails to make out the contours of smaller characters. This elaborate script eloquently spells out entire tomes, which describe the inner, hidden dimensions of life.

In summary, Hashem's involvement with Torah translates into His Awareness of the progress and order of the world. It is a refutation of His having walked away from it. Hashem must be seen as connected to the conceptual nature of all things.

◄§ Patterns of Involvement

It does not end here. Hashem is described as spending the next segment of time in judgment of the world. This connotes a stronger sense of attachment to the world. Like a king who addresses his subjects, the judgment of G-d means that He relates to them as distinct creatures, not just to the master plan that stands behind them.

---

75. *Bereishis Rabbah* 1:1. See further in this essay.

76. *Bereshis* — usually understood in the sense of "In the beginning," or "In the beginning of G-d's creating of the heavens and earth."

77. In the manner of *Proverbs* 8:22, where the Torah itself is called "the beginning of His way." The sense of the first verse of *Chumash* would then be: "With Torah, Hashem created heavens and earth."

78. *Ethics of the Fathers* 5:26.

In the third quarter of the day of our passage, the relationship intensifies. As a Judge, G-d looks at His creatures from a position of detached objectivity. But now He is seen as Provider and Sustainer. He turns towards each individual; He approaches closely, and lovingly gives what is needed.

The fourth set of hours is spent "sporting" with, or "laying" with *Leviathan.* We play, or make merry, with something by engaging it fully.[79] For the moment, we focus our active attention on it, identifying with and attaching ourselves to that object or situation. Describing G-d as "playing" with something of this world is therefore an endorsement of a position diametrically opposed to that of the philosophers mentioned before. We understand Hashem's Will to be as connected to our world as could be imagined.

Another opinion shifts the agenda of the first two periods. Hashem is seen as judging in the first hours of the day, and studying Torah later. This opinion notes that the arbiter of justice must respond to issues, rather than people. He removes himself from people, and addresses principles. His actions towards the litigants are depersonalized. Studying Torah, the science that maps out the proper place and itinerary of everything, leaves room to consider people as unique individuals, all having their appropriate niche in the Grand Order of Things.

Both opinions share a common understanding. They both see a consistent development in the passage. Through its various images Hashem's involvement with the world is seen as growing and intensifying in quality. A passage in *Bereishis Rabbah*[80] adds more depth to our premise. The first time that the Torah uses both of the chief Names of G-d together — *Hashem Elokim* — comes only after G-d completes the work of Creation. "He attaches a Full Name to a full world." G-d cannot bind Himself to something incomplete. Because we understand Hashem as "renewing Creation each day" (as we say each morning in the *Shacharis* service), every day must be regarded as a new world, a new creation. Hashem cannot join Himself to it until it has had the chance to bear its potent fruit. This occurs only with the maturing of the day in its closing hours. Only then does *Leviathan,* the symbol of G-d's approval of and identification with the world, win Divine pleasure.

---

79. This is explained at greater length later in this piece. See page 139.
80. 13:3.

Noting the connection between Creation and our passage, we are ready for a variation on the above theme, a new approach that is really not that different. The four-part structuring of Hashem's day, we quickly realize, is a reenactment of Creation itself.

✑ Retracing the Steps of Creation

Creating anything viable requires steps of planning, execution, and maintenance. Each day, Hashem revisits the processes of Genesis upon an existing world that He once created *ex nihilo* — *yesh mei'ayin.*

Just as He "looked into the Torah and created the world,"[81] Hashem "begins" His day by studying Torah. Here, G-d looks to the blueprint, the game plan, the script. During the genesis of antiquity, the next step was the actual molding and forming the world from primordial nothingness. In the daily re-creation of the already extant world, God's judgment is the analogue. Hashem's original Creation brought forth a world consistent with the Architect's plans. His daily judgment maintains the consistency of the global machine. He keeps it in line with His expectation — pulling behind the scenes here, nudging there, prodding and tweaking. (Judgment is, after all, comparing reality with a desired standard. This is what G-d does each day, using the standard of His own Torah. It is also what a human judge does in the courtroom, comparing behavior with the norm that G-d mandated for us. This is why the Gemara maintains that "every judge who sits [even] a short while in judgment becomes a partner with G-d in Creation."[82])

In G-d's opening address to Adam, He informed him that "every herb ... every tree ... shall be yours for food."[83] Having designed and executed plans for the world, the next priority is *parnasah,* providing for its maintenance. The third set of hours in our passage parallels this step of Creation.

When the Torah gives its retrospective to the six days of Creation, it introduces a new element, as mentioned above. For the first time He is called *"Hashem" Elokim.* Creation does not draw to a close without

---

81. *Bereishis Rabbah* 1:1.

82. *Shabbos* 10a, with a slight difference in the text.

83. *Genesis* 1:29.

G-d confirming His approval; the day concludes with Hashem showing that His Will is satisfied with the world. Therefore, He "sports" with *Leviathan.*

⋴§ *Leviathan*

Why *Leviathan*? Examine the name for a moment. It is related to the expression, "For they shall be an attachment[84] of grace (*livyas chein*) to your head, and a chain around your neck."[85] *Leviathan* is no ordinary physical being, but a special entity that is appropriate to the fullness of Divine Will.

Don't think for a moment that the position has already been filled by Man, or by the *tzaddik,* Man's most perfect representative. It is quite true that Man is the choicest of all beings created by God. It does not follow at all that Man is the recipient of unrestrained Divine pleasure and Will. Man was put here with a mission. He fulfills his destiny only through effort and exertion. Were God to attach His Will to Man, the battle would be over! Man would have nothing to accomplish. Smothered by the beneficence of God's Will made manifest, Man would not need to struggle. Without struggle, there is no growth — and no need for human life! G-d does not generally lavish the signs of unstinting affection upon the *tzaddik.* His lot, says the Gemara,[86] is most often a good deal less than Divinely dished out peaches and cream. The typical *tzaddik* meets up with a hefty share of obstacles and disappointments. Hashem holds back many gifts available in His trove of available treasures. These are hardly the kinds of thing you would expect to find in a relationship of complete satisfaction and joy.

So we understand all too well that the full light of Hashem does not accompany Man in his journey through this world. Much of that light is obscured, withheld from him. The upshot of this, it would seem, is that nothing receives an unqualified display of Divine Will. If Man, the most deserving and precious, must continue without the benefit of its full impact, all other things must suffer the same fate.

---

84. Thus in *Rashi, Ibn Ezra, Metzudas Tziyon.*

85. *Proverbs* 1:9.

86. *Kiddushin* 39b.

This is not the tradition of *Chazal.*

HaKadosh Baruch Hu does find complete favor with aspects of this world. It can, theoretically, win over Hashem's perfect pleasure. This capacity was incorporated within the world from the time of Creation. In our lifetimes, we have not witnessed displays of complete Divine acceptance, where every possible good that we could conceive of occurred to all possible people at all possible times.[87] Yet the world can draw this kind of response, and not because of something that still needs to created. Hashem stocked His big pond with *Leviathan,* a part of Creation with such sublime promise, that it can take hold of a fuller measure of His Will. Hashem can attach Himself to it without holding back anything at all.

Despite all the obvious deficiencies of the moment, the world is a better place than we could ever imagine. As the day "matures," G-d's discerning glance can pick out the *Leviathan* factor from amongst everything else, and give the world a vote of confidence.

We should be much more at ease regarding our passage. The words "sport" and "play" and "delight" still make us uncomfortable. How can we use such banal, trivial terms in reference to Hashem?

⋅§ More Than Relaxation

We must recognize what stands behind these words. "Playing" and "sporting" really mean throwing ourselves fully into something that pleases us. Our worries and distractions evaporate. For a short time, we focus on something that shuts out weightier concerns,

---

87. Many of us sense why. Ironically, when things are too good for Man, they are less good. We have a very poor record managing the blessings Hashem bestows upon us. We quickly turn many blessings into curses through our greed and misuse. Others make us slothful and complacent. We hardly seem prepared to live with too much G-d-given good! Unfortunately, we do much better responding to adversity and hardship than we do to unrestrained plenty.

Livyasan may indicate that we need not accept our current state of affairs. Boundless pleasure in this world is not an impossibility. We fail to detect it because of our own shortcomings in utilitzing it, not because Hashem shortchanged the world. G-d created the world in a way that one day He would let out all stops! The bounty of physical pleasure He readied for us will be manifest. And we will share in it, without experiencing any of the ill effects that too much good have visited us with till now. This is the intent of the Gemara's (*Bava Basra* 74b) description of future *tzaddikim* dining on a sumptuous repast of *Livyasan.*

and pretend that we are part of a different reality. We bind all of our will to some diversion or form of entertainment, and submit to a different set of rules than those that often irritate us. These are rules that are easier to master than the bigger game of life.

This process need not have negative connotations. Again, at the core is nothing more than attaching our will to something or other. There is nothing negative about this. Imagine if we could truly "delight" or "sport" with *mitzvos* and acts of kindness!

◈§ The Uglier Side of *Sechok*

Practically, however, humans rarely engage in this process except in regard to the trivial. Anything serious seems to burden us and make us more concerned. We lose ourselves most easily to things that are immediately pleasurable, and whose "lightness" does not make too many demands upon us. We need to relax, not to intensify.

Often, our need to uncouple from rigor and stress leads us not only to things that are light, but even lightheaded. We lighten our load even further by throwing off some of the heavy shackles of propriety and moral discernment. We can understand why *Chazal* looked disapprovingly at *leitzanus* — at lightheadedness and mockery. We have a strong need to find something with which we can bind our wills without reservation. If we hit on the answer of sacrificing moral bounds and limits that are important to us, there is no telling where things will end. And because the process is so inviting, because we throw ourselves into it with ease, we can ironically take the jokes and merriment quite seriously! They can easily become more important to us than the humdrum reality we wish to escape.

Stripped of the negative aspects that our own hangups have imposed on the idea of *sechok*/playing, there is nothing at all unseemly in the term. In the days of *Mashiach,* we are told, "our mouths will be filled with *sechok.*"[88] Clearly, *sechok* must be something positive, not comtemptuous and immature.

The *sechok* of Hashem with *Livyasan* must be taken the same way. It is not, G-d forbid, disparaging of Hashem, but a laurel around the neck of the world. It is a more important place than we realize.

88. *Psalms* 126: 2.

VIII. G-d's Moment of Anger

It has been taught: "God is angered every day."[89] ... [And when is He angry?] A baraisa was taught in the name of R' Meir, "When the sun shines [in the morning] and all the kings of the East and West place their crowns on their heads and bow to the sun, *HaKadosh Baruch Hu* immediately becomes angry."[90]

Rambam[91] claims that the Torah attributes "burning anger" to Hashem only in regard to idolatry. There are many examples of this. "Then Hashem's anger will burn against you."[92] "What is the meaning of the heat of this anger?"[93] "Why, Hashem, does Your anger burn against Your people?"[94]

✦ Idolatry and Associates

There are also quite a few counter examples. "And Hashem's anger was inflamed against Moses"[95] when Moses balked at acting as G-d's representative to Pharaoh. "The wrath of Hashem flared up against them"[96] who participated in the rebellion against Moses. "My wrath shall blaze"[97] at those who take advantage of the widow and orphan.

What *Rambam* really meant was that Divine anger is linked only to idolatry and to offenses that are cut from the same cloth. Hashem's anger is inflamed by outrages that directly oppose His Honor. Idolatry,

---

89. *Psalms* 7:12
90. *Berachos* 7a.
91. *Moreh Nevuchim* 1:36.
92. *Deuteronomy* 7:4.
93. Ibid. 29:23.
94. *Exodus* 32:11.
95. Ibid 4:14.
96. *Numbers* 12:9.
97. *Exodus* 22: 23.

of course, frontally challenges His Honor, by replacing Him with other objects of devotion. There are many other (and some not so obvious) ways of directly opposing the Honor and Will of G-d.

Moses was reluctant, for a variety of reasons, to assume the role of Hashem's spokesman to Pharaoh. He didn't realize that Hashem willed this role completely, and his refusal set himself up in stark opposition to G-d! This caused Divine anger.

On the other hand, so did those who spoke negatively of Moses. Since he had become seasoned in the role of Hashem's representative to *Klal Yisrael,* those who challenged and opposed Moses were guilty of affronting G-d. He reacted with anger.

Greed, ego, cruelty, indifference can all contribute to oppression. Targeted, patterned oppression is different. An oppressor of only the weakest and most vulnerable shows that he is afraid of retribution from the strong, and only dares to take advantage of those who cannot protect themselves. He takes no risks. The possibility of intervention by G-d Himself does not disturb him in the slightest. Clearly, he rules out G-d as an active Force in human affairs. This also occasions Divine anger.

◄§ Bad Gods and Worse Gods

People here and there place their expectations, faith — even devotion — in many things. Most of these are silly and nonsensical. While they certainly deflect from the attention and focus the rest of us give to Hashem, they are not as pernicious as other forms of devotion. Shallow thought, superstition, and desperation will often lead some people to seek help and comfort from ridiculous and contemptible sources. They are little threat to the clear thinkers. And eventually, even shallow and fuzzy thinking can be cured through forceful, logical demonstration.

Ideological opposition to the notion of G-d is far more dangerous. Here is where the sun comes in. The Torah describes the sun as "ruling" over this world. It is not difficult to see why. If you view the world entirely as a natural, mechanical system, the sun easily is its most important element. We rise to it, and diminish our activity when it bids us farewell each evening. It bathes the coldest winter day with enough heat to maintain life, relative to the frigid recesses of the solar system where its rays do not reach at all. Photosynthesis takes simple building blocks and transforms them into the free lunch that nourishes all occupants of the food chain. Sunlight provides the energy.

When the sun was deified, it was not just because it has presence and power. Because it is responsible for so many of Nature's activities, it could be seen as an ultimate source, replacing the Ultimate Source. Standing at the apex of a complex system that provided for everything, the sun was as far as Man had to go. In time, the system over which it presided would be expected to yield the answers to all questions. Meanwhile, Man could live in a world of Nature, and focus on nothing higher than the sun.

The sun rules, indeed. It rules over Natural law, the world of *teva*. G-d rules over it, because He is above *teva*, and created it as His tool. Man is expected to remind himself that while the sun is king, it answers to the King of kings.

Man has a nasty habit of forgetting about what is above. He likes to think of himself as beholden to no one and no thing. Consciously and unconsciously, Man tends to exaggerate his importance.

⋞ Authority Can Point to G-d

Authority — even human authority — effectively counterbalances some of this tendency. Within civilized circles, the most strident libertarian is aware that he must live by certain rules and regulations, or face harsh consequences. This puts a bit of a damper on thinking of himself as a demi-god. He is aware of restrictions and limitations. Sobered by such fetters, he has a better chance of reminding himself where it all begins. He can pinch himself and remember that there is a *Ribono Shel Olam* Who created and maintains everything.

Temporal rules, then, are a useful string-around-the-finger, reminding us that there is something above. The human figures who control us can be a valuable link to the Authority that empowers them. We stand subservient to them, and they show themselves to be subservient to G-d. In turn, we get the message of Who is really in control.

What, though, if the rulers themselves reject that Authority? What if they serve the wrong being?

The effect depends on what they serve. It is bad enough if they busy their devotional side with vacuous nonsense. They have lost an opportunity, and their subjects will be worse off for it. They will not, necessarily, have mounted an effective assault on the Being of G-d.

What happens, however, if they build a ceiling over their heads, blocking out what is Above? What if their words and actions indicate to all that they have come to grips with the issue of ultimate authority, and that it lies in Natural law? Nothing else. No other applicants need apply. Man is bound, is indeed restricted, but the buck stops not at the gates of Heaven, but at the forces of Nature.

◄§ Serving in the Temple of Nature

This is a global tragedy, not individual silliness. Temporal rulers can keep large populations rooted in the world of *teva*, oblivious to the connection between *teva* and G-d Who empowers it. They do not need to actually prostrate themselves to the sun. All they need do is ignore the Place from which their own authority derives, and their constituents will get the message. The sun — and the natural order that is associated with it — becomes an idolatrous object. No priests, no temples, no ritualistic mumbo-jumbo need be associated with it. Human authority figures need simply disregard the Divine, need only to distance it from Man's consciousness. The masses will in time become sun-worshipers, in the sense that they will serve at the altar of Nature.

In a world of many options and many nations, it is inevitable that significant parts of the population will fail to respond to the notion of real Authority, of the Oneness of G-d. Whatever they fill in under "religious affiliation" is largely irrelevant. *Chazal* tell us here that these people live by a potent and pernicious form of idolatry. This variety is so ubiquitous that it guarantees a display of Divine anger each day.

We would like to believe that we are the perfect antidote to their provocations. After all, we remain tenaciously loyal to Hashem, admitting no distortion of His Oneness and no dilution of its consequences. Shouldn't this be enough to firmly enthrone G-d in His world?

✑ We Don't Live Here Any More

Alas, no. This "solution" ignores the profound secret of our success. We remain so close to G-d because He gave us an unusual gift. Hashem assigned us a special nature, propelling us above ordinary Nature.[98] Our history is saturated with transcendence; our collective *neshamah* senses that it goes beyond *teva*. We cannot join G-d with this world, because we are not really citizens of it in the first place! The Kingship of G-d still requires *this* world to recognize Him!

That job remains for the other nations. They are the ones to whom this lower world serves as home. They were given a wonderful gift, in the form of planet Earth. It comes with a layer of *teva* surrounding it. The Gift-Giver watches with dismay as the recipients never get to the contents, refusing to peel away the attractive wrapping. His anger is problematic for us all.

IX. Dancing with G-d in *Olam Haba*

> Ulla Biraah said in the name of R' Eliezer, "In the future *HaKadosh Baruch Hu* will make a circle of all the righteous, and He will sit among them [in the middle of their circle] in the Garden of Eden, and each and every one of them will point with his finger [towards Him], as it says,[99] 'He will say on that day, "Behold! This is our G-d; we hoped to Him and He saved us; this is Hashem to Whom we hoped, let us exult and be glad in His salvation." ' "[100]

---

98. See *Rashi* on *Genesis* 15:5. When Hashem tells Avraham that he is destined to have a son, He takes him "outside." *Rashi* tells us that Hashem took Avraham outside of the natural, predictive system in which he could not, in fact, have children, and lifted him (and his descendents) "above" it.

99. *Isaiah* 25:9.

100. *Taanis* 31a.

Our critics wag their fingers disapprovingly. How could the authors of this passage so profane the *kedushah* of *Olam Haba*? The World to Come has nothing in common with our limited, temporal world. It transcends the physical. Coarse human activity like dancing is entirely incompatible with the lofty plane of existence in *Olam Haba*.

As usual, they have missed the point. *Chazal* teach us here, in subtle allegory, about the great good that awaits *tzaddikim* in *Olam Haba*.

Let us examine the elements of this passage one by one, starting with the dance circle. Most of the time, we keep the bulk of our happiness close to the chest. Some of it may ooze out in the form of a smile, or an expression of satisfaction shared with a friend. Rarely does our jubilation take the form of shouting from the rooftops. Our joy remains muffled and muted. We don't express more than a fraction of our ecstasy.

✑§ Rejoicing Set Free

We have a hard time abandoning ourselves to happiness. We rarely exult about everything in general. Almost always, it is some particular that delights us for the while. One of the reasons is that we think too much. Our minds are trained to fill themselves with many issues at one time. They nag us with reminders of unhappiness that compete for our attention!

In the image of the dance circle you will find complete rejoicing. It is sometimes linked specifically with young girls,[101] and with good reason. Dancing is the joy within externalized, turned into action. The casual, worry-free lifestyle of the young girl knows of nothing to dampen her enthusiasm. When she dances, she actualizes the energy of the joy within, and turns an inner state into fluid motion.

The chief point of our passage is that the joy and happiness of *Olam Haba* is rich, unrestrained, and fully actualized. It cannot be depicted as an inner state, because inner happiness is repressed by too many reservations. The dance figure moves our understanding of *Gan Eden* to a different plane. We see *tzaddikim* whose happiness is not tentative but active. They point to Hashem with their fingers, identifying the reason their happiness is complete.

---

101. *Jeremiah* 31:3,12.

We can take this thinking further. Happiness is an inner state, and ultimately more a matter of the spirit than of the body. Contrary to the common assumption, we don't really achieve happiness with the physical aspects of ourselves. In fact, physicality actually impedes happiness. True happiness comes from a sense of completion and perfection. While the spirit can know of such things, the body cannot. The physical is never perfect, because it is always limited by dimensions of time and space. Therefore, it cannot know real happiness.

While alive, the *tzaddik* cannot experience full happiness. Although his spirit is firmly in control of the physical side to which it is wedded, his physical attributes always add drag to the spirit that would soar. His progress through the journey of life is always a bit sluggish.

Upon entering *Gan Eden,* the *tzaddik* can actualize the *simchah,* the joy that his *neshamah* has long grown towards. Since the *tzaddik* leaves his physical side at the door, his unencumbered *neshamah* is finally in a position to feel the completion of his rejoicing. Moreover, the physical part of him intervened throughout his lifetime between his *neshamah* and *HaKadosh Baruch Hu.* It shrouded Him, obscuring the *tzaddik's* view of the limitless and infinite. Now that the veils have parted, he can "point" clearly to G-d! His joy is magnified. The dance shows it to be complete. Each leap and pirouette shows him to be free of the coarse burden of his physical self.

The evil person, however, sits out the dancing. While the *neshamah* of the *rasha* may depart the body, the body never departs from his *neshamah.* Living a life in which the body so often prevailed over the needs of the *neshamah* takes a heavy toll. The *rasha* passes on to another existence, but he hobbles rather than flies. He is bent under the weight of an enduring physicality, a shriveling of his scope that is his perpetual burden.

✌§ Relating to All of It

There is a reason why the dance takes the form of a circle. A circle surrounds. It encompasses from all sides and directions. *Chazal* teach us here that the *tzaddik* in *Gan Eden* attaches himself to Hashem, as it were, in all His aspects. We might imagine that getting close to any "part" or aspect of Hashem is cause enough for infinite rejoicing. Perhaps coming close to Hashem is a group effort, with each individual relating to one facet of Hashem? Perhaps each *tzaddik* in his lifetime exposes a different manifestation of Hashem, and attaches himself to it alone?[102]

The circle is here to teach us otherwise. A circle is a path described by points all equidistant from one crucial, central point. It is that one all-important point that gives significance to all the others. The *tzaddik* in *Olam Haba* is a point on the circle. His being is completely animated by the Origin. Gone are all the factors that intervened between him and Hashem in his lifetime. Absent are all the issues that competed for his attention and devotion. He is now truly transcendent, tied to Hashem[103] by an eternal tether. Through it, he circumnavigates all the greatness of Hashem that a *neshamah* can know.

X. The Death of Sennacherib

R' Abahu said, "If the [following] were not [actually] written in Scripture, it would be impossible to say it! For it is written, 'On that day the Lord will shave with a hired razor — the king of Assyria — [his] head, and the hair on [his] legs; his beard, too shall also be destroyed.'[104]

"**H**aKadosh Baruch Hu came [and appeared] to him [Sennacherib] in the guise of an elderly man. He [G-d] said to him, 'When you go [back] to [your allies] the kings of the East and the West, whose sons you brought [to battle] and [caused] their deaths, what will you say to them?' He replied, 'I myself live in fear of this. What [then] shall I do?' 'Go,' He replied, 'and disguise yourself.' [Sennacherib then asked] 'How shall I disguise [myself]?' He [G-d] said to him, 'Go [and]

---

102. See the First Well (pp. 18-20), where Maharal describes the process of studying Torah in *this* world in just such terms.

103. *Michtav MeEliyahu*, vol. 4 p. 150 maintains that the points of the circle are connected not only to the origin, but to each other. The *tzaddik* can relate to the Whole of G-d by his association with the work of all other righteous people.

104. *Isaiah* 7:20.

bring scissors to me, and I will shave you.' 'From where should I bring [these scissors]?' 'Go into that house and bring them [to Me].' He went and found them.

"[But this is how he found them:] The ministering angels came [before Sennacherib arrived], and appeared to him in the guise of men. Now, [the angels] had been grinding palm kernels. 'Give me scissors,' said he [Sennacherib]. '[First] you must grind [for us] a measure of palm kernels,' they replied, 'and we will give them to you.' So he ground a measure of palm kernels, and they gave him the scissors.

"By the time he came [back], it had grown dark. 'Go and bring some fire,' said He [G-d, appearing as the elderly man]. [So] he went and brought a fire. While he was blowing on it [to increase its size] the flame caught hold of his beard. [In this way,] he shaved off the hair of his head and his beard [even though he had not initially planned to cut the latter]. They [the Sages] said: 'This is [the meaning] of that which is written, "His beard, too, shall also be destroyed.' "

"He [then] went [and] found a plank from Noah's ark. 'This', said he, 'must be the great god who saved Noah from the flood.' [He addressed the plank,] saying, 'If I go [to battle] and prevail, I will offer my two sons [as a sacrifice] before you.' [But] his sons overheard this, and they killed him, as it is written,[105] 'And it came to pass that he was worshiping in the house of his god Nisroch, that his sons Adarmelech and Sharezer smote him with the sword.' "[106]

Many readers are confounded by this story. First and foremost, describing G-d as shaving someone's beard is lamentable. Even if the evil Sennacherib deserved such a fate, the dirty work could certainly be done by another, and not by Hashem Himself! Besides the near-blasphemy, the point of the story is also problematic. Should nothing worse befall Sennacherib than a trip to the barber?

❧ The Lone Survivor

When we analyze this passage, we will understand that it really deals with the equity of Hashem's justice. Along the way, we will find solutions to other problems associated with this text. Why, for

---

105. *II Kings* 19:37.
106. *Sanhedrin* 95b.

instance, was Sennacherib among the literal handful of people[107] spared from the miraculous destruction of his huge armed force? We understand why Nebuchadnezzar and his general Nebuzaradan survived. Both figured prominently in important events that were foretold by Jewish prophets. Sennacherib, however, had exhausted his usefulness. No longer would he serve as Hashem's tool. He would be quickly killed by his sons. Why did he seem to cheat the Angel of Death, walking away from one of the greatest military debacles of all times, only to die a short while later?

Our passage provides the missing pieces of the puzzle. Sennacherib had to be humbled and ridiculed before he died. He had surpassed the transgression of other sinners in his scorning and mocking of G-d. He authored the infamous boast, "Which among all the gods of the lands saved their land from my hand, that Hashem should save Jerusalem from my hand?"[108]

Sennacherib did not deserve to die together with his troops. Divine justice demanded that he pay for his arrogance before being allowed to exit from this world. For this reason his two sons survived the battle with him. His ultimate disgrace was that he was killed by his own flesh and blood. This is the meaning of the passage in brief. The rest are details.

Walking away from the carnage caused by the angel on the battlefield-that-wasn't, Sennacherib quickly realized that his survival could be short-lived. What could he possibly tell his military allies, who had committed huge forces to what had seemed a certain victory? How would he explain the loss of the entire army?

⇝ The Fugitive

Sennacherib had no choice but to go into hiding. The man who had enjoyed the adulation and worship of an empire had to disavow his own rank and station. All his honor and respect evaporated in an instant. Actually, they didn't quite vanish in a moment. He had to make them disappear by actually running from them. This is the meaning of the "shave." A bearded man who doesn't want to be recognized

---

107. *Sanhedrin* loc.cit., following the opinion of R' Yochanan.

108. *Isaiah* 36:20.

will change his appearance by shaving. Sennacherib's abdication of the throne, his fleeing from his previous role, was the equivalent of shaving. Sennacherib suffered far more than a quick death among his devoted soldiers. He lived for a while with nowhere to turn, denying himself everything that he had taken for granted for so many years. His world lay in ruins, and he was forced to roam the territory as a haggard shell of his previous existence.

All of this is telescoped by the *Navi* in the image of the "hired razor." *Chazal* simply took the imagery of the verse, and fleshed it out further. The razor is "hired" because Sennacherib was forced to act with desperate speed, much as someone who cannot wait until he returns home will seek out a razor to rent. His hair is cut from head to toe, emphasizing the enormity of the loss in his mind: He had been stripped of the vanguard of his supporters, down to the last man.

The *pasuk* continues: "his beard, too, shall also be destroyed." We labor to make our faces attractive and presentable, more than any other part of our bodies. People recognize and react to us chiefly through the "face we show the world." The beard, therefore, always took on special importance in male grooming. Cutting away Sennacherib's beard indicates his complete and utter disgrace. Sennacherib did not even enjoy the luxury of brooding over his fate in privacy. He could not simply drop out and disappear, hermit-like, prisoner to his memories and his misery. Try as he did, he could not escape the intrusion of others. Wherever he turned he was met with derision and scorn.

ᴥᴥ Held Like a Puppet

HaKadosh Baruch Hu appears to him as an old man. The latter is symbolic of the hoary sage, or human wisdom. Sennacherib believed that he had studied all the options, and that good sense dictated that he had to disguise himself. In fact, Hashem was the source of Sennacherib's strategy. Sennacherib had far less control over his choices than he thought. His circumstances had been meticulously engineered by Hashem to offer him only one solution.

His game plan demanded that Sennacherib act with desperate haste. His attempts at escape were difficult to execute. For this reason he is described as having to grind palm kernels, something accomplished only in laborious drudgery. G-d heaped shame upon shame upon him.

This is the darkness mentioned in the passage. The absolute darkness, the reaching of the nadir of his depressing experience, caused him to seek a way out — the "fire" to light a path before him. This path, this "fire," though, resulted in his "haircut" — the removing of all traces of his previous honor, and the destruction of any vestigial sense of self-worth. The pride of Sennacherib had not only been brought low, it had been obliterated, causing him far more well-deserved anguish than a quick death on the battlefield.

‏‎ The Delusion of Specialness

Did Sennacherib recognize the Hand of G-d in all this? Did he realize that Hashem was punishing him measure for measure for his pride and arrogance? Not at all. Searching for an explanation for his predicament, he found it in Noah's ark. Look at the similarities, he said to himself. Noah alone survived a catastrophe visited from Above. So did he, even if he was suffering. There had to be some significance to his surviving, while everyone else had perished. It only remained for him to uncover the secret of their shared "success."

Sennacherib saw it in the ark itself. Surely the exact measurements of the ark held the answer. They must have invested the ark with special properties, compliments of some deity or other, that allowed the vessel to weather the storm. If he, Sennacherib, also survived, then most likely he had been spared by the same force, the same deity. If he hadn't ridden out the storm in the comfort of a cabin, he had at least been thrown a life-preserver. He had found a plank of the ark!

Alas, the gods were a demanding bunch, according to the ancient idolaters. If Sennacherib had been rescued by some sponsoring deity, that god now could claim him as his own. Sennacherib owed him his life — and the loan could be recalled at any time.

Sennacherib decided to pay back the debt. Nothing comes closer to us in our personal orbits than our children. To many people, children are extensions of themselves. Sennacherib had to sacrifice himself to his protector-god. He reasoned, as did many in the pagan world, that children made convenient substitutes. Offering them would be seen by the gods as the ultimate sacrifice, tantamount to offering oneself.

✺§ Completing the Circle

It seemed like the right thing to do. (The ancient idolaters didn't get finicky over the murder issue. It took our Torah to demonstrate to the world that G-d detests bloodshed, and would never be pleased by human sacrifice. When Man would feel the need to offer something to Him, Hashem would only accept tribute by way of property over which the giver had full legal control.)

Unfortunately for Sennacherib, his thinking was predictable. His sons read the desperate mind of their father, and anticipated his plan of action. It met with something less than enthusiasm on their part. Not sharing his religious zeal, they killed him before he could do the same to them.

The story is complete, and with it we have a fuller appreciation of how Divine Justice suitably dealt with Sennacherib. The short life he led after surviving his great defeat was no great gift. Everything he had cherished was taken away from him — including his sense of self-worth — and replaced with humiliation and derision. He lived as a fugitive — from others, and from his previous self. Unlike so many others, he did not succeed in turning failure into triumph. He could have acknowledged the Hand of G-d in his defeat, and perhaps turned around his life. Instead, he attempted to give meaning to his ordeal by hiding from the truth, and paying homage at the altar of a new god. He had not known this god of Noah, but he discovered him in the temple of his own desperation. Surely this god had saved him, and he must now offer himself up to him. He would kill his own sons, if he had to, rather than admit to the presence of the real Hand that had touched him. His pigheaded denial cost him his life. Sennacherib the Proud ironically stayed involved in guiding his destiny — even causing his own demise, failing to recognize to the very end the real Force that led him.

XI. Man's Blessing to G-d

R' Yishmael ben Elisha said, "One time I entered inside [the Holy of Holies] to burn incense, and saw *Achteriel Kah, Hashem Tzevakos,* seated upon a high and lofty throne. He said to me, 'Yishmael, My son, give Me a *berachah*!' I replied, 'May it be Your Will that Your mercy conquer Your anger, and Your mercy overcome Your [sterner] attributes, and that You behave toward Your children with the attribute of mercy, and that for their sake You go beyond the boundary of judgment.' He nodded to me with His head." And [R' Yishmael comes to] inform us that the blessing given by an ordinary person should not be unimportant in your eyes.[109]

The skeptics are astounded by this depiction! How can a common mortal give a *berachah* to Hashem, when it is from His *berachah* that everything is blessed?

We explained earlier[110] that deficient human beings cannot relate to the full Honor of Hashem, but only to a limited refraction of it. This passage is no different. G-d did not, and could not, seek from R' Yishmael a *berachah* to His essential Self. Rather, He indicated that He would like to relate to His creatures in a *berachah*-like manner, opening up more of His fullness to them.

ᴇᴈ Anatomy of a *Berachah*

First we must explain what *berachah* is. Simply defined, *berachah* is enrichment, enhancement, providing beyond the necessary and expected measure. It does not mean filling a need, but adding on in excess of what is needed, or what is usually appropriate.

---

109. *Berachos* 7a.
110. See above, p. 115.

HaKadosh Baruch Hu set up "rules" governing His relationship with the world. While His ultimate nature is inscrutable to human beings, His behavior is predictable to some extent. His actions are neither arbitrary nor haphazard. G-d arranged that different "parts" of Himself are shown to the world in discrete measure, according to our needs, our readiness, and our behavior. Loosely, we refer to this system as the *middos,* or observable characteristics of Hashem. Displays of compassion, of strength, of healing, of generosity — all manifestations of His inner Self — are part of a complex system that He created to insure the continuity of the world, and its progress towards the goals of history. There is a formula that governs just "how much"[111] of the different characteristics of Hashem we will get to see, depending on many variables.

If *berachah* is going beyond the ordinary, if it is ignoring the limits, then so it is with Hashem Himself. *Berachah* to Him means that He adds on to the portion that His own standards and rules allocate. *Berachah* to G-d means adding to the *middos*! Nothing can add to the perfection of G-d, of course. He can, though, choose an alternate formula of relating to the world, in which differing "amounts" are assigned to each of the *middos.*

R' Yishmael did not contribute anything new to Hashem. Rephrased, what he really said is the following. "You, Hashem, in your infinite Wisdom, have different ways of relating to the world. They are all just and fair and appropriate. In one of these ways, You show Your attribute of *rachamim,* of compassion, beyond the conventional. You exceed Your own self-imposed bounds and limits. May it be Your Will that You should always choose this enhanced mode of dealing with your creatures." R' Yishmael was not giving something, so much as asking for something!

Why, you may ask, was R' Yishmael called upon to make this request? Why would G-d need him? If He wills it, it is! If He decides to conduct Himself towards us in an enriched manner, what is going to prevent Him?

---

111. It is no coincidence that *middah* - the word for characteristic - is also the word for measure and quantity. We see the different "personalities" of G-d according to how "much" of Himself He reveals to us at the moment.

·ᜫ Berachah and Tefillah

We can answer this if we pursue the notion of *berachah* to the next level of meaning. *Berachah* and prayer are opposites, in a way. *Berachah* is always conveyed by another. Abraham gave a *berachah* to Isaac; Isaac gave one to Jacob. Nowhere do we find a *berachah* that someone gave to himself.

The opposite is true of *tefillah*. The most effective prayer is offered by the petitioner himself. The Midrash says, "The prayer of the sick person for himself is better than anyone else's prayer for him."[112]

Our treatment of *berachah* above is the first step in understanding the reciprocal relationship between *tefillah* and *berachah*. When we *daven*, when we ask Hashem for things, we are conscious of our deficiency and vulnerability. We ask Him to give us what we *need*. Focusing on Him, understanding that only He can grant our request, is the most important element of prayer. There are only two elements that figure in our prayer: us, and Him. Even when we *daven* for a third party, we chiefly focus on these two elements. It is as if we were saying, "Hashem, healing *Ploni Almoni* is important to me. I could turn to many sources for help. I realize, however, that all of those are just your surrogates. Their success depends entirely on Your Will. I therefore turn to You as the only address that I can approach that has the wherewithal to deliver." *Recognition* of Hashem as Giver and Provider stands behind successful *tefillah*.

This is not the language of *berachah*. *Berachah* is not need-fulfillment, but the act of reaching out beyond. If *tefillah* is predicated on understanding the all-encompassing, general importance of Hashem in everything, then *berachah* stands on relating to a particular subtlety about Him. Not only does He provide generously, but He sometimes exceeds His own prescribed generosity. *Berachah* is not the cake, but the icing on it.

It is a truism that we deserve a special dose of some characteristic of Hashem only when we can utilize it properly. It will only do us real good if we can acknowledge where it came from, thank Him for it, learn something about Him from it, and use it according to the

---

112. *Bereshis Rabbah* 53:14.

conditions we sense are attached to it. In other words, a special revelation of G-d is justified only when we are mentally and spiritually prepared for it.

◄§ The *Berachah* of the Commoner

If a *berachah* from Hashem implies that He exceeds His self-imposed rules, we need to be in a framework of "going beyond" to take it all in. This is why *berachah* always comes from another party. We understand Hashem when we imitate His ways. In every *berachah* from a human being, a giver attempts to reach out beyond himself to the intended recipient. When we receive a human *berachah,* we become more aware of the notion of going beyond. It does not even matter so much just who is reaching beyond his own ego. This is why *Chazal* urge us to take seriously the *berachah* of even a simple, common person. The efficacy of his *berachah* is not fixed by his merit, but by his reaching out beyond himself. When we offer *berachos* to each other, we ready ourselves for G-d's going beyond Himself. We merit *berachah* by entering the motif of reaching out!

Hashem's *berachah* is facilitated by human beings for another reason as well. We can make a contribution to the process of *berachah* even in a passive manner. By our own nature, we "invite" Hashem's *berachah.* All of us are, after all, excellent examples of Divine *berachah.* Creation itself was an act of Hashem going "beyond" what preceded it. Our existence is the extension of Hashem beyond His infinite Self into the realm of our spatial and temporal world. Our entire existence addresses G-d's *berachah* mode, and invites more of it.

Seen in this way, G-d asked of R' Yishmael to dwell on the specialness of *berachah.* He wanted R' Yishmael to grasp the distinction between *tefillah* and *berachah.* Hashem challenged him with a riddle: Give a *berachah* to the Source of all *berachah.* R' Yishmael responded perfectly. *Berachah* to Hashem can only be an enhancing of the power of His *middos,* of going beyond the letter of His own law. As the delegated agent of *Klal Yisrael* in the Holy of Holies on Yom Kippur, R' Yishmael grasped the essence of *berachah,* and laid claim to more of it in the coming year.

◄ঙ Names of Significance

The Names of Hashem in this passage are significant. Taken together, they describe a panoply of characteristics of G-d. The *aleph* in *Achteriel Kah* tells of Hashem as First. He precedes everything, including time. He is the beginning of everything. The next few letters[113] form *keser,* or crown. The crown on the head of a king indicates his lofty position, or how distant he is from his subjects. Hashem's crown reminds us that no matter how close He acts to us, His ultimate Being transcends all of us and all we can imagine. The word *el,* or power (and by extension, god), follows. G-d's crown is no ordinary sign of dominion. He is not King of kings because the rest agreed to be ruled by Him. His kingship is Divine, of a different and supernal nature.

The words *"Kah"* and *"Tzevakos"* add two more dimensions. Traditionally, Hashem employed this Name to create the world, utilizing its component letter *yud* to create *Olam Haba,* and its letter *hei* to form our familiar world.[114] This name, therefore, adds G-d's role as Creator of the Universe. It is followed by the Name of four letters, which expresses the notion of existence, in the past, present, and future. Once created, all things require the Will of G-d to empower their continued existence. Finally, *Tzevakos,* or hosts, points to the innumerable tributaries of Creation, the idea that G-d vested powers of growth and reproduction in this world, and did not leave it static. Taken together, these Names are a summary of the pathways through which the Absolute *Aleph,* the inscrutable, undifferentiated Oneness of G-d, takes different forms until it expresses Itself in myriad concrete manifestations in the physical world.

One day a year, and then only shrouded in a cloud of burning incense, *the Kohen Gadol* is allowed entry into the Holy of Holies. As the agent *of Klal Yisrael,* his welcome into Hashem's holiest place on earth indicates that the source of the Jewish soul is in the most profound, inner place within Hashem. R' Yishmael, performing the *avodah* that Yom Kippur, achieved a prophetic vision. Hashem revealed Himself to him, at least through the attributes of the long Name we just discussed.

---

113. כתר.

114. *Menachos* 29b.

R' Yishmael realized that one aspect of G-d was apparently missing. Hashem revealed Himself for the way He typically is, but showed him nothing of His ability to go *beyond* His own imposed limits, of adding to His usual *middos.* He therefore understood the challenge Hashem gave him. *HaKadosh Baruch Hu* was about to seal the fate of the world for the coming year. In his vision, R' Yishmael sensed the presence of G-d and how He interacted with the world. He did not sense, however, that Hashem was exceeding His *middos.* He did not feel that Hashem was prepared to flood the world with the overflow of His attributes. G-d was with the world, but not with as much *berachah* as he would have liked.

It is a tall order to change the Mind of G-d, as it were, and to do so globally. R' Yishmael was emboldened by the realization that, ironically, we have more power to attract Hashem's *berachah* than we realize. After all, we are all embodiments of Divine *berachah:* We are the "something other" that Hashem reached out to. We are the most important manifestation of Hashem's *berachah,* and He is disposed to continue the process of *berachah* towards us.

⋖§ The *Aleph-beis* of Creation

R' Yishmael understood that the Torah begins with the letter *beis* for this reason. The Ten Commandments, by way of contrast, begin with the letter *aleph,* the first letter of the alphabet. *Aleph* can mean "one," which is a number appropriate to this most important legal part of the Torah. The law is monolithic. It does not change from person to person, and disregards different needs and backgrounds. The law is blind to everything but its own logic.

Creation, though, is not served well by the number one. Hashem wants to shower the world with abundance and bounty. The number "two" stands almost in opposition to the simplicity of "one." The letter *beis* offers a brilliant introduction to the story of Creation. It conjures up associations with words like "plurality," "more," and "extra," reminding us of how Hashem would like to relate to us, if only we would allow Him to.

Happily for R' Yishmael's generation, Hashem was prepared to give the *berachah.* He only wanted to be asked.

In the final analysis, we have a trump card to play in calling down Hashem's *berachah.* When we ourselves act in the *berachah* mode — when we reach out to the other — we invite reciprocation from G-d. The blessing of the commoner should never be taken lightly, because wherever it is offered, His own *berachah* follows behind.

XII. G-d the Matchmaker

From the six days of Creation and on, what does *Ha-Kadosh Baruch Hu* do? He makes matches: The daughter of such-and-such should marry so-and-so . . .[115]

People find it strange that we should envision Hashem occupying Himself with matchmaking since the time of Creation. Upon reflection, however, we find that the statement is not only appealing, but its logic is compelling.

Chazal do not contest, of course, that Hashem is responsible for all phenomena. They understood that He graced the world with such Wisdom, that all the wonder of life that we observe is just a *continuation* of the work of the days of Creation. "The world continues on its customary path,"[116] they tell us. Even the birth of new individuals is not truly new, but part of a process that Hashem designed into the fabric of the world order. We do not see any new creation, so much as the playing out of an old but beautiful script.

✑ True Creativity

Marriage is the exception. In it we come closest to seeing Hashem as Creator. In pairing each couple, G-d forges a bond between two unique individuals, creating a perfect match that would not work with anyone else. Every match is different and special — a new creation. Hashem cannot simply dip into a reservoir of available choices, and scoop one out for the next available single. Each marriage is, as it were, hand-crafted.

---

115. *Bereishis Rabbah* 68:4.
116. *Avodah Zarah* 54b.

The Hebrew words for "man" and "woman" point to the Divine role in arranging marriages. Sandwiched within the words *ish* and *isha* are the letters *yud* and *hei,* which together form a Name of G-d.[117] Marriage is not a "natural" phenomenon, in the sense that the right people will gravitate towards each other and build successful relationships. Hashem's creative intervention joins together what Man's nature has left asunder.

This is what *Chazal* really mean when they observe that making matches is as difficult as splitting the Red Sea.[118] By its nature, water flows together. To split it, Hashem had to subvert water's customary manner, and cause the sea to rigidly divide and separate, and assume the posture of granite cliffs. Marriage is the other side of the coin. Every unique personality resists being lumped together with others. Each person's individuality tends to keep him somewhat separated from every other person. Only Hashem can overcome this "natural" resistance to pairing and bonding, and form the amalgam of husband and wife.

We can pursue this more deeply. A deep fissure seems to separate Hashem's role in the world of Creation with that of the post-Creation world. During Creation, Hashem relied upon no messengers. His direct, unmediated Will brought all things into existence.

The post-Creation world contrasts sharply. Many events are now predictable. To a certain extent, the job of maintaining many of the diverse elements of our world has been delegated away. It was assigned to a system of natural Law that He established precisely for this purpose. The intervention of His "direct" Will is not something that we observe in abundance. G-d seems, as it were, to have moved to the back seat.

In fact, though, His role in the post-Creation world really upgrades the quality of His involvement. The visible consequence of Creation seems to be a world of multiple forms and options, rather than singular instances. Difference and disparity seem abundant. The pendulum now swings in the opposite direction. Hashem takes charge of uniting the hodge-podge diversity around us.

---

117. *Sotah* 17a. As *Maharal* himself cited above, it was with this Name that G-d originally created the world.

118. *Sotah* 2a.

To a large extent, the greater occupation of Man is to unite this world. While much apparent *disunity* seems to stare us in the face, we proclaim — in word, and through our faithful obedience to Hashem — that behind the facade we recognize the absolute Oneness of Hashem. By obeying His laws, we reunite all things, all elements of this world that we touch. Everything in the macrocosm of the universe and the microcosm of Man's inner life is touched by the word of Torah. By heeding it, we bring all of variegated Creation back home to the Source, reclaiming every nook and cranny of existence for the One Who created them.

◄§ We Can't Do It All

But we can go only so far. Man cannot bring all things together, because he himself is not together. The most profound part of himself is lacking and lonely. He is not one — at least not until he finds his life's companion, the lost side of himself.

Man, in the course of history, unites all of the world, but cannot unite himself. His hopeless inability reminds him that he is far less of a "partner" to Hashem than he might imagine himself to be. He is no demi-god. He is but a tool of Hashem's Will and plan. It takes Hashem to help him along in his work. Man is the single most important tool in piecing all of the bits of the puzzle together. But the tool doesn't work without G-d putting it together.

In doing so, Hashem Himself completes the job of uniting the world.

We now see the Gemara's question in a new light. It did not question the role of Hashem in our world. All of the activity around us is traceable to the Will and design of G-d. Moreover, there is no shortage of intervention by G-d against the natural law He authored! All of our prayers ask for Hashem to intervene against the "expected" flow of events! Yet all such interventions are really just continuations of the state of affairs that Hashem left in place at the end of Creation. The Gemara questions what fundamentally *new* activity Hashem involves Himself with. Once we understand the real meaning of the Gemara's answer, we appreciate its elegance. Hashem's post-Creation occupation is indeed an exalted one — moving beyond Man's inability — to confer the final forms of oneness upon a waiting world.

THE FIFTH WELL

Taming

the

Extreme

The challenge: The Sages at times write about utter fantasy, about events and objects that have no basis in reality.

The response:

Introduction: Open Debate and Closed Wisdom

Our critics should have realized that there are tools readily available to help make sense out of passages that seem remote and incomprehensible. Works such as the *Zohar* and the *Bahir*,[1] although not so well known to the masses, are cherished and valued by the wise. They are invaluable aids to further explicate the Torah's secrets that the Sages merely hint at.

◄§ How to Conduct a Debate

Just as love often causes you to overlook deficiencies, hatred can make you discover imagined faults, and summarily dismiss other viewpoints. This is a consequence of a jaundiced eye and a warped mind. Even the great secular philosopher wrote[2] about how inappropriate it is to contemptuously dismiss the position of your opponent in order to shore up your own position. The truth is the best defense against the barbs and criticism of your enemies. Producing clear evidence is the necessary and sufficient refutation of your adversary's position.

In addition, your arguments will have far greater appeal to people who truly seek the truth when you calmly and rationally consider your opponent's position, rather than dismiss it with contempt and hatred. You will protect yourself from the accusation that your arguments are self-serving, rather than a serious attempt at arriving at truth.

---

1. Two key works in the Kabbalistic tradition.
2. Aristotle, *De Caelo,* chapter 10, 279b.

You should not provoke your adversary to anger, or show hatred to him, but show compassion, conceding his correct points, and speak softly and calmly with him. "Hatred annuls the standard of propriety."[3] Disputants should show the same courtesy and understanding to each other as they do to themselves; it is never appropriate to strong-arm your adversary into submission.

All of this is reflected in a passage in the Gemara:[4]

> Because of [what] reason did Beis Hillel merit to fix the halachah according to their view? Because they were easy and forbearing, and they would study their opinion and the opinion of Beis Shammai . . . and they would [even] mention the matters of Beis Shammai before their own.
>
> How does this follow? Beis Hillel's humbling themselves would seem to have nothing to do with deciding the Law! Halachah accords with the Truth, not with a humble demeanor!

✑§ Decoupling Emotion from Reason

Rather, this passage uncovers the reasons that they were able to arrive at the truth. Because they were calm and easygoing, they were not angered. The power of one's anger betrays an emotional need to prevail by force, if reason will not suffice. Similarly, their humble spirit contributed to their discovery of the truth, because it precluded any possible attempt to artificially rise above the other. People with such needs prematurely reject their opponents' line of reasoning. And going so far as to study the arguments of Beis Shammai before their own shows that they would not allow personal animosities to cloud their reasoning. They were never driven by the need to triumph. Only the pursuit of truth was important to them.

Many people have fallen into the pitfall of sacrificing their vision and objectivity to some emotional need or compulsion. Their hatred clouds their minds' eye, turning the straight path into the crooked; their love replaces majestic peaks of greatness with valleys of mediocrity.

---

3. *Sanhedrin* 105b.
4. *Eruvin* 13b.

Were our critics only to rid themselves of their jealousies, they would remember how strongly our Sages abjure us to be accurate and truthful about ordinary, everyday events. How could these same Sages create the remarkable fiction they are accused of, even about Hashem Himself?

It is quite proper to think that wise men make mistakes. Errors growing out of, or in spite of, wisdom are not unthinkable. But our complainants indict the Sages for gross falsification, for creating tall-tales that even simple-minded folk avoid!

You will understand why the *Chachamim* spoke so mysteriously when you consider the importance of keeping deep wisdom demurely covered and protected. The wise author of *Proverbs* accurately described the way of all sagacious men: "To understand parable and epigram, the words of the wise and their enigmas. . ."[5] We see that the hidden, sometimes mystifying, language of metaphor, analogy, parable, and riddle is a trademark of wisdom. How could it be otherwise? Wisdom, by its nature deep and hidden, must be expressed in a roundabout and somewhat inaccessible manner, lest it be cast before the feet of every passerby. There are terrible consequences to making profound ideas available to people who are ill-prepared to grasp them. Wisdom itself is disgraced when it is misunderstood and distorted. Misshapen notions spring up, often replacing valuable insight with senseless nonsense. Every person who understands the preciousness of wisdom relates to it protectively.

This style is common to the writings of all the prophets. They did not communicate in plain, forthright language because their prophetic experience — and their message — was not an ordinary human one! A Heavenly message deserves its own special medium of expression!

This notion was common even in the secular world. Many of the literary works of the ancient world were treated to commentaries and super-commentaries, because it was taken for granted that the author sunk far more meaning in his work than met the eye.

In truth, there is no real comparison between great literary works and the contribution of *Chazal*. Whoever failed to unlock a secular author's metaphor simply walked away from his reading, gaining nothing of value. The words of our Sages are entirely different. Because

---

5. 1:6.

they are connected to, and extensions of, words of the Torah and the Prophets, they share an important property of Scripture: the guarantee of two levels of significance.[6] Like golden apples carved onto silver plates,[7] the words of Torah and of the Sages have an inner core of profound, golden value. But even taken superficially, they are of sterling worth, pleasing and good to behold.

We find all of this pithily expressed in a mishnah in *Chagigah*.[8]

> [The laws of] forbidden unions may not be expounded among three [people]. Nor [may] the account of Creation [be expounded] between two [people], nor [may] the account of the [Heavenly] Chariot[9] [be expounded] by [even] one [person] — unless that person was a scholar who could arrive at an understanding [of the issues] on his own.

There is a definite hierarchy here. The areas that are more inherently profound demand more secrecy and cover.

⊷§ Keeping Knowledge Under Wraps

The Divine Chariot touches on issues closest to the nature of Hashem Himself. (The Chariot refers to that which bears the Honor of G-d Himself, like the heavenly beings closest to His Throne.) It requires the most hiding.

Creation occupies the next niche below. Here we do not deal directly with G-d, but with His interaction with a limited, physical world. We study G-d's actions, not G-d Himself. Not being quite as profound, this area of study can tolerate a bit more openness.

Finally, we come to illicit unions. Here we look at combinations of elements within this world, rather than the interface between G-d and His handiwork, as in the step above. There is still secrecy here. Hashem bans certain relationships because of a Divine order and plan that He wove into the fabric of Creation. Because He is the Creator, He

---

6. For a similar but fuller treatment of the idea that Torah can be studied on two levels — the superficial and the comprehended — see *Derech Hashem* 4:2:2-3.

7. A reference to *Proverbs* 25:11.

8. *Chagigah* 11b.

9. Based on the prophetic vision in the first chapter of *Ezekiel* that describes the beings and activities closest to G-d.

recognizes which associations, which pairings, which marriages are going to work, and which will be improper or ineffective according to Wisdom hidden from the human mind. Studying these laws is tantamount to studying the Mind of G-d — as applied to human needs.[10] It is still the study of G-d, albeit less directly. Hence, an even greater latitude in the number of participants who may study together.

Earlier, we explained some passages in *Chazal* that seemed to many to be troublesome. We showed them to be deep, profound, and beyond reproach. We showed that all criticism directed against them was unjustified. Those exercises should serve as testimony to the integrity of other such passages.

In this Fifth Well, we turn to selections that elicit legitimate questions. Even unbiased readers will greet them with incredulity. We will provide the answers they deserve. In doing so, we will be forced to probe and explore more deeply than is generally proper. We are hesitant and unwilling participants in this search, recognizing the sanctity of the ground upon which we tread. Two factors should atone for our trespass. One is that we intend purely to enhance the Honor of Heaven. And even here, where we must go further, we will still hold back. We will uncover one measure, while hiding 10 others.

---

10. The *Rishonim* dispute the reasoning behind the ban on incestuous and other forbidden relations. On the one hand, *Rambam* (*Moreh Nevuchim* 3:49) sees the ban as completely rational. *Ramban* (Leviticus 18:6), on the other, concludes that there is no clear rational basis for the prohibition, and that we relate to it as a Divine edict (*chok*) that we must simply accept.

Maharal steers a middle course here, although much closer to the position of *Ramban*. While we cannot understand the reason for the prohibition, and cannot assign a rationale as readily as *Rambam* did, we know that the ban is certainly not arbitrary. Surely Hashem forbade these unions because His infinite wisdom knows that they are injurious to us and the world. The very fact that we cannot easily understand why, even after much examination, indicates that the reasoning is deep, indeed. This arena, then, must also remain guarded and private, removed from the scrutiny of an uncomprehending public which will not be able to appreciate the depth. (For a fuller development, see Maharal's first introduction to *Gevuros Hashem*, p. 4.)

I. Monsters and Freaks

> Rabbah bar bar Chanah said: "I myself saw a certain frog, [and] it was the size of the [the city of] Akra of Hagrunia." And how big is Akra of Hagrunia? Sixty houses. "A sea-monster came and swallowed [the frog]; a female raven came and swallowed the sea-monster. It flew up and perched on [the branch of] a tree." Come [and] see how great the strength of the tree was! Rav Pappa bar Shmuel said, "Had I not been there, I never would have believed [it]." [11]

This passage in particular has come under attack by both early and recent non-Jewish sages. It appeared to them to be a perfect example of an old wives' tale.

Our critics regard this passage as so much insufferable nonsense. We will show that this selection is indeed extreme — extreme in its elegance! It is a rather strong example of the depth and profundity of *Chazal,* not, G-d forbid, of any foolishness.

❧ The Unity of Creation

Our Sages teach us here about the essential unity of Creation.[12] They maintain that all things are linked and interconnected, forming a single, unitary system.

---

11. *Bava Basra* 73b.

12. The *aggados* of Rabbah bar bar Chanah, dealing with fantastic creatures, have long been regarded as some of the most difficult and elusive in the entire Talmud. One approach is to assume that they are a series of commentaries on various contemporary kingdoms and governments. Because the upshot of much of it is uncomplimentary to those countries and their rulers, the authors had to disguise their intentions in order to avoid reprisals. Much of the symbolism would be lost to future generations, just as we might imagine that readers a few hundred years from now might not understand the point of an American political satire dealing with donkeys and elephants, not knowing that they were the colloquial symbols of Democrats and Republicans. Such an approach is cited in Dov Katz's *Tenuas Ha-Mussar,* (3rd ed., volume 1, p. 219, note 2) in the name of R' Yisrael Salanter.

Maharal does not take this route. He treats these passages to the same rigorous

It is crucial that we understand this, because when we don't, we quickly become mired in an ancient heresy. Many argued that the varying, disparate phenomena of this world point *away* from a Creator who is One. How can plurality proceed from an Absolute Unity? If, at the core and essence of what G-d is, there is a wonderful Unity and sameness, why are His creative outgrowths so varied and different? How does so much difference flow from Something that knows no differences or fragmentation? In fact, some of these creations are so different, that the Torah brands them as forbidden and impure. Effectively, the Torah assigns them negative value, and insists that we banish them! How can the negative come from a Being Who is entirely positive? These heretics conclude that it takes *multiple* forces to explain all the disparity that we observe.

Job already hinted at this problem, as well as our response to it. "Who can produce purity from impurity? No one!"[13] Job suggests that G-d actually *demonstrates* His real Unity when *tahor* comes from *tamei*, when we see polar opposites relating to each other, both connected by G-d.[14] Our human minds, seeing only the chasm that separates the

---

analysis as all other *aggados*, refusing to see in them anything less than profound lessons accessible to all generations. As he indicated above, the stranger a passage seems to us, the more likely it is that we will uncover messages of great sophistication.

13. *Job* 14:4. The translation follows *Rashi*. Maharal seems to take the last phrase of the verse as a rhetorical question, rather than a statement: "Is it not the One [G-d, Who alone can overcome the apparent incompatibility, and] draw the pure out of the impure?"

14. Most of us are familiar with a variation on this theme: that the existence of good and evil refutes the notion of a single, good Deity. It was for this reason that the ancient Zoroastrians created two gods, one presiding over good, and the other over evil. According to one reading, we make direct reference to this heresy in our *davening* each day in the first *berachah* before the *Shema*, when we proclaim that Hashem crafts both light and darkness — symbols of good and its opposite. In contradistinction to those who need two gods to account for good and evil (or the popular modern heresy of assuming that evil exists on its own outside of G-d, Who is somehow powerless to intervene), we assert that Hashem leaves room for both.

The importance of the problem — and its solution — cannot be overstated. See in particular the argument of R' Moses Chaim Luzzatto in *Da'as Tevunos* (section 40 s.v., *amnam*) who says that part of the function of evil is to *demonstrate* the Unity of G-d. The fact that extreme evil is unable to thwart Hashem's plan for the world increases our appreciation of His Unity. In fact, he reasons, evil and the revelation of Hashem's unity are related. The more that evil is allowed by G-d to exist, the greater will be the display of His Unity when he ultimately abolishes it.

opposing positions, are impressed only with the differences between them. It became the task of *Chazal* to remind us that this impression is ultimately illusory, and that the world is one, mirroring the Oneness of its Creator.

So why, then, does the Torah rail against certain objects and activities? Does this not show that the Torah regards them as foreign, as *outside* the useful handiwork of G-d? Can we escape the essential difference and incompatibility that is frozen into much of our world? Doesn't the world's polarity argue against a single Creator?

◆§ Two Tiers of Creation

Our Sages here provide an answer to this thorny problem. We cannot admit to a deeply divided world. Doing so might indeed lead to the assumption of another deity, or a competing set of forces. Rather, all phenomena, whether we can grasp this or not, are part of a unitary whole. Within that whole, some things are closer to the essence of the world's purpose and function, while others are further removed. It behooves a holy, pure people to attach itself to phenomena that relate to the holy and pure root of existence, to the front-runners in the race for significance, not to the stragglers lagging far behind.

We will explain further. *Chazal* here divide the world into two tiers. Some phenomena are best described as primary Creation,[15] or the

---

15. Maharal has already commented on the distinction between primary and secondary Creation. The "secondary" Creation described in the First Well (p. 10), however, did not have a negative connotation. To the contrary, the secondary there directly serviced and contributed to the primary.

In the Second Well (pp. 42-43), Maharal expanded the concept to include negative spiritual phenomena like demons. Here, Maharal returns to the world of tangible, observable phenomena. He reasons that once Hashem decides to create various elements of this world and entrust them to fixed, predictable laws of nature, some unpleasantness will inevitably ensue. The bad and the ugly are the industrial wastes of the elegant systems that produce their bounty of good.

A down-to-earth example is in order. Imagine that you are throwing a party in honor of a great *simchah*. You start to compile a guest list. First come those with whom you really want to share your joy. These are the people to whom you feel closest, including family and good friends. You cannot imagine having a good time without them. You quickly realize that you cannot limit your list so much. There are many people who will be insulted if you do not invite them as well. These may be business associates, good clients, coworkers, and friends with whom you are not so close. So the list grows. There are some people whom you really dislike. But they are spouses of people you have already included, and they cannot be left out either. The night of the party, a process server representing a litigious customer sees an opportunity to surprise you. He shows up to hand you a subpoena.

Clearly, you made the party for those who mean the most to you. They are the "primary" targets of your plan. Others, like the clients and coworkers are the "secondary" elements. Still others are even more distant. You never would have asked the process server to come. You did not invite him to the party; in a sense, the party itself invited him. His unwelcome presence is a consequence of the party, but certainly not part of its primary design. The analogy would seem to break down when we deal with G-d. After all, He can do anything He wants. He can throw the party, and keep away the unwelcome guests. Why would Hashem be constrained to create things in a way that produced less than perfect by-products?

The natural world provides us with a possible model that might help us understand. Behind all systematic study of the natural world lies a notion that we are comfortable with, both experientially and theologically. We are able to study the natural world only because phenomena are lawful and predictable. While we have perfect faith that nothing — including the laws of nature — occurs without Hashem's active Will, we are not fazed by the unchanging patterns of behavior through which He expresses that Will.

Regularity and lawfulness serve many purposes, not the least of which is providing room for human beings to choose freely. Natural law gives G-d a facade behind which to hide. If Man wishes to deny, natural law gives him a place on which to hang his disaffirming hat. This was discussed at length in the Fourth Well in note 67.

We pointed out there that once G-d develops certain natural laws, there are consequences. We will offer a few more examples. Take, for instance, the behavior of water. If asked to guess why Hashem endowed water with certain well-known performance oddities, many of us would be quick to point out the important consequences for human life. When we consider the fact that the solid phase of water (ice) is less dense than the liquid (a phenomenon that is quite atypical of solid/liquid differences), we are quick to applaud Hashem's wisdom. If ice were more dense, then it would sink to the bottom of the ocean during cold periods, snuffing out all life in the ocean's depths. Because the food cycle begins with plant life in the ocean, human nutrition would be eliminated. Instead, the lighter ice collects on the ocean surface, where it actually helps to insulate the water below, providing a hospitable place for ocean life through the harshness of winter.

We have no complaints about this. We rarely consider, however, that the collection of ice on the ocean's surface also spells doom to an occasional ship that encounters an unexpected ice floe.

Which is the "primary" intention of Hashem in creating ice? Most of us would guess that it is the continuity of life, rather than the sinking of ships. But once G-d settles on the laws that He does, the unfortunate loss of ships is a secondary, predictable consequence that comes with the territory.

Or take the intricate way in which cells use the information they contain to carry out the complex missions that "Nature" expects of them. Our cells translate the information contained in DNA at a dizzying pace, and with accuracy that human beings cannot directly imitate. While people often ask why G-d allows something as

essentials of Creation. Other phenomena follow directly from them. They are offshoots and tag-alongs of the primary. Because they are related to the primary elements, they are united with them to the point that they form one seamless system. Their existence is less significant, however, in that they are not the chief objects of concern in Hashem's plan for the world.

One of the functions of the Torah is to differentiate between the important and the unimportant; between the choices that can attach us to ultimate significance, and those that involve us only with the earthly and immediate.

⸲§ Real and Ersatz Existence

When we contrast the eternity of G-d with ephemeral, here-today-gone-tomorrow earthly existence, we might easily reach the conclusion that we don't really exist! What sort of "existence" is ours, stacked up against that of G-d? A mere parody, at best! It becomes easier to understand that only those options that connect us somehow with the Eternity of G-d really "exist." The Torah is a document of this real "existence." It insists on focusing the lives of Jews on things that really count, on the issues and activities most closely linked to His Will. Phenomena that are furthest removed from the primary objects of Creation are the most irrelevant and injurious to the Jewish spirit and earn the designation "tamei."

---

ugly as cancer to exist, we might point out that it is more amazing that there is so little cancer, owing to the remarkable efficiency of DNA transcription! It takes approximately five million replication generations to miscopy one percent of the DNA code. This is about 450 times the accuracy of a human typist, and applies to more rapidly changing molecules. Other molecules change at a much slower pace; their replication efficiency beats the human typist by a factor of half a billion! Actually, some 5,000 DNA letters per day randomly degenerate in a human cell, but built-in repair mechanisms take care of most of the damage [Richard Dawkins, The Blind Watchmaker, ps. 125-126]. As incredible as the accuracy is, the process still relies on apparatus that is inherently fallible. (Only Hashem is entirely infallible and perfect; nothing outside Him can ever evidence absolute reliability.) This means that every now and then there will be mistakes. Some of them will have catastrophic consequences, like the cancer caused when the cells' replication system runs away with itself. Maharal might argue that cancer doesn't "exist" on the same plane as the life that the DNA system is meant to serve. It is, however, a secondary consequence of that system.

~§ Freak Phenomena

These non-essential elements are found everywhere. That is why this passage describes a frog, a snake, and a bird. Between the water, land, and air that the three of them frequent, all earthly habitat is included.[16] The three act as symbols of all the parts of Creation that we sense are not the key players. Whether within the animal kingdom or outside of it, we realize that in the cast of billions of characters in the drama of global history, some things are not even auxiliary players. They include all the monsters that Nature sometimes produces, and all that our Torah-developed sensibility tells us is monstrous.

We will turn now to some of the symbolic detail of the passage. The frog is the size of 60 houses, corresponding to the size of a particular fort. Apparently, the fort was not particularly well known, since we have to be told that it was as large as 60 houses!

Chazal often use "60" to mean a very large, inclusive number. Large numbers, though, usually mean collections of disparate items. This monster-frog didn't represent an individual phenomenon to our Sages, but the entire class of such phenomena. The fort is a collective that includes the individual members it contains. It is large, but it is a single unit, or grouping.

Continuing the analysis, we learn that three assorted beasts swallowed each other serially, and the last moved to a tree. It is the tree that unlocks the hidden meaning of this passage.

~§ Trees and Branches

A tree typically has many branches, which spread out into many more smaller branches, which further split off into even more twigs, covered with innumerable leaves. All this growth proceeds from

---

16. In order to grate less on the modern reader, I have substituted these three realms for Maharal's original formulation: the four elements of water, fire, air, and earth that were held until modern times to be the basic building blocks of all matter. Maharal relates the three animals of our passage to three of the four, and provides a reason why none of them is related to the element of fire. The upshot is much the same: Whichever framework you chose to use, the three beasts encompass the entire orbit of earthly existence.

a common trunk and its hidden roots.

Nothing could speak more eloquently about the nature of our world. Everything comes from a single trunk and its roots, a single Source, which is partially manifest and partly hidden from us. (A heretic is often termed a *kofer be'ikar,* a denier of the Source/Trunk of all existence.) From this source spring a number of chief branches. They represent the key elements of Hashem's plan and design. From them, less important, smaller branches also shoot forth. These are elements that are positive, but progressively less important as the "distance" between them and the source increases.[17]

Some things are so distant from the trunk that they are really not attached to the tree, although there is no doubt that they also arose because of it. They are almost accidental or chance consequences of the tree's existence. Not of the same flesh and substance as the tree, they are nonetheless related to it; without the tree, they wouldn't be there. In our passage, they ultimately come to rest *on* the tree, rather than become part *of* it.

There is one more important detail. The three beasts do not all happily sit on neighboring branches. Two of them are swallowed up by their strange colleagues, one after the other. This runs parallel to the tree itself. The larger, primary limbs support and accommodate others that branch from them. Everything is connected and ordered. Even in the realm of rejected, freak phenomena there is systematic order.

---

17. It is tempting to see an allusion here to another famous tree. The *Sefiros* (the ten emanations of G-d so important in Kabbalistic literature), divided according to the chief attributes of *din* and *chesed,* and arranged hierarchically, form a pattern which is sometimes called the *Ilan,* or *Eitz,* both meaning "tree." This pattern describes ways in which the Will of Hashem takes the active form that it does, often after successive transformations by the individual characteristics of different *Sefiros.* Looking at the *Ilan,* or at the *Sefiros* system as a whole, we observe the way in which all events of this world originate in the Will of Hashem, and wend their way through complex spiritual pathways until they take their observable, concrete form. Every detail, no matter how small, is connected to that tree, and owes its existence to the sustenance it draws from its Source.

Maharal may very well do here what he seems to frequently do elsewhere. A master Kabbalist himself, he takes Kabbalistic concepts, and distills them into a form that is stripped of Kabbalistic vocabulary, and accessible to people with no background in Jewish mysticism. (It must be added, however, that it is not known whether Maharal had access specifically to the Kabbalah of the *Ari,* who lived in Israel not long before the Maharal wrote.)

These strange creatures occupy different levels, with one accommodating — or swallowing up — the next. They are not outside the pale of Hashem's vision and supervision. Even these chance, orphaned events and objects have discrete places. While only peripherally related to the tree, their apparently random association with it is not as chance as we might believe. Without exception, everything is foreseen — and precisely measured — by Hashem.

Indeed! How great is the tree that connects G-d's Will to the complexity of this world! And while the ideas and concepts we have discussed are accessible to all wise men, Rav Pappa bar Shmuel could not help but exclaim that had he missed the fuller development of the concept from Rabbah bar bar Chanah, he never would have properly grasped it.

In conclusion, the observable world is certainly not always full of happiness and harmony. There is much that is ugly and dangerous.[18] *Chazal* wish us to understand, however, that G-d did not limit His work to things we sense are positive, useful, and good. Surely, He created a universe that is positive, useful, and good. But the system that He used to translate Divine energy into earthly phenomena, the laws He utilized to spawn the myriad phenomena of our world, form by-products as well. The monsters, the *tamei* — these are not essential to G-d's design of the world. But there is a place for them. Their existence should not be laid at the doorstep of other gods, or forces, or Fate, or arising unsupervised from an area of the universe from which G-d has absented Himself.

To think that anything could exist outside of the Will of Hashem is the most monstrous idea of all.

---

18. In some belief systems, the harmony and symmetry of Nature were the strongest indication of the work of G-d or the gods. Others, like Maharal here, own up to the fact that Nature does not always paint such a pretty picture. R' Yehudah HaLevi in *Kuzari* (3:11) notes that the believer has a real advantage in dealing with the observed inelegance of Nature . The cruelty and violence so often found in Nature can profoundly disturb the non-believer, because they demonstrate a reality to which he is chained, but powerless to change. The believer, while taken aback by these events, can nonetheless appreciate that a good and just G-d has compelling and valid reasons for including what our myopic human vision perceives as problematic.

Maharal suggests that our (perhaps futile) quest for understanding may be misplaced. Instead of trying to comprehend the justice of individual phenomena, what we really need to understand is the larger picture. We should aim to understand why Hashem made certain laws and pathways part of the fabric of Creation. We need to understand why this set of protocols meant the best for the most. Once this regiment was put into motion, however, monsters — little and great — would appear in its wake.

II. How Good is *Olam Haba*?

Rabbah bar bar Chanah said: "Once we were going in the wilderness, and we saw certain geese whose [wing] feathers fell out because of their [excessive] fat, and streams of fat were flowing beneath them. I said to them, 'Will we have a portion of you in *Olam Haba*?' One [goose] raised its wing [in reply], and another raised its thigh. When I came before R' Eliezer, he said to me, 'In the future, Israel is going to be held to account because of them.' "[19]

W hat seems to be a bizarre travelogue is really a commentary on a profoundly disturbing problem — the good that the righteous deserve in this world, and the deficient state in which they actually find themselves.

Know this: *Chazal* use eating as a metaphor for the good that will be the lot of the righteous.

Eating means receiving. We frequently find ourselves hungry, or sleep-deprived, or otherwise lacking. Without receiving what we require, we soon cease to exist. As physical beings, not natives of Hashem's upper worlds, we are needy in many ways, and only gifts from Above sustain us. Eating is the most common activity that demonstrates our need to receive.

In *Olam Haba,* the "eating" will continue. The righteous will receive from Hashem all that they could possibly need and want.

৵§ Soul Food

T here is a crucial difference between our meals in the here and now, and the "eating" of *Olam Haba*. When we get up from a well-set table, we only shed our deficiency for the moment. We remain beings of incessant dependency. No sooner do we receive, than new

---

19. *Bava Basra* 73b.

needs develop. Each breath of life-sustaining air that we breathe requires an encore. The food we eat is quickly utilized, leaving us hungry and in search of our next meal.

This is not the case in *Olam Haba.* The food that we receive will be spiritual, not physical. We will receive it without being caught in an endless cycle of want and replenishment. We will receive without being prisoners of need.

ᴥৡ Spiritual High-flyers

C *hazal* point to all of this in the form of the fat geese. We often use terms like "above," and "higher," and "upper" to refer to things that transcend this world. Because birds soar aloft, they are an apt earthly symbol for things that aren't quite earthly — in this case, for the spiritual. Putting bird on the menu signifies that the main entrée is "elevated" fare, feeding the soul, not the body.

The goose was chosen because of its famed store of fat. Fat is always a symbol of fullness, richness, plenty. In our passage, the fat of the geese serves as the antidote to the inherent leanness of our present condition, in which we are constantly aware of being needy. Things will be different on the other side. When we take in this world, we always quiet some hunger, be it large or small, acute or chronic, native or acquired. And there is always an upper limit to how much we can take. In *Olam Haba,* even the sky is not the limit. And we will receive not because we sense need or deprivation, but because Hashem will turn us into beings of real fullness and completion beyond our present comprehension.

Rabbah bar bar Chanah finds these friendly geese in the wilderness, an unlikely place for domesticated birds. The wilderness is often associated, though, with Hashem's *din,* His attribute of judgment. The harsh, demanding conditions of the wilderness make it inhospitable to geese, people, and all but those creatures specially adapted to its extremes.

The scrutiny of G-d's *din* has a similar effect. When untempered by His *rachamim,* His attribute of mercy, *din* makes it very difficult for physical, temporal beings to exist. (The physical state always implies limitation, and therefore leads to fallibility and deficiency. These are

all anathema to pure *din*.) Because *din* is so inhospitable to the physical, the wilderness is often the place in our tradition where we encounter *non-physical* things, like the giving of the Torah, and the falling of
the manna (a spiritual food).

Din is neither negative nor distasteful. It merely describes things the
way things are meant to be. Since we so often fall short of its exacting
demands, we survive through Hashem's *rachamim*. This itself is not
quite the way it should be. Through Hashem's *din,* there should be an
uninterrupted flow of wonder and delight to *this* world, a continuous
torrent of Divine beneficence. Bestowing this good upon us is, after all,
the whole point of Creation in the first place. In a sense, it is the Great
Law upon which many others are predicated.

Unfortunately, we cannot say that we always feel and witness all of
this kindness. We somberly note many places that seem to have
stayed relatively dry during what is supposed to be a shower of good.
Chazal want us to know that, despite our frequent reality checks, there
is nothing wrong with a model of incessant flow of blessing. To the
contrary, Hashem's *din* mandates it. We do not observe a deluge of
pleasure and happiness because we are inappropriate recipients of His
good.[20] A stream of fat flows from the geese, because *din* calls for a
constant flow of good to us, even in this world. Most of us, though, will
discover the full extent of this good only in *Olam Haba.*

When it comes, it will be distinguished in the two ways hinted at by
the geese. One bird showed Rabbah bar bar Chanah its leg. A leg
supports what rests on it, allowing something to stand in place for long
times. It is a symbol of permanence. The bird assured Rabbah that
what the righteous will receive in *Olam Haba* will not be ephemeral
and short-lived, but eternal.

---

20. There are theoretical and practical benefits to this knowledge. It blunts a "complaint" many people can't help but harbor. Why did G-d stop short of giving the
world and its inhabitants what they really want? Why does He seem to pull the plug
so often? *Chazal* here tell us that we are mistaken. We have turned the tables.
Hashem doesn't withhold good from us by design or principle. We — not He — set
the limits on what we receive.

There are practical benefits for us in this realization. Having a more upbeat view
of what the world — this world — potentially offers, can motivate us to make better
use of it. While we cannot instantly launch *Olam Haba,* there to eternally taste of
Hashem's delights, we can make ourselves more deserving recipients of the bounty
that potentially is ours to claim.

The second goose answered Rabbah's question with a very different insight. It presented its wing, the part of it that enables it to take off and fly, the symbol of transcendent, spiritual power. It promised Rabbah that the tribulations of the righteous will not only end in *Olam Haba,* but the pleasure they experience will be of a much richer variety than people can readily imagine.

Between the two birds, the message is clear. *Olam Haba* will be a place of unending pleasure. All of this was already hinted at by David in *Psalms,* [21] when he wrote, "You will make known to me the path of life, the fullness of joys in Your Presence, the *delights* that are in Your right Hand for *eternity."* Both factors are underscored: the pleasure that is in store, and its eternity.

Once again, what at first seems to be a trivial story aims at raising our consciousness of important and profound ideas. At the same time we see how *Chazal* compact much meaning in an economy of expression. We learn about their masterful use of words and symbols, and the clever and subtle ways in which *Chazal* employ everyday language to teach us matters of enduring worth.

III. Accusations Against Moses

"They were jealous of Moses in the camp."[22] It teaches that everyone [every husband] suspected Moses of [an illicit relationship with] his wife.[23]

O ur critics are galled by this seemingly preposterous and uncomplimentary treatment of Moses. As usual, the true, deep meaning evades them, and is the opposite of what they assume. This passage actually pays tribute to the lofty stature of Moses. Only *Chazal,* who understood the secrets of the Torah, and comprehended Moses' significance, could do justice to his greatness.

---

21. 16:11.

22. *Psalms* 106:16.

23. *Moed Katan* 18b. The word "jealous" in Hebrew also connotes the formal procedure through which a husband warns his wife not to seclude herself with another man whom he suspects is involved in an illicit affair with her. The Gemara here assumes an allusion to this second sense.

We begin by noting another difficult claim that *Chazal* made about Moses. Moses, they say,[24] was the equal of all the rest of the Jewish people taken together. This is no bombastic exaggeration. They do not mean that Moses' *mitzvos,* or his worth in the estimation of Hashem, were the equivalent of millions of his fellow Jews. Moses was their match in the sense that he fully *complemented* the existence of everyone of his generation.

◄§ Form and Substance

We can often learn about the relationships between things (and sometimes about the complex functioning of a single object) by looking for differences in roles. Since ancient times, people have found it useful to distinguish between "form" and "substance,"[25] On its simplest level, the clay that a sculptor uses is the substance of the sculpture; the image that the artist executes is its form.

We can apply this dyad to more subtle relationships as well. Wood, brick, plaster, metals and plastic contribute to the substance of a new building. You might say that the craftsmen who construct the building impart the form. Each takes raw material and shapes it into something specific.

When you step back, though, you see that each craftsman is given precise orders from a supervisor. Relative to that overseer, you might argue that the craftsman is a "substance" person, since he is almost only a tool in the hands of the supervisor who really determines what processes should be implemented.

Looking a bit further, you learn that the supervisor gets his orders once a day from his superior, and that this subcontractor was in turn given detailed instructions from the major contractor. Behind all of this, though, is someone who may never appear in person at the construction site: the architect. Without ever taking a hammer in hand, or speaking to the carpenter who does, it is his or her design that determines what the new building will look like.

---

24. *Shir HaShirim Rabbah* 1:65.

25. While the terms are quite old in Jewish and secular circles alike, Maharal uses them in a somewhat idiosyncratic manner. He applies them not only to physical, material things, but to concepts and relationships as well. This will become apparent later on.

You might say that the architect is the real "form" giver, while the others are all "substance" people, since their contributions to form all grow out of his vision.

You can apply the same analysis to more complex relationships: between friends, between communities, between cultures. For these more subtle distinctions, we will use the Hebrew forms: *tzurah* (form) and *chomer* (substance).

◆§ Moses' Pervasive Influence

Now we are ready to return to our passage. Moses was the equal of *Klal Yisrael* because he was the *tzurah* of the people. His vision and his presence constantly shaped the way his flock lived their lives. He crafted a raw and malleable group of individuals into a functioning nation. His instruction transformed the individual lives of his charges. Since every complex must have both *tzurah* and *chomer,* he complemented everyone else by fully doing half the job! In this way, he was the equal of everyone else. (This, by the way, is the meaning of the *midrash* [26] that asks for the identity of a woman who gave birth to 600,000 babies at one time. The answer, of course, is Moses's mother. By complementing every individual of a large nation, Moses would become the equal of 600,000 people.)

◆§ Moses' Unusual Marriage

This principle will unlock many other doors in the thought of *Chazal.* Consider Moses' marriage. We can assume that Moses was no worse than any other Jew, about whom a heavenly voice cries out at the time of conception, "The daughter of such-and-such will marry so-and-so."[27] Even Rebecca's unrighteous brother understood the extent of Divine intervention in pairing marital partners, and exclaimed, "The matter stemmed from Hashem!"[28] Shouldn't Moses have had the same Divine assistance in finding his match?

---

26. *Shir HaShirim Rabbah* 1:65.

27. *Sotah* 2a.

28. *Genesis* 24:50.

It comes as no surprise that Aaron found a spouse entirely appropriate to his rank. Elisheba came from a distinguished family; her brother was a *Nasi* (prince). Moses, on the other hand, reached outside the ranks of his people to marry Zipporah. Why did Divine Providence bring about this unusual match? Was there no Jewish woman appropriate for him?

Truth be told, there wasn't. Every proper wife is an *ezer kenegdo*, [29] a helpmate opposite her husband. "Opposite" implies some sort of equivalence, of occupying a similar plane. A true spouse is the half of you that is missing, that makes you complete. No individual human being could be the complementary half to fit Moses, because he was the equivalent of the entire community!

It would take an entire group to weigh in opposite Moses. Hashem matched Moses with Zipporah, the daughter of Jethro, a stellar figure of the non-Jewish nations of the world. We need not assume that Zipporah towered spiritually over the Jewish women of her day. We need only note that, to all the other Jews, she *represented* the entire non-Jewish world. Marrying an individual Jewish woman would have diminished Moses, by implying that he was just an individual, albeit a remarkably great one. Marrying the representative of an entire group, of an entire culture, stressed that Moses, too, subsumed an entire group.

✑§ Complementary Roles in Marriage

We draw closer to understanding the accusations against Moses. Loosely speaking, husband and wife behave in many ways like *chomer* and *tzurah.* Men often seize a disproportionate amount of the decision-making of the family, of the pointing and orienting to its major and minor goals. (This is especially true through their teaching the Torah in which they have become proficient.) This is a *tzurah* role. Women, on the other hand, often spend more time than their spouses producing and delivering the finished, usable products of family life. This is much more a vocation of *chomer.*

In a successful marriage, each spouse knows that he or she can depend on the other for the missing half of the picture. By consistently complementing each other, each spouse comes to regard the other as

---

29. Ibid. 2:18.

an extension of self. Moses' presence in the Jewish camp potentially threatened this relationship. His effect on all others was so important, and so overwhelming, that husbands sensed that they were not the actual *tzurah* in their own marriages. Women were not really leaning on the strength and direction of their husbands, because Moses' example provided the same. In a sense, Moses was each man's competitor. Moses' persona interfered with the bonding between husband and wife. Quite different from an act of infidelity, it was nonetheless similarly intrusive.

✑ Adultery and Mathematics

Were they wrong in complaining? Completely. Only something or someone cut from the same material competes and intrudes. Another person, one who could substitute for a spouse, cannot. Concepts, disembodied ideas do not challenge in the same, personal way. A husband will go into a jealous rage if he learns of an amorous relationship his wife is carrying on with his neighbor. If she invests the same passion in the study of mathematics, he might be inconvenienced — but he won't become insanely jealous of her beloved equations.

This is where the men erred. They didn't fully grasp Moses' greatness. Mindful of Moses' effect on all their lives, they saw him interfering with their marital relationships. Moses' *tzurah* activities interfered with their own. They failed to realize that Moses' *tzurah* was a disembodied, transcendent one. Its power and might went far beyond what is typically contained in a human being, even a great human being. The full force of Moses' presence did not owe so much to his personality as to the Word of Hashem that he bore. His *tzurah* was not self-made, but on loan, as it were, from the greatness of Hashem.

✑ Jeremiah Accused

A similar passage regarding Jeremiah further bolsters our approach. The Gemara[30] reports that people suspected Jeremiah

---

30. *Bava Kamma* 16b.

of either adultery, or of a relationship with a prostitute. Jeremiah also occupied a position that reached beyond the bounds of individual significance. In the Torah's section on prophecy, Moses foretells, "A prophet, from your midst, from your brethren like me, shall Hashem your G-d establish for you."[31] A *midrash*[32] sees an allusion to Jeremiah in particular, since both Moses and Jeremiah prophesied to the entire Jewish people (rather than to the Northern or Southern Kingdom alone).

Note that the people made no claims of impropriety regarding anyone else — not against any other prophet, and not against any king. It was Jeremiah's overarching role as a master prophet that made him a potential *tzurah*-competitor. No other prophet was so much of a presence. And kings were certainly not candidates. The regal demeanor of kings insured that they were seen as aloof and above the rest of the people, and therefore not direct competitors. The effect of the prophet on everyone's own growth and development was intensely more personal, and more likely to be seen as intrusive.

Note, too, how the obvious difference between Moses and Jeremiah shows itself in this latter passage. Moses was accused of adultery, in the general sense, because his *tzurah* was felt across the entire community, without exception. Jeremiah's influence, powerful as it was, was still far more muted than that of Moses. Therefore he was charged by some only with consorting with a prostitute. The prostitute is an individual woman — not the whole community. And a relationship with one is usually far more casual than an illicit affair with a married woman.

⋰⋰ The Other Marriage

A very different approach to our passage takes us to virtually the same conclusion. We showed earlier that relationships between people often include *chomer/tzurah* separation. This is particularly true in marriage, but there is no shortage of other parallels. The

---

31. *Deuteronomy* 18:15.
32. *Yalkut Shimoni, Jeremiah,* p. 256.

Jewish people proudly stand as *chomer*, eagerly accepting Divine input and imprint in all facets of their lives. Our outward behaviors as well as innermost thoughts are forever soft to the touch of Hashem's demands.

Our ultimate *tzurah* is Hashem Himself. Throughout *Tanach*, Hashem is called *"Ish"* — husband — in relation to His people, because He confers *tzurah* upon us.

Korah proclaimed this as the battle cry of his rebellion. "For the entire assembly — all of them — are holy and Hashem is among them; why do you exalt yourselves over the congregation of Hashem?"[33] *Chazal* explain: All of us stood at Sinai and received the Torah directly from Hashem. On such a lofty plane, who needs a Moses as a leader? Why should we resort to intermediaries to rule us, and to determine Hashem's Will? We are all great in our own right! Each of us can lay claim to G-d Himself as the source of his or her *tzurah*. Our relationship with Hashem is close, strong, effective, and intimate. Hashem is the *Ish,* the husband to *Klal Yisrael.* Anyone who comes between us commits an act of adultery.

Moses, people claimed, had done just that. He had interposed himself between G-d and us, and made himself felt forcefully and dramatically. (The claim would be repeated years later in regard to Jeremiah, although in diluted form, as explained above. Jeremiah's generation could not claim a bond with G-d as strong as the one enjoyed by the generation of the Exodus. Nonetheless, they cherished their connection with Hashem. And they were so overwhelmed by the influence of their leader, that they viewed it as an intrusion.)

Moses' response stressed that real competition and intrusion were impossible. Had he led as a conventional ruler, their wrath would be justified. A people once led by G-d should not have to settle for the active leadership of a mere mortal. But Moses' own mortality, his personal humanness, was inconspicuous in his role as *tzurah*-provider. Moses' attainment was so elevated and transcendent that he should not have been seen as a human interloper.[34] The *tzurah* that

---

33. *Numbers* 16:3.

34. The *tzurah* that he provided was not of his own making, nor was it changed or diminished in any way through his own personality, words, or preferences. Adultery involves the disturbing of the privacy and intimacy of a relationship through the

he provided was not of his own making, nor was it changed or diminished in any way through his own personality, words, or preferences.

"Not a single donkey of theirs did I take, nor did I harm any one of them," Moses responded. In a real human relationship — even between a powerful, but honest and caring, ruler and his subjects — people need each other. It is inconceivable that at some point Moses would not have needed and accepted the assistance of a fellow Jew. It is quite impossible that Moses would not have inadvertently harmed some citizen.

Remarkably, Moses did neither of these. The greatest impact of his leadership was his message, one that was forged out of the encounter between Man and G-d. This created the *tzurah,* and this — the teaching, not the teacher — was an elevated and transcendent gift. It could only enhance — but never intrude on — in the relationship between *Klal Yisrael* and Hashem.

---

intrusion of *another.* Moses was no "other." The gifts that he had, the message he radiated that worked so profoundly upon everyone else, were emanations of Hashem himself.

A gift of flowers from a male to a married woman is in bad taste, and on a continuum with adultery. If a husband sends flowers, and they are clearly marked as such, no one will fault the delivery boy for presenting them. Moses' *tzurah* contribution was an extension of Hashem's relationship with them — something welcomed by each and every man and woman — not a substitute.

We can only speculate about the intended impact of Maharal's lesson. Did he wish to instruct us only about the nature of Moses? Or perhaps he wanted the reader to realize that, to a lesser extent, the arguments and counterarguments continue through time. People sometimes complain that their dependence upon teachers, *poskim,* or rabbis detracts from the "personal" relationship they have with G-d. They are unwelcome intrusions, they claim. There is a sure antidote: recognizing that what they take from these human figures is not manufactured by Man, but merely passed on from G-d through our *mesorah.*

IV. Pharaoh's Grotesque Stature

> Avitul the scribe said in the name of Rav: "The Pharaoh of Moses' days was [one] *amah* [tall]. His beard was [one] *amah* long, and his male organ an *amah* and a *zeres*, to fulfill that which is stated[35] '[G-d rules over the kingdom of man], and He appoints the lowest of men over it.' "[36]

To our critics, this passage is a joke and a mockery. No human being could possibly look like this! Those, however, who are familiar with words of wisdom see no problem at all.

Every person has two images. One is manifest. It obeys natural laws that apply to the entire human species. It describes the general form of their bodies, number and size of limbs, and so on. All human beings share this general description, and no one escapes its limitations.

Individuals show much greater difference than their physical forms and dimensions let on. Each person has a unique form generated by his own potentials and actions. It is this second form, hidden and more personalized, that *Chazal* speak of in our passage. And they speak similarly in many other places.

This second image describes what the person actually is. It shows what he or she has that differs with others, not what they have in common. The first, species-wide form casts the mold into which all must fit. It dictates the shape that the outer person must take, regardless of what the inner person looks like. If the inner person is horrifically evil, his misshapen features are not externally visible, because their expression is tempered and limited by the common factors of the first image. (The opposite can also be true. *Chazal* will sometimes describe someone's *greatness* by seemingly exaggerating his physical propor-

---

35. *Daniel* 4:14.
36. *Moed Katan* 18a.

tions.[37] Here, too, they refer to the inner person, or what he would look like if there were no constraints imposed by the natural-law image.)

Chazal give us a glimpse of the real Pharaoh. They show us what he would look like if bone and sinew would accommodate the inner reality of the person. Because he was a human being, he was fortunate enough to be blessed with the standard apparatus of his species. Thus, he had two eyes, and legs, and arms, and a single torso — all of them arranged in much the same proportion as everyone else.

Lucky for him. The inner picture showed only a few hideous features, dwarfing the rest.

"Dwarfing" may be the wrong word. He was exceedingly short, no taller than his beard. There is nothing unseemly in being short or even a midget. On the contrary, compacting the force of his determination and personality in such a small body would have shown him to be a rather powerful person. Reducing him to the size of his beard, though, shrinks his substance to a fraction of what it ought to be.[38] Contemptuously, Chazal tell us that there was nothing to the man, except for the negative, with which he was richly endowed.

Private parts are always kept covered among decent people. Exposing them brings shame. In Pharaoh's case, they were even larger than the rest of his body! Chazal want to tell us that beyond having nothing of real worth, his true possession was degradation and shame, in unusual quantity.

Does any of this tell us anything about what Pharaoh actually looked like? As we said, anatomical realities common to all humans preclude someone from visibly matching Chazal's description. They speak only of the inner man.

Alternatively, there might have been some expression on a visible level. Pharaoh could not have been that short, because grown humans simply can't be compacted into such a small package. But Chazal may

---

37. See Gevuros Hashem, p. 91, where Maharal deals with Moses' reported height of ten amos (Shabbos 92a). He refers the reader to his discussion here.

38. See Fourth Well p. 150, where the beard is associated with the prideful face we turn to the world. If Pharaoh's beard was as long as his body, Chazal may mean that his pride was immense relative to his real substance.

be indicating that Pharaoh was very short, as short as biology will allow.

৶ From the Depths

They certainly mean to comment on the nature of our national redemption. *Klal Yisrael* earned much more than physical freedom at the time of the Exodus. They attained, for themselves and for all generations thereafter, a lofty rank and station. They became Hashem's people — by His choice, and by their substance.

It is characteristic of Hashem to elevate something specifically from the greatest depths. Rising to a high level is a wonderful attainment. Getting there from the starting point of the polar opposite points to the Hand of Hashem.

The Jews in Egypt wallowed in the depths. They were completely subjugated by their captors. Their time, their property, their bodies were not theirs. They lived at the lowest sub-basement of the structure of human society.

Presiding over their degradation was no great, all-time hero. Pharaoh, when appreciated for what he really was, turns out to be a nobody. Stacked up against others, even ordinary people who are forgotten to history, he was an exceptionally small person. Today, we would consider him "off the charts."

This contributed to the redemption, to the drama of Hashem raising us up from one extreme to the other.

It also solves one of the psychological mysteries of the redemption. History produced no shortage of evil leaders who defied Hashem. None of them, though, saw a sustained march of miraculous signs, tailor-made by G-d to bring anyone to his knees. How did Pharaoh resist? How did his resolve last past the first of the plagues?

৶ Dealing with Inadequacy

Had Pharaoh fallen within what we call the limits of normality, he could not have resisted. He would have reached his breaking point. But Pharaoh was not within the norm. He was a very, very inconsequential being inside. People who are troubled by low self-esteem, who fear that they are not what they should be, often have a need to prove that they are significant. They want to demonstrate — to others, and to themselves — that they have real worth, and real power.

Pharaoh had such a need. He had it much more than others, because at his core, he was a much smaller person than those others! This translated into a defiance of G-d that makes no sense to the rest of us, but was compelled by his need for recognition. It, too, contributed to our redemption.

Pharaoh, say Chazal,[39] was a sorcerer. Magic attempts to "defy the edicts of Hashem's court."[40] It fits perfectly with the personality profile of someone so desperate to prove himself that he would attempt to do battle with Hashem Himself.

V. David, Bathsheba, and Sins that Weren't

R' Shmuel bar Nachmani said in R' Yonasan's name: "Whoever says that David sinned is simply mistaken, for it is stated, 'David was successful in all his ways, and Hashem was with him.'[41] Is it possible that [David] sinned [so grievously], and the Divine Presence [remained] with him? Then how do I interpret, 'Why have you despised the word of Hashem, to do that which is evil in My eyes?'[42] [It means that] he sought to do [evil], but did not."

Rav observed: "Rebbi, who is descended from David, sought to expound [the verse] in defense of David [in the following manner:] 'This "evil" [mentioned] here is different from all the "evils" in the

---

39. *Moed Katan* 18a.
40. *Sanhedrin* 67b.
41. *I Samuel* 18:14.
42. *II Samuel* 12:9.

Torah. For regarding all [other] "evils" in the Torah it is written, "He *did* (that which is evil)," whereas here it is written, "to **do** (that which is evil)," [which teaches] that [David] sought to do, but [in fact] did not. "You struck Uriah the Hittite with the sword."[43] You should have judged [Uriah] by the Sanhedrin, but you did not. ". . . and you took his wife unto yourself for a wife."[44] You may [legally] take her [in marriage].' "

For R' Shmuel bar Nachmani said in R' Yonasan's name: "Whoever goes out to [fight] a war of the House of David writes a bill of divorce for his wife, for it is stated, 'And bring these ten cheeses to the captain of the thousand, and look into your brothers' well being, and take their pledges [*arubasam*].'[45] What is meant by *arubasam*? R' Yosef teaches: 'It [refers to] matters that are commingled between him and her.'[46] 'And you have slain him [Uriah] with the sword of the Ammonites.'[47] Just as you are not [to be] punished for [the killings effected by] the sword of the Ammonites, so too you are not [to be] punished for [the death of] Uriah the Hittite. What is the reason? He [Uriah] was [considered] a rebel against the monarchy, [for Uriah] said to him [David], 'And my master Yoav, and the servants of my master, are encamped in the open field, etc.' "[48],[49]

---

43. Ibid 12:9.

44. Ibid. 12:9.

45. *I Samuel* 17:18.

46. The marriage ceremony commingles the lives of husband and wife. The verse can therefore mean that David's father instructed him to find his brothers at the front and to take — or take back and annul — the force of their marriages to their respective wives. He was to do this by having them execute writs of divorce for their wives, to free them to remarry if they disappeared in battle.

47. *II Samuel* 12:9.

48. Ibid 11:11.

49. *Shabbos* 56a.

The sin of David is so well established according to the plain sense of the story that our critics react with disbelief. They refuse to pay any attention to this attempt to clear David's reputation, at the expense of seemingly mangling the text.

There is no mangling, no distortion, no garbling, no falsification. To the contrary, it is our critics who are insensitive to the nuances of the text. They ignore the overwhelming evidence of the verse that *Chazal* selected to introduce this passage: "And Hashem was with him [David]."

Chazal understood that such a statement is not an exaggerated way of saying the David enjoyed a spate of good luck, or that the wheel of fortune always landed in the right position for him.[50]

◦§ Relationship with Hashem

When Hashem is with someone, he enjoys more than success in his enterprises. Being "with" means togetherness, attachment, connection, relationship. When Hashem "invests," as it were, in a relationship, He wishes it maintained. He will take steps to insure that the connection is not severed.

Sin is guaranteed to negatively impact a relationship with G-d. Virtually by definition, sin creates barriers and distance between the sinner and his Creator. David was selected for a relationship with G-d in large part because of the roles for which he alone was most suited. He was to be the linchpin to some of the most important projects in the unfolding of human history: the building of the *Beis HaMikdash*, the establishment of the Davidic line of kings, and others. To make sure that David would remain "with" Him, Hashem intervened to prevent David from sinning.

More accurately, Hashem prevented David's sin, although David was completely unaware of this intervention. The description of David's misadventures with Bathsheba, and with the execution of Uriah, are entirely accurate at the same time! David allowed himself to falter, and to disregard the terrible sin involved in both these incidents. In his mind, he was prepared to sin. What he did not realize

---

50. The phrase is repeated in several other verses in regard to David. It is used but once in all of Scripture in regard to another: David's son Solomon (*II Chronicles* 1:1).

is that, ironically, he never committed the heinous acts that he intended!

As the Gemara explains, the soldiers of David's army handed bills of divorce to their wives before departing for battle. Bathsheba was no different. Every husband who executed such a document, however, had one purpose in mind: The divorce should be effective only if he did not return at the end of the war. He wanted to free his wife to remarry in the event that he would remain unaccounted for at war's end. There was no other reason to grant the divorce.

When David first took Bathsheba, he had no way of knowing that Uriah would not return. In his mind, he sinned. At best, he knew that she *might* have the status of a married woman, were her husband to survive the war. He continued on, unfazed by the possibility of transgression. Similarly, when David dispatched Uriah to the front lines, he did not justify it as the execution of a treasonous soldier. Had he thought of that, he would have turned the matter over to the Sanhedrin for adjudication. David, in his mind, did what he did.

◆§ Sin in Mind; Sin in Deed

Hashem, however, wanted to retain a closeness with David. He would not allow David to compromise his past achievement — and his future accomplishment — through two terrible sins.

In effect, He stopped David in his tracks. While we cannot overestimate the importance of intention,[51] a sin intended is not the same as a sin committed.

An analogy might be in order. Shimon watches as Reuben readies himself to snatch some valuables from his house. Shimon argues, "Look, the money is lost anyway. I cannot stop him before he runs out. What do I gain by Reuben having to shoulder the guilt of theft for his entire life? Let him have what he wants as a gift!"[52]

---

51. Maharal does not relieve David of guilt for his role in these incidents. That would indeed fly in the face of the plain meaning of the narrative. David spent the rest of his life both repenting (as is obvious from many of his contributions to *Psalms*), and facing a string of tragedies that were part of his punishment. Maharal's intention is not to whitewash David, but to protect *Chazal* from the charge that they would subvert the obvious meaning of the text in order to advance their agenda.

52. The reader will recognize the story as behavior attributed to the Chafetz Chaim, who ran after a shoplifter shouting that he renounced ownership of the article!

Is Reuben a thief? Technically, no. You cannot steal what is yours. Should he be *thought of,* morally, as a thief? Certainly. Only his intended act of theft turned the property into a gift. His own thievery unwittingly rescued him! This cannot absolve him of blame. At the same time, though, a subtle nuance peeks through the argument. The perpetrator's thievery has helped him, indirectly, from escaping the legal designation of thief.

Hashem salvaged the relationship by foreseeing what David would choose, and then intervening behind the scenes. He nudged things along so that there would be a divorce, and so that Uriah would have his opportunity to rebel. As it turned out, David killed a dead man, someone who fully deserved to die. And his wife was retroactively released from her state of matrimony. David neither violated a married woman, nor murdered an innocent man.[53] (This is supported textually as well. Why does the verse underscore, "You disgraced the Word of Hashem *to do* evil," rather than directly state, "You disgraced the Word of Hashem and *did* evil"? We must conclude that David's *willingness to do* evil was disgraceful in its own right, not the commission of the act.)

⋘§ Uriah's Indelicacy

You might still object. Was Uriah really guilty of rebellion against the crown? The answer is an unqualified "Yes!" The crime was not so much in referring to Yoav as "my lord." Yoav *was* Uriah's lord, his superior. Uriah was required, however, to be sensitive to the honor of

---

53. As serious a moral failure as this was, apparently it did not sound the death knell to the close and special relationship Hashem had with David. David's repentance would soon commence, and mend the broken bridges. If he had sinned in deed, this would not have been possible.

The great stress that we place on deed, even above intention, is an important theme in a Judaism which places so much importance upon actions and deeds. We do not get to the World to Come by believing or thinking, but by doing. While our inner life is important, Hashem designed that inner self to respond strongly to our actions. G-d also willed that those actions bring important consequences, "facts on the ground," that thoughts alone do not automatically yield. Sinning in deed is inherently more problematic than intending to sin. See *Nefesh HaChaim* (1:22 and Chs. 4-5 between the third and fourth *shaarim*) for a cogent argument for the primacy of the act over the intention.

the king. The faithful subject would have handled things differently. He would have called Yoav "my lord, your servant — Yoav." This is especially true in the context of battlefield performance. The allegiance of subjects is particularly vulnerable during wartime. A hero who outperforms and outshines the king in combat can sway large parts of the population. David himself experienced this in his earlier years, when his own exploits in battle threatened and enraged King Saul. David would certainly recall the nation's victory song: "Saul has slain his thousands, and David his tens of thousands."[54] He would remember the prophet's terse description of Saul's reaction: "Saul grew very angry,"[55] and how Saul was then set against David, with near-catastrophic consequences for David and his followers.

There is no legal minimum, no threshold of tolerance in detracting from the honor of the king. A small amount of rebellion is still rebellion. Not for this, though, did David want Uriah killed. He could not have sent the matter to the court even had he wanted. It would have raised eyebrows. The members of the court were well aware of David's own personal tolerance. It was not his style to prosecute every technical violator of his honor. They would have suspected that something was amiss, while David was intent on maintaining secrecy.

David did what he did. Hashem stood behind His otherwise faithful and devoted servant. He gave David a chance to recover, to rebound without shattering his greatness. In doing so, G-d not only restored a great king and leader to the Jewish people, but added another accomplishment to David's lifetime. David would forever serve as a model of the depth of remorse and regret that must accompany true repentance.

---

54. *I Samuel* 18:7.
55. Ibid 18:8.

VI. Noah and the Curse of Ham

> "And Noah awoke from his wine, and realized what his younger son had done to him."[56] Rav and Shmuel dispute this. One of them says that he [Ham] castrated him [Noah]; the other says that he sodomized him.[57]

The critics complain. How are we to imagine that such disgusting things became Noah's lot? How could such befall the *tzaddik* who, alone among all the people of the earth, was saved by G-d from the Flood?

This objection is the product of rank superficiality. Our critics are bothered by this point only because they have inadequately looked at the source *psukim*. *Chazal* treated the text to proper, thoughtful analysis, and came to very different conclusions.

Assume, as the critics obviously do, that Ham's misdeed was to look at the nakedness of his father. Would Noah have cursed him so strongly and bitterly for that alone? People sacrifice so much for their children, even when they disappoint their parents. Would ordinary, decent parents lash out against a child after an unprecedented, isolated incident of relatively minor importance? Did Ham deserve such fury for a moment of disrespect?

⌐§ More Than Meets the Eye

You will note that the *pasuk* says that Noah became aware of what "his younger son had *done* to him." If his sin were in looking, then he hadn't really *done* anything. *Chazal* understood that Noah responded proportionately to the seriousness of the crime. A major outrage provoked a major response.

---

56. *Genesis* 9:24.
57. *Sanhedrin* 70a.

It is hard to imagine more despicable behavior than sodomizing one's own father. Was Ham capable of such despicable behavior?

The Torah makes the effort to warn us about the flaws of only a handful of nations. In the arena of sexual impropriety and moral decay, the Torah takes aim at two peoples. "Like the deeds of the land of Egypt where you lived, do not do; like the deeds of the land of Canaan that I will bring you to . . ."[58] There are no coincidences in the Torah. If both of the nations that became the Torah's examples of moral degradation are descended from the same ancestor, then Ham, the family progenitor, had much to do with it. Ham's personality just have had its fill with sexual license and base coarseness.

⮢ Two Ways to Earn a Curse

How did Ham evidence these leanings towards depravity? What did he do, that his descendants would be so flawed? Both opinions address precisely this point.

One opinion sees Ham sodomizing his father. If this was what he did, then the curse, a statement of moral emptiness, is entirely deserved. Ham showed himself to stop at nothing for a moment's gratification. His activity could only point to an empty abyss, a yawning chasm where moral worth should ordinarily reside. Noah's curse of Ham, according to this view, was not a wish, or a call for Divine retribution. It was a restatement of Ham's nature. Ham was *already* a curse, a low person, who would have nothing to contribute to humanity. His offspring were therefore destined to occupy the lowest strata of human society.

The other position sees Ham as castrating his father. Pleasure could not be the motivation for the crime. Rather, castration was a calculated response to Cham's selfishness. He enjoyed the prospect of inheriting a full third of the world, alongside his two brothers. The prospect of having to share with future siblings galled him. Noah's drunken stupor afforded Ham an opportunity to take re-solute action, and he prevented his father from ever siring a fourth son.

Responsible parents see their children as their greatest *berachah*. In

---

58. *Leviticus* 18:3.

the infancy of the world's population, in the years after the decimation of the Flood, each child born would be a potential *berachah* for all of mankind. Looking only at his narrow self-interest, Ham spurned the *berachah* that additional siblings could have meant to human history. Noah's reaction was a moral *quid pro quo*. Deny me — and the entire world — the *berachah* of a fourth child, and no *berachah* will come from your fourth son. A curse is the opposite of a *berachah*. According to this opinion, Noah did not describe what Ham already was, so much as what was appropriate for him (and his heirs who would bear his legacy) to be. *Berachah* would not be distributed equally across the face of the globe and across history. *Berachah* would attach itself to people who had some connection and receptivity to blessing. By turning his back on *berachah* that could benefit others, Ham showed himself to be the antithesis of *berachah*. *Berachah* would cross the street before darkening Ham's doorway.

✌§ The Essence of Sexual Immorality

Having arrived at this understanding of Ham's proclivities, we can reexamine our original assumptions, and offer an alternative approach. It is quite possible that Ham never touched his father. Noah reacted to the incident as if Ham had sodomized him, as if Ham had castrated him. Noah, in his wisdom, understood the potency of a look, a stare.

Let's start with the opinion that Ham sodomized his father. While the mechanics of the sexual act are obvious enough, the Torah relates to them differently. In describing one type of illicit sexual union, the Torah writes, "And he *saw* her nakedness, and she *saw* his nakedness." The verb "see" is *not* used as a euphemistic substitution. "Seeing" is an apt synonym for forbidden sexual activity. You can only see something by focusing on it, by attaching yourself to some extent, even from a distance. Ultimately, violating the ban on forbidden relationships means attaching yourself to, connecting with objects that are improper, either by their nature or because of the mindset of the participant. The Torah expects our focus to be oriented at higher places. In forbidden unions, we throw ourselves bodily into relationships that are distant from the holiness that the Torah demands of the Jewish people.

✒ The Power of a Glance

We can make these connections in other than the obvious manner. By using the verb "see," the Torah suggests that there are many ways in which we can lose ourselves to complete abandon, some less active (and less obvious) than others. Seeing, watching, is usually not equivalent to doing. That can change, though, depending on how much of the inner person is invested in that seeing. We can attach ourselves *visually* to places and people that are inappropriate; we can put so much of our energy and interest into the things we watch, that we attach our very souls to them.[59]

Noah understood his son all too well. As we developed above, Ham's leanings towards moral turpitude and crudeness were extreme. The untrained observer looking at Ham saw nothing more than someone gawking and staring. Noah knew better. He understood Ham's leanings. He considered Ham's behavior, and realized that there was more behind Ham's lecherous gaze than curiosity. Ham *identified* with vulgarity and license. Noah did not have to be a mind reader to know that *visually,* Ham had done nothing less than sodomize him. Noah saw himself used and abused. Ham's behavior exposed his worthlessness, and fully invited the curse.

We can similarly explain the other opinion. The generative faculty of Man, his ability to reproduce, is a Divine gift of great power. Perhaps because it is so common throughout the animal kingdom, we take it for granted, and see nothing unusual in it. In truth, however, capacities that we share with lesser organisms become much more important when Hashem gives them to intelligent souls.[60]

---

59. Compare *Mesillas Yesharim,* Ch. 11, which states that sexual transgressions can be performed with many organs of the body. Looking at the improper is a visual *zenus* (lewdness); obscene speech is *zenus hapeh* (lewdness of the mouth), etc.

60. The Gemara (*Shabbos* 31a) lists the six questions that are addressed to each individual on his or her judgment day. One of them is, "Did you involve yourself with procreation?" Maharal explains that part of us leans towards the limitless existence we call spiritual, while another part pulls towards the here-and-now that we call physical. The common thread uniting all six questions is how much the person preferred the former as a model over the latter. Having children, raising a family can be an exercise in the spiritual model, when a person sees it as a way of transcending

Chazal teach us to prevent these gifts from becoming common-place. One way in which we preserve the specialness of reproduction, in which we elevate it above the animal realm, is by taking care to keep certain body parts covered and private. The uniquely human component of reproduction is a gift with a price. If we fail to treat it with respect, Hashem withdraws its power. Inappropriately exposing private parts will reduce the power of a person's generative potential.

The type of exposure makes a difference, of course. Here is where Ham comes in. Noah, the faithful ally of Hashem, had a more elevated view of all human gifts and potentials. He understood that every part of the human psyche could be, must be, put in the service of Man's Creator. Ham's mind, at least in regard to sexual pleasure, was at the other end of the spectrum. Ham's look, Ham's lascivious stare, was decidedly unholy. There was a dark strength in Ham's gaze. It meant the polar opposite of what we try to do when we keep something hidden and covered, to preserve its specialness. Ham's was a stare so potent that it reduced his father's potency. In effect, he castrated his father, and deserved the curse because of it.

Chazal, in their profundity, opened up a Heavenly Gate for us to arrive at the real intention of the Torah. For all the words of our Torah sit at the highest pinnacle of meaning. For the undeserving it may be said, "The righteous go in them [the paths of Hashem], and the transgressors stumble in them";[61] for them, light is turned to darkness.

You must know that I have explained only a small part of what they teach here — just enough to quiet the wagging tongues of the intellectually blind. In the merit of this, may Hashem enlighten our eyes with wisdom, and uncover for us the treasures of His Torah.

---

the limitations of being a very small cog in a very large machine. Regenerating ourselves beyond the confines of our own life and times ties us in with existence in general, with the non-restriction that characterizes the spiritual.

61. *Hosea* 14:10.

VII. *Mashiach's* Birth in the Six Days of Creation

"Back [or last] and front [earliest] You have restricted me, and You have laid Your hand upon
me."[62] R' Shimon ben Lakish said, "He [Adam] was
the last in the work of the last day, and the earliest in
the work of the first day." That is consistent with the
view of R' Shimon ben Lakish, for he said, " 'And the
Divine Presence hovered'[63] refers to the soul of
Mashiach the King, as you read, 'The spirit of Hashem
shall rest upon him.'[64] If Man merits, they say to him,
'You preceded the ministering angels.' If he does not,
they tell him, 'Before you came the fly, the gnat, the
worm.' "[65]

"How could this be so?" they ask. What possible reason could
there be for creating *Mashiach* within the six days of Creation? And what has he been doing up until now, with so much time
on his hands until the day (may it come speedily!) of his revelation?

The key thought here is that it is insufficient for us to see Hashem
as just the Creator of the universe. A creation that never makes it to
the finish line shows inadequacy on the part of the creator. True
creation is married to *purpose*. It leads to a goal, to the accomplishment of an objective.

We needn't puzzle over the purpose of G-d's Creation. "Everything
Hashem made [He made] for His sake."[66] Or, as *Chazal* teach,[67] "All

---

62. *Psalms* 139:5.
63. *Genesis* 1:2.
64. *Isaiah* 11:2.
65. *Bereishis Rabbah* 8:1.
66. *Proverbs* 16:4.
67. *Ethics of the Father* 6:12.

that G-d created in this world He created for His Honor, as it says, 'Everyone who is called by My Name and whom I have created for My glory, whom I have fashioned, even perfected.' "[68]

It should now be apparent to you that the world as we see it today is a far cry from its goal. It reflects the act of Hashem's creation, without fully evidencing the purpose of its creation.

When will Hashem's intended purpose become manifest? In the words of Zechariah, "Hashem will be the King over all the land; on that day Hashem will be One and His Name will be One."[69] Such a society will do justice to the Honor of Hashem! As the Gemara succinctly states, "The world was made for *Mashiach.* "[70]

A purposeful creative act focuses on its goal throughout all stages of its execution. It follows that arriving at the end point — achieving the epoch of *Mashiach* — was woven into the fabric of Creation. Hashem created the world assuring its success; He began unraveling the scroll of history with the final chapter already written. The tension-filled opening movements were scored so that the melodic line would give way to the symphony's triumphant coda. The end, the last, was already fixed in place at the beginning. History, one way or another, would wend its way to a satisfactory conclusion.

We return to our passage. Man was created both first and last. On the one hand, he had to be created last. Everything that we know is complex, in the sense of being formed by simpler objects coming together. The simplest things that we use are made of yet smaller things that fit together synergistically.[71] We know of nothing that cannot be further subdivided.

We divide living organs into pieces, or more elegantly, into different organs and organ systems. Each of these have component parts, which in turn can be reduced to cells. On the cellular level, we know of an entire universe of complexity, with various chemical factories churning out a myriad of products. We can thus reduce life to a catalogue of inanimate, chemical components.

---

68. *Isaiah* 43:7.

69. 14:9.

70. *Sanhedrin* 98b.

71. This was explained in detail in the First Well, p.18-20.

We can further reduce inanimate objects to their constituent molecules. We see these molecules as composites of different atoms. The atoms, in turn, we know to be collections of particles and sub-particles.

It makes sense that in the design of things, the order is reversed. The primary building blocks are the most basic elements, and must be present, at least from a human perspective, before the construction of anything based upon them.

Viewed this way, there is no gainsaying that Man stands at the opposite end of the continuum from simplicity. He is the most complex object of all creation. We need not even debate the capabilities of Man in relation to other creatures.

One unique ingredient of Man's recipe puts him on a different level of complexity — sechel. Assemble all the building blocks of all the infra-human species, and you still do not have Man, until you add the element that defines him as human. This — the merging of the physical with the spiritual/intellectual — is a whole order of complexity apart from anything else. When Man lacks this element, there is indeed little to distinguish him from the lowly fly.

In the intuitive progression from the simple, Man has to be seen as last. And indeed, chronologically he was created that way. Concurrently, Hashem insured from the beginning that the culmination of Man's history — the era of Mashiach — would come about in due time.

There is another subtle point we must add. In the progression from simple to complex, the soul of Mashiach eclipses even the creation of Man, which merged spiritual and physical. His soul is so sublime and pure that it doesn't occupy a place on the same continuum as anything else in Creation. Completely transcendent, it wasn't part of the gradual development of the six days of Creation. Hashem shaped it on the very first day.

But why, you will ask, was it created even before the angels? Surely Mashiach is no holier, no more transcendent than the angels?

There was reason enough, says the midrash, not to create the angels on the first day. Had Hashem done so, we would forever remain confused about the Unity of Hashem. People would somehow suspect a collaborative effort, and argue that "Michael stretched [the world] from the south, while Gavriel pulled at it from the north."[72]

Enlarging the number of primordial entities deflects from the Unity of Hashem in Creation. To avoid this, Hashem allowed nothing else to compete with His absolute Unity on the first day of creation.

He made a single exception. The soul of *Mashiach* has the very opposite effect than that of the angels. Angels introduce the notion of plurality, even if only on the spiritual level. After all, they are divided in name and in function. Michael is not Gavriel, and Gavriel is not Michael.

Mashiach does the opposite. He is the one that brings all the loose pieces together. He unites the world and all its disparate pieces under the leadership of Hashem. He belongs, like nothing else, to the absolute unity of the first day.

---

72. *Bereishis Rabbah* 3:8.

THE
SIX WELL

Reasons

for

Reasons

challenge: *Chazal* lacked the wisdom and knowledge commonly available to educated people. *Chazal* seem not only to ignore the wealth of human understanding and science, but they replace it with strange assumptions.

The
response:

I. *Chazal* and Science

Were this charge true, it would be a very serious indictment of *Chazal.* It would indicate that they were deficient in wisdom and distant from the truth.

Nothing, however, could be more inaccurate. To the verse, "Say to wisdom, 'You are my sister,' "[1] *Chazal* append the following thought. "If a matter is as clear to you as [the fact that] your sister is forbidden to you — then speak about it. If not — don't."[2] Now, the Torah forbids a number of incestuous unions, in all of which there is a certain closeness between the partners involved. Several of these are fairly obvious to us, almost intuitive. None of them is based on a relationship as naturally close as brother and sister, who occupy a single generational plane. Even the relationship between parent and child is, at least in one sense, more distant. The two parties are separated by generation and by role. Brother and sister remain the most perfect example of close relatives, separated by nothing other than their individual identities.

Without *Chazal* invoking the incest prohibition, we might have read this verse differently. We would have seen an exhortation to get close to and comfortable with wisdom, much as a person enjoys a close relationship with a beloved family member. Our Sages detected something more in it. They noted that the text specifically chose brother

1. *Proverbs* 7:4.
2. *Shabbos* 145b.

and sister, the metaphor *par excellence* for obvious and manifest closeness. They caught an allusion to the confidence we should have in our grasp of a matter before we offer an opinion. Prudence dictates that a wise person refrain from speaking about matters he knows nothing about. We don't really need a Torah to tell us that. *Chazal* here go further, urging us to remain silent unless we have moved well beyond familiarity and competence. Lacking perfect clarity, we are advised to retreat into silence.

This is an exacting call to excellence. It is inconceivable that the same authors were guilty of a general lack of intellectual rigor and sloppiness of thought, and that they disregarded all that science had to offer.

◈ *Chazal* and Science

Our critics arrived at their conclusion because they noted many places where *Chazal* provided reasons for natural phenomena that are simply unbelievable. Herein lies the essence of their mistake. They assumed that *Chazal* were providing the natural causes for these phenomena. *Chazal,* however, were not so interested in the immediate, natural cause for different phenomena. They left this inquiry to empirical scientists. Their concern was the cause *behind* the expression of natural law. They knew that for every explanation, for every rationale, there is a reason behind the reason.

◈ Apparent Causes and Real Causes

To deny this is to deny proper belief, and to deny Torah itself. Does the Torah not tell us that the rainbow was placed in the sky as a reminder of G-d's ancient covenant with Man? Yet scientists have no problem explaining the multicolored refraction of light that we call the rainbow. Clearly, the Torah wants us to go beyond the scientifically obvious. It expects that we understand that there were multiple ways that Hashem could have structured the interaction between light and water droplets. He chose the configuration He did in order to remind us of the ancient Flood. *Chazal* aimed at the ultimate causes of reality; in no way did they deny the apparent and proximal scientific ones.

Human anatomy provides us with another example. Every limb, every organ, every structure within the human body has some important function. Scientifically, we have no need to go beyond the natural role and function of any body part to understand why it is there. Yet the Torah teaches us otherwise. "So G-d created Man in His image; in the image of G-d He created Him."[3] Man's physical body shows more than good engineering. It has something to teach about Hashem and His attributes.[4] There is a G-dly set of considerations and causes that determine how the "natural" causes should take shape.

Our critics miss out on two counts. They accuse *Chazal* of ignoring or being unaware of well-established scientific explanations. In this, they seriously underestimate the knowledge of our Sages. And because they do not appreciate how deep the thought of *Chazal* is, they fail to uncover the hidden meaning within their words. Thus, the real sense and import of the reasons offered by *Chazal* — the ones that deal with the cause behind the cause — remain obscure to them.

---

3. *Genesis* 1:27.

4. Note that Maharal treats Man's "image" of G-d in much more concrete terms than many of the earlier commentators. Some saw this "image" as either the gift of a rational faculty (*Rambam, Moreh Nevuchim* 1:1; *Abarbanel* to *Genesis* 1:26 states that all the early commentators embrace this approach), or of the ability to make free, non-determined choices (*Malbim*). (Interestingly, *Rambam* himself, *Yad HaChazakah, Teshuvah* 5:1, although citing a different verse, sees free-will as the factor that man holds in common with G-d.) Maharal, however, seems to follow the approach of some of the Kabbalists, who saw parallels between the physical structure of Man and the organization and structure of the different attributes with which Hashem relates to the world.

II. The Four Causes of Eclipses

Eclipses of the sun occur on account of four reasons: because of an *Av Beis Din* (Chief of the Court) who dies and is not eulogized properly; because of a betrothed woman who cries for help [during an attempted rape] but no one assists her; because of sodomy; and because of two brothers who are killed together. The darkening of [other] luminaries occurs for four reasons: because of forgers; because of those who give false testimony; because of those who raise small animals in the land of Israel; and because of those who cut down fine trees.[5]

A ll of these reasons are contradicted by the observable, complain our critics. We know quite well that eclipses and the like depend on the paths that various heavenly bodies take through the sky, and how they occasionally cross each other. These events can be calculated; they are entirely predictable. Man's transgressions have nothing to do with them.

As we wrote above, *Chazal* in no way deny the natural explanations for these phenomena. But they are not satisfied with such arguments. Why would G-d create a universe in such a way? Why do the paths of some of our closest neighbors intersect, plunging them at times into temporary darkness? Wouldn't it be more elegant for those steady and reliable outposts of illumination to be a tad *more* steady and reliable?

All that Hashem created is meant to serve Man. His conduct is the single most important determinant of how the laws of nature perform. There is no question that Man's actions are the cause of the not-quite-perfect elegance we observe.[6] Would Man not sin, the laws that govern the heavenly bodies — and everything else, for that matter — would be slightly different. There would be no eclipses.

---

5. *Succah* 29a.

6. See "Earthquakes and the Fuzziness of Creation" in the Fourth Well for a parallel consideration of this theme.

This is all apparent in the story of Man's creation. Had we not transgressed G-d's word, we would all still live in *Gan Eden.* Its ample produce, flourishing without any human toil, would sustain us — a state of affairs which is a delight to imagine, but hardly consistent with a few millennia of human experience. Our shortcomings created the need for Hashem to craft a completely different style of living for us, one in which we would have to strain and strive to eke out subsistence from the earth. Hashem refashioned the world appropriate to the spiritual level of Man.

⊷§ Children of a Lesser Light

This applies to the orbits of heavenly bodies as well. In a theoretical, sin-free world, no heavenly orb would ever lose any of its light. We human non-luminaries, though, are not all perfect. A byproduct of allowing Man free-will is that in a large society, we can predict with certainty that some people will make poor choices. We cannot even hope for a world populated only by the righteous, at least not until the fulfillment of Hashem's promise for the future, "Hashem your G-d will circumcise your hearts and the heart of your offspring."[7] At that time, Hashem will provide a new constancy of illumination, as it is stated, "And the moon will be humiliated, and the sun shamed."[8] "Never again will your sun set, and your moon will not be withdrawn; for Hashem will be an eternal light for you."[9]

Chazal express this thought in a *midrash*:[10]

> It is a bad sign when the sun is eclipsed. It is analogous to a king who arranges a feast for all his servants, and places a candelabrum in front of them. If he is angered with them, he instructs one of his servants to remove the candelabrum, leaving the rest sitting in darkness.

We honor guests with bright, cheerful lighting, by providing more light than is absolutely necessary. When the servants slight the king,

---

7. *Deuteronomy* 30:6.
8. *Isaiah* 24:23.
9. Ibid. 60:20.
10. *Succah* 29a.

he responds by eliminating the light meant to honor the feast and to honor them. Hashem does the same to us. The light He provides our world honors us. When we sin and deserve lesser honor, He substitutes a lesser light.

Having come this far, we really have answered our critics, and could move on. The reader will still be curious. Granted, it is the imperfection of a sin-mired world that ultimately causes inconsistencies in the luminaries. But why are some sins singled out? What makes them the culprits?

As far as our intent here (which is only to dull the sword of our critics), the question itself is much of the answer. Had *Chazal* pointed a finger at, say, illicit relations, we would have concluded that they took an educated guess. We would have argued that they weighed the severity of different offenses, and chose one of the worst.

This is clearly not what happened. They did not specify the obvious. Their motley list of human failings confounds us at first reading. We can only conclude that much more wisdom lies beneath the surface! Even without an explanation, our confidence in them should increase, rather than the opposite!

We have really succeeded already in overcoming the objections of our opponents. Nonetheless, we will go further, and explain *Chazal's* intent in this passage. We have previously explained[11] that light and dark are appropriate symbols for existence and its negation. (Perhaps because of the strong impact that the day/night cycle has upon us, we associate light with the presence of something, and the extinguishing of that light with its removal. By extension, light becomes a symbol of existence itself, or the most important presence. Darkness, on the other hand, represents any diminution of existence, or any deficiency and need.) This is borne out by the story of Creation, which deals with light before anything else, conveying to us that existence itself was willed and created by G-d.

Now, we understand that this world cannot be an uninterrupted flash of fierce, bright light. All things in our physical, limited, unperfected world show some signs of deficiency. Some darkness attaches itself to everything. If this were not the case, we would perforce be residing in

---

11. See, for example, his linking of *Gehinnom* with darkness in the Second Well, p. 52.

Gan Eden! This darkness is expected, and quite normal. Its representation in natural law is the expected passage of each day into the darkness of night. Nothing unusual there.

There are, however, unusual lapses of light, such as eclipses. To be sure, they are scientifically predictable. But they are unusual in the sense that they are not everyday occurrences. And they mirror the spiritual state of a world that tolerates unusual deficiency.

◄§ Law Enables Existence

We will turn to *Chazal*'s list of deficiencies, one by one, beginning with the death of the Chief of the Court. As the head of the judiciary, the *Av Beis Din* oversees the administration of Law. As light is to the notion of absolute existence, Law is to the idea of human and societal existence. Without Law, there is only chaos. Without the security and order it brings, society cannot be said to fully exist. For this reason, the name *Elokim* (which is always associated with Hashem's attribute of Law and Justice) is used throughout the account of Creation. For the world to come into true existence, its features must be fixed and predictable, fixed by some immutable Law. For a similar reason, *Chazal* emphasize that one who sits in judgment, even for a short while, becomes a partner with Hashem in Creation.[12]

We can now understand how the death of the *Av Beis Din* means an end to an important kind of existence. We can also appreciate why his death might yield a lessening not only of the intellectual light of the world, but even cause the light of the luminaries to wane. In fact, though, *Chazal* do not point to the *death* of the *Av Beis Din,* but to the way he is treated *after* his death.

Death, after all, is not unusual. It is part of the general deficiency of unperfected life that we mentioned before. In truth, the "loss" that death introduces is a sham. The *neshamah* of the *Av Beis Din* continues to shine. If anything, it shines brighter in *Olam Haba,* unencumbered by the darkening elements of physical existence.

In an absolute sense, then, the "light" of the *Av Beis Din* is never extinguished. It changes addresses, but never disappears. Human sin and

---

12. *Shabbos* 10a.

failure, however, can truly snuff out the light of the *Av Beis Din.* When they do, they create the unconscionable loss and deficiency that dull the luminaries.

∽§ Vintage Soul

Here do they do this? Take the process of aging, for example. If you are fixated on strength and vitality, the weakness, infirmity, and frailty of old age can be either frightening, sympathy-provoking, or even contemptuous. How different is the Torah's perspective! It teaches us to prefer the inner grace of the *neshamah* over the outer graces of strength and agility. We submit that a quiet, confident, considered voice says more about the real inner person than the frenetic activity of youth. We know that Man is a composite of body and soul, and that they are both important to us in our years in this world. But if we are pushed to choose between them, we should not hesitate to opt for the spirituality of the soul above all competing values.

We make such a choice whenever we encounter an older person. Without the Torah's instruction, we might easily pity the waning of strength and loss of vitality. Instead, we are instructed to rise before, and give honor to, the older person. Where others only notice the terrible, enfeebling toll that time takes on the human body, the Torah provides us with a different lens. We catch a glimpse of a *neshamah* that has broken away from the vise-grip of the body! Body and soul ordinarily live in uneasy accommodation to each other, neither deferring to the other. In the older person, though, we detect a balance of power that has shifted. The *neshamah* has begun to break away, asserting its independence. Rather than turning our backs on a reminder of physical mortality that we do not want to face, we rise to honor a display of the ascendance of the immortal soul.

We strikingly indicate how much we value the soul-component of Man when we mourn and eulogize. We could simply reminisce about the deceased's interests and personality, what made him or her different. Especially, we might reflect upon what the deceased meant to us, feeding our sense of loss and self-pity. The more we value the *neshamah,* and the eternity of its accomplishment, though, the more we will focus on other things as well. We will spend far more time exploring, cherishing, and even celebrating the mitzvos and spiritual accomplishments of the deceased. This constitutes proper mourning, from a Torah perspective. It honors the successful passage of a *neshamah* through the journey of earthly existence, and marks its return to the place where it was meant to live eternally.

By upholding the Law, the *Av Beis Din* was a primary torchbearer for the community, providing one of the essential underpinnings of communal life. His work should have greatly illuminated the lives of many. If he is not eulogized properly, if his worth and contribution are not appreciated and noted, then no one really ever sensed that light. It may shine ever strong in *Olam Haba.* But in this world, his light was effectively snuffed out well before.

Here Man introduces unusual deficiency, not the expected, hardwired kind. The darkened sky in an eclipse mirrors this deficiency. Not that sin "causes" the darkening of the luminaries. Rather, Hashem created them in a way that the curious intertwining of their paths gives mute testimony to a world that doesn't properly appreciate light, a world in which obscuring that light is tolerated and accepted.

We have considered so far the first of the four examples given by *Chazal.* In his response to the *Av Beis Din,* Man introduces deficiency through his failure to see clearly, and to appreciate what he sees. Man's shortcoming here is passive. The remaining three examples deal with shortcomings directly wrought by Man's activity.

Every sin, every transgression brings deficiency to the world. This is almost a tautology. By definition, a sin is something that Hashem determined should not be there, that has no place. Each time we commit one, we attach ourselves to non-existence, to a counterfeit, ersatz reality. Nothing could be more deficient than sin itself.

The examples *Chazal* chose in this passage are particularly outrageous. In several places, when they wish to point out just how evil someone is, they argue that he violated a betrothed woman. We use the word *kiddushin* for marriage, and it relates to *kedushah,* or holiness. The marital agreement between two people generates a form of holiness, which is negated by the transgressor's sin. (Note that *Chazal* do not point to the violation of an ordinary married woman, but to a betrothed one. While the state of *kiddushin* continues unabated throughout marriage, the *kedushah* element is most obvious when it is

newly created, when it is young, fresh, and full of energetic commitment. Violating the betrothed woman is a more diabolical form of
nullifying *kedushah.*)

Similarly, homosexuality and the murders of two brothers show the
world to be a place of great deficiency. (The punishment for all three
of the active failings here is death, or the negation of the life of the
perpetrator. This itself should reassure us that we are on the right track
— that we are looking at actions that negate proper existence, and that
are therefore inherently deficient.) Homosexuality is an extreme example of human deficiency and failing because not even animals practice
it. The deficiency in an act of murder needs no elaboration. The double
murder of two brothers adds outrage to outrage; it points to a deficiency intensified and redoubled.

Once again, we have more than adequately responded to our critics,
and need go no further. We will, however, not refrain from explaining
whatever is appropriate.

✍§ Searching at the Top

C*hazal* employed four examples of deficiency, of a world clinging
to non-existence. If we were unaware of any terrible shortcomings
in this world, but knew that Hashem found things terribly deficient,
where would we look for signs of weakness? The most reasonable
place to search would be at the pinnacle of G-d's Creation, at its most
important product. We would look to the condition of Man himself.

It is useful at times to divide Man's sense of himself into different
parts. We will now show through one such division that Man's propen-
sity towards deficiency has spread to every dimension of his life. In
effect, if Man becomes thoroughly deficient, so will the world.

The most obvious division we make within Man is between body and
spirit. Animals, though, also share these two parts to some extent. In
Man's case, the precise and exact combination of these elements
amounts to a third dimension — the Image of G-d. The richness and
fullness of the individual is not in using the first two elements sequen-
tially or even together. There is rich potential in their merging; the
whole here is greater than the sum of its parts. But there is more. As
we grow into adulthood, we discover that we are still not complete.

The "whole" person is still lacking without a partner, another perspective at his side. Bonding with one's spouse fills the remaining gaps.

Let us now consider our passage's four examples. By improperly marking the death of the *Av Beis Din,* people fail drastically in their appreciation of what the *neshamah* really is, and how much more important it is to its possessor (and to the cosmos!) than any other part. If such events can transpire, then the world is a place generally deficient in one of the four elements of Man. The *neshamah* is undervalued and compromised.

Violating the betrothed woman demonstrates that the bodily part of Man malfunctions, badly. The body is meant to be a tool of the soul, a vehicle for translating will into positive, mitzvah activity. The mind and soul must always retain control, keeping the body on a short leash. Without that control, the body, the physical part of Man, has its own agenda. In the worst case, the pecking order is reversed. Man can lose himself so thoroughly in the physical that his mind and soul are left as second-class citizens.

This is what forbidden relations is all about. *Chazal*[13] see a parallel between the barley-offering of the accused adulteress, and what we put into an animal's feeding trough. "Just as her deeds are the deeds of an animal, so is her offering the food of an animal." Whatever spirit animals have serves the physical and bodily, not the other way around. Illicit relations in general indicate that a person has submerged himself to his purely physical wants and desires. When a person capitulates to the physical part of himself, he shows the body to be deficient in subverting the lead role that the higher functions of mind and soul were meant to play.

So go the others. Murder is the absolute extinction of a life, of the ability of one unique form of the Image of G-d to leave its mark on this world. The double murder increases the outrage exponentially. Homosexuality represents the final compromise of Man's fourth component — his capacity for completion through bonding with a spouse. By perverting this need for completion in such an unnatural manner, Man shows that in this area as well he is deficient. The set is thus complete. Every aspect of Man — the culmination and goal of Creation — operates deficiently. No wonder the lights go out.

---

13. *Sotah* 14a. Barley was commonly fed to animals rather than people.

All that remains is the final part of the passage, dealing with the dulling of other luminaries. These phenomena cannot be as significant as the eclipsing of the sun, which is the all-important source of light to the world. All the other luminaries make only a small contribution, sparkling from the periphery. We should not be surprised, then, to observe that the shortcomings that *Chazal* link to them are also more peripheral, rather than wounds festering at Man's essence. Like the first set, though, all of them concern denial of existence.

⊷§ Forged Reality

Forgers create reality where there is none. The purpose of a document is to solemnize a commitment to some small part of reality — a transaction, a contract, etc. Counterfeiters elevate non-existence to an art form by forging an impressive testimony to something that does not exist. False witnesses do the same, not in writing but orally.

The final two are more subtle. The flip side of creating a false reality is destroying an existing one. Small cattle, like sheep, are not fed in place. They roam, they forage, they graze where they find vegetation. When they exhaust one hillside, they move on to the next. Shepherds in the times of *Chazal* were notorious for allowing their charges to graze wherever they could, paying no heed to ownership of property. (Grazing sheep cut paths of destruction in other people's property. We might say that they destroy the land as it was meant to be settled; they negate the land of Israel, choicest of all places.)

⊷§ Missing the Fine Points

Their partners in crime are those who destroy fine trees. These people close their eyes to the special *berachah* that Hashem put in some trees and withheld from others. Needing the wood that most trees can provide, they cut without discrimination. It does not occur to them that some trees should be spared because of their greater value and utility. Their view of the world is monochromatic. They miss all the color — all the subtlety of the world Hashem gave us, its richness and nuance and variegated gifts. By destroying the gift of fruit that the tree could have provided (had another been cut in its place), they too destroy and negate the *quality* of existence that Hashem created.

If Man acted as he should, he would be a king. His palace would be adorned with chandeliers that would never fail. Servants would accompany him bearing bright torches. Regrettably, we are not so regal, and we have turned the palace into something much less majestic. We are quite privileged that Hashem provides adequate and reliable illumination nonetheless. But we shouldn't be surprised if the lights flicker every now and then.

III. What the Earth Rests Upon

R' Yosi says: "Woe to those people who see but do not realize what they are seeing, who stand but do not realize upon what they are [standing.] What does the earth rest upon? Upon the pillars, as it says: 'Who shakes the earth from its place, and its pillars tremble.'[14] The pillars [stand] upon the waters, as it says: 'To Him Who spread out the earth upon the waters.'[15] The waters [stand] upon the mountains, as it says: 'The waters stood above the mountains.'[16] The mountains on the wind, as it says: 'For behold, He forms mountains, and creates wind.'[17] The wind [stands] upon the storm, as it says: 'The wind, the storm does its bidding.'[18] The storm is suspended from the Arm of *HaKadosh Baruch Hu,* as it says: 'And from beneath are the Arms of the world.' "[19]

But the *Chachamim* say: "[The earth] stands on 12 pillars, as it says: 'He set the borders to the nations according to the number [of the tribes] of the children

14. *Job* 9:6.
15. *Psalms* 136:6.
16. Ibid. 104:6.
17. *Amos* 4:13.
18. *Psalms* 148:8.
19. *Deuteronomy* 33:27.

of Israel.'[20] Some say on seven pillars, as it says: 'She has carved out its seven pillars.' "[21] R' Elazar ben Shamua says: "It rests on one pillar, and its name is *tzaddik,* as it says: 'And *tzaddik* is the foundation of the world.' "[22],[23]

Our critics took all of this at face value. They thought that *Chazal* understood the world to literally stand upon columns, a depiction they found to be highly implausible.

The passage, of course, is an allegory. *Chazal* want us to know that the world has no permanence or continuity of its own.[24] Our image of *terra firma,* of bedrock-like stability, is inaccurate. One thing alone keeps it from slipping into oblivion — its connection with Hashem.

On the other hand, we cannot fathom how our world can conceivably maintain any connection with Him! We know our world to be the polar opposite of everything we attribute to G-d. It is limited, physical, time-bound. What possibly can create an ongoing association across a chasm that is infinitely wide?

◆§ Small Jumps

Chazal here suggest replacing a single-span bridge with a chain of many small links. The distance, as it were, is traversed in small steps, moving away from the insentient coarseness of the earth, and ultimately moving within range of the supernal qualities of G-d.

---

20. Ibid. 33:8.
21. *Proverbs* 9:1.
22. Ibid 10:25.
23. *Chagigah* 12b.
24. Some of the ancients, of course, believed in the eternity of the world, in an existence that was "just there," part of some essential nature of things. Modern proponents of a steady-state approach to cosmogeny are not far from this position.
   On the other hand, Deists always saw the masterful brushstrokes of a Divine Hand behind the creation of our world. They thought that G-d did such a good job, though, that the world was quite capable of continuing on its own, without requiring further intervention by G-d.

It starts with Man. The earth was intended for Man's use, and is therefore connected to him. The words of *Psalms* spell this out clearly: "The earth He has given to mankind."[25]

The Stature of Man

What is it about Man that inches the earth a bit closer to the ineffable Holiness of Hashem? (We are not dealing with great men or their deeds yet. More on that later. Here we speak of generic Man, the race to which Hashem entrusted the entirety of the earth.) *Chazal* hint to the answer by using the word "columns." Columns stand tall, stately — and erect. Man distinguishes himself among the animals by standing straight and erect. He stands tall because nothing in his world stands above him, humbling him and diminishing him. He bows before nothing of this world, while all its elements serve him. A Divine mandate urges him to press his dominion to all realms of this earth. ("Fill the land and subdue it. Rule over the fish of the sea, the birds of the sky, and every living thing that moves on the earth."[26])

The Image Not Used

Standing erect is the single most powerful image that points to the *Tzelem Elokim,* the image of G-d within Man. This anatomical feature speaks more forcefully for Man's lofty level than his ability to speak intelligently![27] Ponder this some more and you will see that the image is borrowed from another place — a law that prohibits the use of this image.

---

25. *Psalms* 115:16. Maharal does not cite the *pasuk* at the beginning of *Genesis,* which assigns the name *Adam* because Man was taken "from the earth." The point in our passage is the opposite one. We are not looking at the earth as the place that generates and nurtures Man. We are trying to show how Man sustains the earth! Without Man as an intermediary (linking with yet other intermediaries), the earth cannot connect with G-d, and cannot sustain itself.

26. *Genesis* 1:28.

27. *Ramban, Genesis* 2:7, explicating *Onkelos,* sees speech as the most important factor that differentiates between Man and animal. Maharal cites *Onkelos* in the next Well, p. 244.

The Torah instructs us not to associate Hashem with any form or image. What precisely does the Torah mean to prevent? Were it not for this prohibition, what image would intelligent people substitute for an incorporeal G-d Who cannot be fathomed? The Torah surely doesn't address itself to fools who actually believe that G-d has some physical form!

The answer is fairly obvious. The Torah *does* speak of an Image of G-d, in relation to the Creation of Man. There is something about Man that suggests the closest symbolic representation for G-d available. If we had to depict G-d, we would draw a straight, vertical line. It would symbolize the absolute manner in which absolutely nothing rules over Him, how nothing sways Him or competes with His Power. It would suggest His complete dominion and mastery over everything. This is the image that the Torah instructs us not to use. Ironically, Hashem borrows this forbidden image, and lovingly awards it to every member of Mankind, Jew and non-Jew alike!

This honorable image, we are told here, is not the equivalent of connection to G-d. A sustained association with Hashem requires more than a gift freely granted by Hashem, which Man does not work for or with. The columns themselves will not stand unassisted. They rest on water. The symbolism is obvious. Again and again, Torah is likened to water. "Everyone who is thirsty, go to the water."[28] "Why are the words of Torah compared to water?"[29] The columns, representing all of Mankind, are linked to G-d because of the nation that received the Torah. The transition is hinted at in *Ethics of the Fathers*:[30] "Beloved is Man, who was created in [His] Image. Beloved is Yisrael, who were given a precious vessel." The *Tanna* describes two levels. The first — the Image of G-d — is shared by all mankind, and therefore connects all of it. The second is the privilege of the Jewish people.

The waters cannot go it alone. They rest on mountains, or individuals who tower over everyone else. Every generation has its giants, whose wisdom and deeds majestically are as discernible as tall peaks. (*Chazal* employ this figure in several places. In Rosh Hashanah,[31] for

---

28. *Isaiah* 55:1.
29. *Taanis* 7a.
30. 3:14.
31. *Rosh Hashanah* 11a.

example, they cite a verse in *Song of Songs*:[32] "The voice of my beloved! . . . it came . . . as if leaping over mountains, skipping over hills." They take the mountains as alluding to the Patriarchs and the hills as suggesting the Matriarchs.)

The mountains are supported by the wind. We have moved quite a distance from unrefined earth. We are not yet where we want to be. Many people sell themselves short by training their sights on goals that undervalue their potential. They cannot conceive of anything more lofty than great wisdom and mitzvos. *Chazal* react to this with disappointment. "Woe to those people who . . . do not realize upon what they are standing." There are many, many rungs of greatness to be scaled. New vistas peek out to those who have already scaled the mountains, perhaps invisible to the rest of us still standing at the base. The growth does not stop! Woe unto people! They do not comprehend how much development is possible even for the role models they look up to and revere! Would they understand how valuable Torah and mitzvos are, they would work much harder to achieve them!

The next level up is wind, or *ruach.* It refers to *Ruach HaKodesh* — a spirit of Divine assistance. Here, Man's connection with G-d is manifest, because of the Divine aid and enlightenment that operate within him. The bearer of this spirit is able to perform in ways that others cannot. It is clear to others that a direct power of Hashem is working through him.

A road of infinite length is a long one to travel. At *Ruach HaKodesh,* we have gone well beyond Man reaching out to something Above. We see Hashem reaching down below, acknowledging individual worth. But there are an infinite number of levels of this connection. *Ruach* is only a spirit, and its presence can be still and muted. Much further along the continuum is the raging tempest, the next level up. Here, that Divine connection within works with force and fury. It shows itself as prophecy. The prophet experiences the Presence of Hashem within him so strongly that he is physically crushed by it. He cannot stand. The Torah describes it in several places[33] as "the Hand of G-d upon him."

---

32. 2:8.
33. *Ezekiel* 37:1; *I Kings* 18:46.

That Hand brings us to our destination. We have moved from the pure earthiness of the world to an elevated plane that is responsive to the Touch of G-d. The Hand as well has moved. From its place "beside" Hashem, He causes the Hand to reach out to a person still separated from Him. For humans, the arm extends the reach of the fingers, directing them where they are needed. Hashem is also described as having an Arm — a powerful, outstretched one. The power of prophecy derives from the strength of that Arm, which reaches out to grasp elevated Man. In that grasp, the world finds its connection to G-d, and the continuity of its existence.

~§ The Storm Within the Lull

We could suggest a small modification of the final steps, relating them to the inner spiritual life of all people who come close to G-d, not just the phenomenon of prophecy. In a passage elsewhere which urges a number of positive characteristics upon us,[34] *Chazal* inject a word of caution. "*Yiras Hashem* (fear and reverence of G-d) is [man's] treasure."[35] Without *yiras Hashem,* all other characteristics are ineffective. Like the small amount of preservative added to a large store of grain, *yiras Hashem* preserves and continues the existence of all else.

We might apply this thought to our passage. At the level of *Ruach HaKodesh,* we see connection between Hashem and the world. *Ruach HaKodesh* contributes a confident tranquility of Divine insight and illumination, which belies what you will find beneath the surface of its possessor. No *Ruach HaKodesh* can last, has any permanence unless something rages forcefully within. True *yiras Hashem* constantly bestirs and animates the inner self, always goading the person on. Its possessor will incessantly review and criticize his actions, searching for faults he may have overlooked, and ways in which the good he has done could have been better.[36] Constantly scrutinizing, always preoccupied with the expectation of his Creator, Hashem's immediacy effectively pushes every breath of his life. As cause and effect are related,

---

34. *Shabbos* 31a.

35. *Isaiah* 33:6.

36. See *Mesillas Yesharim,* Ch. 3.

so is Hashem related to him. The relationship enjoys reciprocity: G-d directly sustains him with His outstretched Arm. Thus, the *Ruach HaKodesh* leads to the raging tempest within — which guides the person to the firm grasp of the waiting Hand.

The other opinions in our passage are variations on the same theme. The *Chachamim* specify 12 columns, corresponding to the founders of the twelve tribes. The Jewish people are at the head of the 70 nations of the world; the 12 sons of Jacob stand at our head. This viewpoint emphasizes that ongoing connection and association with Hashem requires a Jewish nation.

Another opinion calls for seven columns. It sees the forefathers as the heads and chiefs of our people. Through the three Patriarchs and four Matriarchs, we stand on seven columns.

R' Elazar ben Shamua posits a single column. Neither the tribes nor the forefathers bear the weight of the world, since they are not of this world any longer, but in *Olam Haba.* We need to find an element of the here and now that creates the first link between the opposing poles of our earth and the holiness of Hashem. In each generation there is one *tzaddik* who clings to Hashem and carries the rest of the world along with him.

Looking back, we have a deeper understanding of the firm footing the world enjoys. We understand that there is a deeper reality behind the one that is apparent to us. In their grasp of this ultimate reality, *Chazal* too were on quite firm footing.

IV. The Value of *Aggadah*

> Regarding the *aggadah*: The one who writes it has no portion; the one who expounds it will be burnt; the one who listens to it receives no reward.[37]
>
> Go and ask of R' Tanchum, who regularly attended to R' Yehoshua ben Levi, who was expert in *aggadah*. [38]
>
> R' Yehoshua ben Levi said, "Anyone who habitually performs [acts of] *tzedakah* will be given sons who possess wisdom, wealth, and [knowledge of the] *aggadah*."[39]

The contradiction between these sources is apparent. Are we to regard the study of *aggadah* positively, or to avoid it? Our critic[40] thinks he found the answer in the writings of R' Sherira Gaon, who offers this assessment:

> Conclusions that derive from Biblical text through the method known as *midrash* and *aggadah* are really just suppositions [rather than received truth].[41]

By citing R' Sherira, this author tries to crown his words with legitimacy. We should not dignify such words by reading them, let alone allow them to pass from our lips!

Our critic compounds the damage he does to the reputation of *aggadah*. He submits that some *aggadic* passages resemble the famed angels of the Dinor river,[42] who sing their swan-song, and never reap-

---

37. *Yerushalmi Shabbos* 16:1(79b).

38. *Bava Kamma* 55a.

39. *Bava Basra* 9b.

40. Azaryah de Rossi, as mentioned in the Introduction.

41. Cited in the Introduction to *Menoras HaMaor*, as originally appearing in a work by R' Sherira entitled *Megillas Sesarim*. *Menoras HaMaor* himself does seem to take R' Sherira Gaon's statement at face value, but writes that it applies to only a small, discrete fraction of the *aggadah*, like reconstructions of events that took place many hundreds of years before *Chazal* lived and wrote.

42. *Chagigah* 14a.

pear. In some cases, he argues, some *aggadic* passages should simply not be taken so seriously. They should be allowed to make their poetic points, and then retire into oblivion. These passages are not based in fact. Treating them as if they are strains the rational mind.

He further argues that besides R' Sherira's characterizing *aggadic* statements as mere supposition, and *Rambam's* position that they are intended to be read as metaphor and allegory, there are some that we must dismiss from serious consideration because they were simple "contrivances." He thus accuses the Sages of misleading the masses through their artifice. Ironically, this is projection on his part. It is this foolish person who interprets the words of our wise men fancifully, in order that *he* can lead the masses astray!

We can learn much from the following passage.

> R' Yochanan once sat and learned: "*HaKadosh Baruch Hu* will one day bring precious stones and pearls which are 30 [*amos*] by 30 [*amos*], and He will cut out from them [an opening of] 10 [*amos*] by 20 [*amos*], and He will place them at the gates of Jerusalem." A certain student mocked him [and said:] "Now, we cannot find [precious stones and pearls even] the size of an egg of a small dove; can [stones of] such [an immense size] ever be found?"
>
> After a time, his [the student's] ship sailed upon the sea, and he saw ministering angels who sat and cut precious stones and pearls that were 30 by 30 [*amos*] and on which were engravings of 10 by 20. He said to them, "For whom are these?" They told him that *HaKadosh Baruch Hu* will one day place them at the gates of Jerusalem. The student came back to R' Yochanan, [and] said to him: "My Master! [Continue to] lecture! You are fit to lecture. Just as you said, so I saw." He [R' Yochanan] said to him, "Empty one! Had you not seen it yourself, would you not have believed? You are then mocking the words of the Sages!" He set his eyes upon him, and [the student] became a heap of bones.[43]

How many piles of bones must have become of our critic, for every passage that he rejects! We see in his writings that every statement that seems a bit strange to him, he dismisses as "contrivance," or the like.

---

43. *Bava Basra* 75a.

◆§ What R' Sherira Gaon Meant

His reading of R' Sherira Gaon is remarkably misinformed. If R' Sherira held that *aggadah* does not present clarified truth, but simply supposition and opinion (which others are free to reject), why does he restrict his remarks to *aggadic* inferences that are made from Biblical texts? Does he lack other examples of *aggadah*? Why not dismiss all the *aggadah* as cut from this imperfect cloth?

He fails to grasp what R' Sherira really means. When you find an explication of a verse, and this exegesis seems quite remote from the simple meaning of the verse, you may indeed conclude that you are looking at opinion. By "opinion" he means the *careful, considered application of Torah thought and process to yield valid conclusions.* If the Torah mind did not independently establish the truth of the thought, the author would never have derived it from the text at hand. Since the *sechel* of the author verifies its truth, the author is comfortable linking the thought to the particular verse. It is not the words of the verse that demand the conclusion, but the truth of the conclusion that suggests the possibility of an allusion in the verse. In other words, the idea came before the link to the *pasuk,* not the other way around. It is in this sense alone that R' Sherira sees parts of *aggadah* as human "supposition" and conjecture.

The passage in the *Yerushalmi* that speaks disparagingly of those who write and study *aggadah* was completely misunderstood by our critic. *Chazal* do not mean, G-d forbid, to denigrate *aggadah,* which contains the secrets and profundity of the Torah. Rather, they criticized those who turned *aggadah* into a fixed written medium.

◆§ Keeping *Aggadah* Oral

The rest of what later became the Talmud — the halachah — had always been studied orally. While many students and teachers were entirely at home with the oral method of studying and transmitting halachah, some were not quite as expert in relying on oral teaching alone when it came to *aggadah.* Many felt a need to commit much of the *aggadah* to a written format. Indeed, there are many references in the Gemara[44] to "books of *aggadah,* " while there is no mention of "books of halachah."

Today, we write the *aggadah* routinely, relying on the verse, "It is time to do for Hashem; they have overturned Your Torah.[45] This was forbidden, however, before *Chazal* specifically sanctioned this writing. At that earlier time, one who wrote down parts of the *aggadah* indeed received no portion in the World to Come, because he acted illegally. In those days, the only works that were legally entitled to be fixed into written form were the twenty-four books of *Tanach.* Writing the *aggadah* was tantamount to adding on to the Torah! Therefore, those who expounded upon a book of *aggadah,* or heard a lecture given from one, received no reward, since the presentation made use of an illicit and objectionable object.

Look at the *Yerushalami,* and you will see that this is the correct interpretation. The passage in question is embedded in a discussion of the propriety of writing different parts of the Oral Law. Our critic did not know how to properly grasp the sense of the Gemara. He therefore found difficulty with the words of *Chazal,* and found refuge in the comment of R' Sherira Gaon. Of course, he likewise misunderstood the sense of R' Sherira Gaon!

R' Nissim Gaon writes:[46]

> This [story] is from the *aggadah.* Concerning it, and all that is similar to it, *Chazal* say, "We do not rely upon the *aggadah.* "

Our critic, predictably, gathers from this that R' Nissim Gaon holds that people authored *aggadic* passages at will, simply to inspire their audiences to understand some point or other. The authors, he believes, did not take what they were writing very seriously.

---

44. E.g., "R' Yochanan studied a book of *aggadah* on Shabbos" (*Gittin* 60a). See also *Berachos* 23a and *Bava Metzia* 116a.

45. A midrashic reading of *Psalms* 119:126. The Gemara (*Temurah* 14b) justifies the writing of *aggadah* with this verse. The Torah initially forbade us from turning the Oral Law into a fixed, written form. With the passage of time, and the catastrophic effects on Torah scholarship of mounting persecution by our enemies, *Chazal* understood the need to violate this detail of the Torah in order to prevent us from losing an even greater part of it. At the proper time, they permitted the publication of the Mishnah, the halachic part of the Oral Law, and later the writing of the *aggadah* as well.

46. Cited in *Hakoseiv,* in *Ein Yaakov, Berachos* 59a.

✒ Attacking Straw Men

A nyone faithful to our religion will tear his heart upon hearing such a charge! How can this person rise up against the Torah of Moshe and the Sages, and reduce the *aggadah* to clever devices to inspire people with chains of falsehood? G-d forbid to attribute such a statement to R' Nissim. What he meant is obvious. *We do not rely on the plain reading of a difficult passage of the aggadah.* [47] R' Nissim addressed himself to the passage we dealt with earlier,[48] concerning Hashem's "tears" upon beholding a fractured world. It is obvious that we cannot attribute tears and deficiency to G-d, and that there is a deeper sense to the passage. This is the intent of the famous phrase: "We do not refute words of *aggadah.* "[49] We can ordinarily refute a statement by pointing out questions and deficiencies. We cannot apply this process to *aggadah,* because we may have simply misunderstood the actual intent of the author! We may be refuting a straw man; the original statement may well stand unchallenged by the questions we have misdirected at it.

Halachah, of course, is different. Halachah calls upon us to act. We dare not act upon a given halachic statement if it is mired in difficulty. *Aggadah,* though, does not always describe what is permissible and what is not. We ought not reject an *aggadic* statement because of the difficulties we have discovered. Rather, we should assume that the author understood quite well what he meant, and it is our understanding that is faulty.

We now understand why our tradition[50] warns that "we do not learn from *aggadah.* " We only draw binding,[51] practical inference from

---

47. A similar approach is taken, at greater length, by R' Eliyahu Dessler in *Michtav MeEliyahu,* vol. 4, p.354.

48. See Fourth Well, pp. 122, 128-130.

49. See, e.g., *Ramban, Yevamos* 61b; *Meiri, Shabbos* 55b.

50. See R' Shmuel HaNagid's *Mavo HaTalmud,* s.v., *haggadah.*

51. Like most rules, the exceptions to this one are legion. R' Zvi Hirsch Chayes (*Darchei Horaah,* pp. 243-251) collects many of them. He also shows that the rule applies only to *aggados* which were originally presented under special circumstances, or contradict halachic sources in the Gemara, or come to us through collections other than the Talmud itself.

sources that can be challenged and refuted. As we just showed, we cannot subject *aggadah* to the same logical give-and-take that we apply to halachic statements in the Gemara. We must always suspect that we have missed some of the author's thrust. Some nuance of meaning may likely have evaded us. Before we even begin analyzing and probing the sense of an *aggadic* argument, we know that we will never be able to satisfy ourselves completely. Whatever challenges or contradictions we bring, we will always shy away from claiming final victory! We simply cannot be completely confident about our grasp of a medium whose expression is so plastic!

◄§ Gaining From the Struggle

It follows, though, that if we cannot disprove some interpretation of an *aggadic* statement, then we cannot prove it either. Halachic opinions are refined and clarified by the careful scrutiny they endure from an endless succession of skeptical students. Any halachic statement is theoretically falsifiable. It can be crushed by the weight of evidence against it. Therefore, the authors of a halachic position must respond to any challenge, and work feverishly to shore it up. Along the way, all involved — proponents and opponents alike — gain new clarity and confidence about the issues. When our questions cannot have this impact, when the dialectic of question and answer does not force greater comprehension, we are left with an imperfect grasp of the intent of the author. This is regularly the case when we study *aggadah.* We rarely gain the conviction to trumpet the call to action that regularly accompanies halachic discourse.

Interestingly, the same holds true of the Mishnah. The terse and conclusory statements of the Mishnah do not instantly yield up the depth they contain. Without the analysis, the probing questions and answers of the Gemara, the Mishnah alone is not a good source for halachic conclusions. No one could argue that the Mishnah lacks authority. Yet here, too, *Chazal* caution that we are "not to learn from the Mishnah."[52] Clearly, neither the Mishnah nor *aggadah* lack reliability. It is we who lack clarity.

---

52. See *Rashi, Niddah* 7b, s.v., *ha kamashma lan.*

◌§ Broad-spectrum Truth

We might look at this issue in yet another way. Halachic statements cannot be half-true. Because they dictate and demand,
they must be thoroughly true to have any validity at all. Expose any
essential weakness in the statement, and you dislodge it altogether.

At the same time, halachic statements need only be true in a very
narrow band of application. They illuminate single points of truth.
Torah, at its real core, is multifaceted and broad-banded. An *aggadic*
statement often addresses an entire spectrum of Torah values, not a
single point alone. Objections might be raised to part of a formulation,
without touching the remainder. Finding a single crack will not tear
down the edifice. For this reason as well, we neither "refute" words of
aggadah, nor learn from them, in a fixed, legal manner. Beyond any
doubt, this is the meaning of the Gemara we cited.

It should be clear, then, that the differences between halachah and
aggadah do not relegate the latter to a lesser, or less authoritative,
role. We proclaim the depth and profundity of *aggadah* without hesita-
tion. Those who are receptive to Divine Wisdom will have no difficulty
seeing this; those who reject it lack authentic understanding, and
relate only to the earthly and physical. And those who argue that
aggadah is somehow not as legitimately and fully a part of the Torah
we received at Sinai have no portion in the World to Come!

Why, then, you may ask, does the Gemara seem to disparage the
study of *aggadah?* "Akiva! What have you with *aggadah?* Desist from
your comments until you reach *negaim* and *oholos.* "[53] If *aggadah* is so
profound and complex, why shouldn't we prefer the study of *aggadah*
to that of halachah?

This is not a difficult matter. Halachah is indeed preferable, since
within it we find the the way to perfect Man's actions. Halachah directly
spells out the way we must live. *Aggadah* does not. The purpose of
Torah is to bring Man to deed, and this goal is best served by halachah.
Aggadah, however, is entirely Divine Wisdom, and the key that opens

---

53. *Chagigah* 14a. *Oholos* and *negaim* are complex areas of halachah dealing with
tumah and *taharah.* In other words, R' Akiva was told to withhold his comments
about *aggadah,* and focus on halachah.

the gates of Heaven. "If you wish to recognize the Creator of everything," urge *Chazal*, "involve yourself with *aggadah.*" One who lacks the key stands from afar and sees, but cannot partake from up close.

V. The Gnat that Killed Titus

Titus took the *Paroches* and formed it into the shape of a wine-carrier. Then he brought all the utensils of the Temple, and put them in it, [and put them on a ship, intending] to go and be praised [for his triumph] in his city. . . . A storm at sea threatened to drown him [Titus]. He said, "It seems to me that the power of the G-d of the Jews is only in water. [When] Pharaoh came [against the Jews], He drowned him in the waters [of the Reed Sea]. [When] Sisera came [against the Jews], he drowned him [and his army] in the waters [of Nachal Kishon]. [Me] too, He threatens to drown in the waters [of the Mediterranean]. If He is [truly] powerful, let Him come up on dry land and wage war with me!" A heavenly voice emanated and said, "O evil man, the son of an evil man, a descendant of the evil Esau: I have a puny creature in My world, and it is called a gnat. Go up on dry land and do battle with it."

When he [Titus] ascended to dry land, a gnat came and entered his nose. It picked at his brain for seven years. One day, [Titus] was passing the doorway of a smithy, and [when the gnat] heard the sound of [the smith's] hammer, it fell silent. [Titus] said, "There is a remedy for me!" Every day they brought [another] smith, and they banged [with their hammers] in the presence of [Titus]. To a non-Jewish [smith] he gave four *zuz* [as payment]. [But] to a Jewish [smith] he said, "For you it is enough that you witness [the suffering] of your enemy." He did this for 30 days, [but] from then on, having grown accustomed to [the sound], [the gnat] became accustomed [to it].

> It was taught in a Baraisa: R' Pinchas ben Aruva said, "I was among the nobles of Rome when he [Titus] died. They split open his head and they found [a gnat] inside it [that was] like a swallow weighing two *selas*." A Tanna taught in a Baraisa: "[The gnat was] like a one-year-old pigeon weighing two *litras*." Abaye said: "We hold [a tradition that] its mouth was of copper and its nails were of iron."[54]

How, our critics ask, could *Chazal* imagine the possibility of such a thing? Everyone knows that there is no void between the brain and the cranium that could accommodate anything the size of a mature bird! And who is to believe that a bird can generate a bronze beak and iron claws?

We earlier[55] explained that *Chazal*'s interest is rarely in what we call the "cause" of things. Rather, they focus on the cause behind the cause, in the ultimate spiritual reason that determines the empirical, scientific laws we observe. It is no different here. *Chazal* in this passage do not describe the "reality" that we observe and feel at home with. Instead, they give us a glimpse of something much deeper.

☙ Function Prededes Form

In a world that randomly comes together, function is a product of form. A tall animal will use its height to eat from the upper branches of a tree, where it has less competition. Another animal, equipped with sharp teeth and vise-grip jaw muscles, will probably include living prey in its diet.

You must reverse all of this in a world engineered and executed by an intelligent Designer. Form follows from function. The role, the purpose for each organism determined what apparatus G-d assigned them when He created them. Simply put, He endowed each organism with the ability and power to accomplish the task He assigned it.

---

54. *Gittin* 56b.
55. See above, p. 209.

In a real sense, then, what distinguishes one living thing from the next is not color, or shape, or eating habits. Such factors are peripheral. The animal essentially is what the animal does. It takes its particular form so that it can perform as it should.

When *Chazal* speak of the small insect that penetrated Titus' nostril, they look to the distinguishing feature of that insect, the characteristic that makes it what it is. They see an insignificant creature that successfully bores through larger and tougher material. From a Torah standpoint, that is what the gnat (or similar insect) is. All other features are merely logistics.

The essential *activity* of the gnat is what entered Titus' brain and faithfully continued its work. It began its work as a tiny, almost unnoticeable object. By the time it finished, it was visible and recognizable. At Titus' postmortem, this tiny force had been transformed into an active agent many thousands of times its original size (or apparent strength), akin to a gnat turning into a mature bird.

The pieces begin to fall into place. Small creatures that penetrate tough material seem to employ two distinct kinds of activities. They bore, pecking away, applying incessant pressure until they gain entrance. They also come equipped with apparatus sharp enough to make fine incisions. We might think of their essential qualities, then, as extraordinary toughness and sharpness. More figuratively, we could depict our tiny creature as having a tough, bronze beak and sharp iron claws. The sense of the passage is that a small force that entered Titus began to assault him with relentless pressure, and agonizing sharpness.

We might point out that this passage tells us far more about Titus than about his death. No one stood up in opposition to Hashem more than the evil Titus, who destroyed and burnt our *Beis HaMikdash*. In this regard, Titus distinguished himself from among all other kings who rebelled against G-d. Titus, according to *Chazal,* refused to simply bask in the glow of his victory, but hurled epithets and blasphemy at Hashem. Not even Nebuchadnezzar, who destroyed the First Temple, behaved this way. He, at least, acted in order to suppress a rebellion. Burning the *Beis HaMikdash* was an offshoot of his military campaign, not his principal objective. What animated Titus, however, was unvarnished resistance and opposition to Hashem.

◄§ Titus' Agenda

Some will object that Josephus described a much more benevolent Titus. Josephus records that the emperor objected to the burning of the *Beis HaMikdash* and did not order its destruction. While this may be true, *Chazal* understood what others did not. Students of true wisdom, they saw through to Titus' real agenda. If he wanted to spare the *Beis HaMikdash,* it was only to better fulfill his desire to disparage and mock it. Because of his venomous hatred for it, he wished to glorify himself in preserving the structure, so that he could later debase it. Hashem frustrated Titus' plan by allowing the Temple to be burnt, preventing the indignities Titus planned to visit upon it.

Chazal knew that it could not have been otherwise. Contrary to Josephus, they understood that the *Beis HaMikdash* was not destroyed because of the whim of an enemy soldier. Events as important as the burning of the *Beis HaMikdash* do not simply "happen," unplanned, at the whim of a lowly soldier on the spot. They are willed and coordinated. The *Beis HaMikdash* burned because Titus was obsessed with defiling it, and Hashem would not allow him to. Titus' diabolical fascination with the *Beis HaMikdash* grew out of utter contempt for the G-d it was meant to serve.

Titus regarded Hashem as a formidable opponent, although completely misunderstanding His nature. As the passage mentions, Titus knew that Hashem had dealt unkindly with His enemies before. He knew that there had been a Flood, that the Egyptians had drowned in the Reed Sea.

Titus detected a pattern. The water is not man's chosen habitat, his seat of power. Man functions best on dry land. Why would Hashem choose water as His selected weapon, if not that He could only prevail where Man was diffident and halting? If he clung to land, to Man's domain, Titus reasoned that he would be able to triumph over G-d. G-d triumphed only where Man acknowledged vulnerability. On turf that inspired human confidence and pride, there was no room for G-d.

✦ A Fitting End

Hashem reversed the tables on this enemy of G-d. Not only would Titus falter and fall, but his death would highlight his puny inadequacy relative to the smallest agent of Hashem's power. The way he died would show that although he succeeded in destroying Hashem's Temple, he only acted as a tool for the Divine Hand that reached out against it. Rather than demonstrate Titus' strength, as he had always assumed, it showed his utter powerlessness and weakness.

If a mortal king dispatches an entire battalion of soldiers to subdue a single opponent, he loses more than he gains. By resorting to vast numerical superiority to crush his enemy, the king acknowledges the enemy's individual prowess. He leaves open the possibility that his enemy is more than the king's personal equal. Thus, he confers nobility upon his nemesis in death.

A better strategy would be to use a relatively unimportant servant of his, who can dispatch the traitor to an ignominious demise. By the same reasoning, fire and brimstone, or an army of heavenly hosts sent after him, would have been the wrong way to address Titus' hubris. Hashem commissioned the smallest of His servants to humble Titus, thus demonstrating His real Power. Hashem could invest the smallest object with some of His awesome strength.

Two opinions dispute the size of the formerly tiny power that felled Titus. We understand the symbolism by looking at the common ground shared by the two views. Both compare it to a different organism, fully developed, rather than just a mass of tissue; both attach a weight of two units to it.

Chazal want us to realize that Titus did not die because his vital life forces were drained from him, nor through general deterioration. While this may be what it seemed to those around him, his autopsy revealed otherwise, at least to *Chazal*.

Hashem had waged war against Titus. G-d's agents are whole and sound, miniscule reflections of the perfection of their Creator. Hence, *Chazal* compare the gnat to some *whole* animal, rather than simply tell us how much it weighed on some scale of measurement.

The insect weighed in at two, either *shekels* or *litras*. We have shown elsewhere[56] that the number two is a common substitution for the concept of division and separation. It is a natural foil to the number one, which stands for wholeness and integration. The ultimate division, or the full extent to which something can be divided against itself, is death. A bird-sized, bloodsucking insect of two units thus conveys the sense of a death-dealing menace that cuts and divides.

Titus richly deserved this. There have been other tyrants in history, other evildoers responsible for much bloodshed. Titus' animus towards G-d put him in a category of his own. We know that the *Beis HaMikdash* serves as the meeting place between our limited world and the limitless expanse of Hashem's world. The *Beis HaMikdash* is the common interface; it is the device that connects heaven and earth. Without a smooth, uninterrupted flow from Hashem through this channel, our world is not the place it was meant to be, neither physically nor spiritually. While everything, of course, ultimately comes from Hashem, without a *Beis HaMikdash,* the direct flow of Divine beneficence is constricted and rerouted. Rather than eating from the King's table, we are forced to make do with packages sent via many slow couriers.

❧ Titus' Legacy

To *Chazal,* then, Titus was the most menacing of destroyers, because he was determined to tear asunder the connection between the worlds. The harm he caused was inestimable. No casualty figures can encompass the dark consequences of that division. *Chazal* find satisfaction in the fitting manner of his death, through a small, insidious force that cuts and divides and destroys well beyond our expectation.

Having come so far, we can even accommodate the views of secular historians. Although they disagree significantly concerning the details of his death, they generally record that Titus died of some illness. We should now understand that this is no contradiction to *Chazal*''s depic-

---

56. See Second Well, p. 43.

tion.[57] The historians describe "apparent" causes and reality; *Chazal* tell us *why* these occurred, and their deeper meaning. Our critics, had they possessed real wisdom, would have understood this.

---

57. Maharal possibly suggests that Titus died of brain cancer. A tumor is consistent with the main thrust of Maharal - that Hashem chose the smallest of His agents to undo the self-assured and bombastic tyrant. He utilized not even a small creature, but a force symbolized by a small creature. The power of cellular replication, invisible to the naked eye, begins to take over some cells in Titus' brain, perhaps through a carcinogen migrating from outside his body. The growth flourishes, and begins to weaken Titus through the pain it inflicts. (Pain, it will be recalled, comes in two main varieties: dull pressure and sharpness.) There is a period of palliation of the pain, or of remission. The growth returns, however, eventually becoming a massive and aggressive competitor to healthy brain tissue. At his postmortem, the physicians marvel at the size of the growth.

THE SEVENTH WELL

Specialness

Chazal disregard the rights and dignity of those who are not scholars. They belittle them in terms so extreme, that we must suspect that they are moved by some hidden agenda. They seem bent on advancing their cause at the expense of others, or even on avenging themselves upon the ignorant! People outside our faith do not fare any better. *Chazal* often speak of them with utter scorn and derision.

None of this is appropriate. All human beings are the handiwork of G-d, and no one deserves to be treated this way.

Our critics pursue this attack fervently. They maintain that impropriety and falsehood must be combated, even if they come from within our own ranks.

The
response:

I. The *Am Ha'aretz*

R' Elazar said, "It is permitted to stab an *am ha'aretz* [to death even] on Yom Kippur which falls on Shabbos." His disciples said to him, "*Rebbi,* say [instead that one is permitted to] kill him through *shechitah*!" He replied, "This [method of killing, i.e. *shechitah*] requires a *berachah,* whereas this [method — stabbing] does not require a *berachah.*"

R' Elazar said, "It is forbidden to accompany an *am haaretz* on a journey, as it is stated, 'For it [Torah] is your life, and the length of your days.' [Since] he lacks regard for his [own] life, how much more so [will he lack regard] for the life of his fellow man!"

R' Shmuel bar Nachmani said in R' Yochanan's name: "One may tear an *am haaretz* [open] like [one would] a fish!" Said R' Shmuel bar Yitzchak, "And [one may do so] from his back."

It was taught in a Baraisa: R' Akiva said: "When I was an *am haaretz* I said, 'Who will give me a *talmid chacham* that I might bite him like a donkey?' " Said his students to him, "Rebbi, say [instead] like a dog!" He answered them, "This [the donkey] bites and breaks bones, while this [the dog] bites but does not break bones." [1]

I t is important that you realize that *Chazal* always spoke words of truth and righteousness. [2] They will bear up well under informed scrutiny; there is nothing here that should embarrass us or them. The *Rif* already explained their real intent in his commentary. [3]

ᥦᱍ The *Talmid Chacham* as the Symbol of *Sechel*

I will offer a different approach, based on a fuller understanding of the *am ha'aretz* of this passage. *Chazal* do not direct their animus simply to the completely ignorant and rail here against bald ignorance. They do not direct their animus against mere lack of knowledge, nor even the unsavory characteristics that are often associated with ignorant people.

---

1. *Pesachim* 49b.

2. If the passage were written as hyperbole, and had been meant as vitriolic condemnation of opponents of *Chazal,* the critics might have had a point. Such harshness and outlandish exaggeration surely is not complimentary to the authors. They would have seemed intolerant and small-minded. Instead, Maharal insists that there literally is no exaggeration! *Chazal* taught a valuable lesson concerning people who throw away the greatest gifts given them!

Although at first glance Maharal would seem to make matters even more difficult to accept, he quickly explains what he means.

3. See *Rif, Pesachim* 49b. *Chazal* certainly did not mean that it is permissible to shed his blood without due cause. There are situations, though, in which it is permissible to kill someone to prevent him from committing a terrible crime, such as murder or sinning with one of the forbidden relations.

The *Ran* (on the *Rif*) cites R' Sherira Gaon (and speculates that this may be the fuller intent of the *Rif*) who elaborates upon this passages. The Gemara instructs us to safeguard the dignity of Man, even in the process of executing the hardened criminal. We choose the method of execution carefully, so as not to subject him to more pain

Chazal address their remarks to a particularly extreme subgroup of the ignorant. These people are so suffused with hatred of Torah, that they, like the young Akiva, would bite a *talmid chacham* like a crazed donkey.

Human free-will allows us to make bad choices. We can choose not only to selectively ignore parts of the Torah, but even to thoroughly distance ourselves from it. Those who do *lose all connection with Torah and its values.* As we shall demonstrate, they are no better than animals.

Chazal do not suggest that only accomplished scholars like them are fully human, while all others should be dispatched to the zoo. It is quite easy to demonstrate that many ignorant people not only rise above the animal-like, but are fully within the orbit of interests and ideas of the *talmid chacham.*

The Torah's depiction of Man's creation bear this out. "And Man became a living being"[4] is rendered by *Targum Onkelos* as "And Man became a talking being." Speech is apparently one of the indicators of human specialness.[5] Now, all of the organs and systems of the body must act in concert to produce a speaking being. We do not think of just the organs of speech as human, or just the brain as surpassing the animal. The entire integrated person sits at the apex of the pyramid of Creation. We do not limit this distinction to the intellect, or to the fullness of its development.

What is true of the individual is true of the community of Man. We would not deny the all-important role of *sechel* in human affairs. However we try to refine our definition of Man's special place in the universe, we come back to the same quintessential concept. Man was created to live by and with *sechel!* But all those who contribute to the furtherance of *sechel* are joined together, just as the various parts of

---

and anxiety than is necessary and appropriate. The *am ha'aretz,* however, doesn't always enjoy this safeguard. Because his ignorance makes it far more likely that he will sin, he runs the risk of major as well as minor failings. Tragically, he may attempt to sin even on the holiest day of the year. If another Jew catches him in hot pursuit of an intended victim, the observer is duty-bound to intervene. Halachah says that he must stop the criminal even if he must use deadly force, employing whatever means are available. Thus, the *am ha'aretz could and may* lose his life in a most undignified manner ("torn like a fish") amidst the holiness of Yom Kippur.

4. *Genesis* 2:7.

5. See above, Sixth Well pg. 222, where Maharal prefers a different litmus test of humah distinction.

the body contribute to speech. As parts of the body work synergistically, so do different elements within the community, as they are
united by the same pursuits. Those who stay connected in some manner or form with the *talmid chacham* fall within the broad sweep of our
definition of a *sechel-*oriented being. It follows, though, that those who
utterly oppose the *sechel/talmid chacham* have no place within the
very definition of the specialness of Man. The condemnation of our
passage is aimed at such a person, and only such a person.

The Gemara itself makes this point as it handles the Torah's mandate
"to love Hashem your G-d — and to cleave to Him."[6] How are we to
cling to the *Shechinah,* whose fiery essence consumes whatever draws
near? Simple, answers the Gemara.[7] Cling to the *talmid chacham.*
Whoever attaches himself to the *talmid chacham,* attaches himself to
the *Shechinah.* This is a simpler restatement of what we said before.
The *talmid chacham* shares a common platform with the *Shechinah,*
through his devotion to, and incorporation of Divine *sechel.* Through it,
he clings to Hashem. So do those who attach themselves to the *talmid
chacham,* who identify with his world and contribute to his work.

But those who oppose him so implacably that they wish to destroy
him have no place in creation at all! They are indeed lower than animals. Animals were created, like everything else, to serve Man. Their
utility gives them some sort of loose connection with Man's specialness, and gives them a place and a niche in creation. The non-*talmid
chacham* who discards his link to the *talmid chacham,* does what an
animal cannot. He squanders his entire reason for existence!

◆§ The *Berachah* on *Shechitah*

The *shechitah* of an animal for human consumption requires a
berachah. When you use the animal fully to satisfy a human need,
the animal points to its purpose as a servant of Man. It is appropriate
to mark this with a *berachah.* The death of the *am ha'aretz* fulfills no
greater purpose to the *talmid chacham* — or to the world — than did
his *sechel*-purged life. No blessing attends his death, just as he brought
none in life. This is what R' Elazar meant.

---

6. *Deuteronomy* 30:20.
7. *Kesubos* 111b.

✺§ Actual and Potential

Another idea will also help you understand the unexaggerated truth of this passage. The *am ha'aretz* does deserve to die — even in a cruel manner, even on Yom Kippur — for being completely devoid of Torah. This does not mean, though, that we are supposed to kill him! Nor, as it turns out, do *Chazal* wish us to direct their contempt to particular individuals.

All of us operate in two modes. Who we are, what we have accomplished so far, defines our present reality. We also exist as potential, for what we are still capable of achieving.[8] *Chazal* aver that Man's potential in Torah is limitless. "If a person declares, 'I have tried [to study Torah], and I have achieved' — believe him."[9] Man is vouchsafed an extraordinary blessing. If he will try, he will accomplish. The *am ha'aretz*, though completely empty of Torah, need not remain an *am ha'aretz*. He can potentially rejoin humanity as it was meant to be. If he wills it, the distance between the abyss and the pinnacle can melt in a short moment. His potential alone makes him special, makes him part of this great species of humanity. For this reason, killing him is unthinkable.

Chazal, however, still want us to know who the *am ha'aretz* is in his present reality. We are mindful of how Hashem takes into account his potential, and we do the same. But we must also know how his present reality is despised and debased. We must understand that our Torah study is not the icing on the cake[10] of the human experience. Without

---

8. At no time are we more conscious of this than during the *Yamim Nora'im,* the days between *Rosh HaShanah* and *Yom Kippur.* When we run out of defenses and excuses, we fall back on a familiar refrain. "We have sorely disappointed you, Hashem. But there is so much that we can still accomplish! All we need is a bit more time, and we will produce for You. Grant us another year for the potential we have, even if we don't deserve it for what we have already done."

Perhaps for this reason R' Elazar underscored that the *am ha'aretz* could be killed on *Yom Kippur,* the day that Jews are forgiven with a Divine Eye on the future. The *am ha'aretz* who lives out his years without ever changing (see on, in the text) turns out to have been completely worthless, even on the day that Hashem places potential before reality.

9. *Megillah* 6b.

10. R' Baruch Ber Lebovitz once heard a speaker declaim that Torah study was as important to us as the air we breathe. The great Rosh Yeshivah of Kaminetz demurred. "It is not so. If medical science figures out a way to give our bodies what they

that study and connection to Divine Wisdom, we are worthless, lower than the animal. Furthermore, the emptiness of the *am ha'aretz* is not completely negated and erased through his potential for future change. What if he never uses that potential? What if he goes to the grave, never mending his ways? In retrospect, his life, his humanity will not have been real. We will realize that he was an insubstantial illusion, a vaporous mist walking among men.

◄§ Why We Eat Meat

R' Elazar ruled that the *am ha'aretz* is forbidden to eat meat. This is quite consistent with a pattern we observe in the Torah. *Adam HaRishon* was forbidden to eat meat.[11] The prohibition continued for ten generations, until the days of Noah.[12]

Adam took his name from his creation from the earth. For all the exceptional intelligence that his Creator gave him, *Adam* remained tied to that earth. It took ten generations for Man to reduce and master the earthiness within him to the point that his *sechel* could predominate.[13] (Noah, in fact, is called *ish ha'adamah*,

---

need without breathing, we will not protest. Torah isn't like that. It doesn't just make life possible. It is life itself."

11. *Sanhedrin* 59b.

12. *Genesis* 9:3 gives Noah explicit license to eat meat.

13. Maharal is not claiming that Noah was greater or more righteous than *Adam*. His point, rather, is whether the higher, *sechel* component within Man could completely outstrip the earthier, more physical part.

Because Adam was created from the earth (and created directly by the handiwork of Hashem), the physical forces within him manifested themselves with particular power. Adam lived much longer than we do today, as did his descendants until the time of Noah. The special physical powers in him were later concentrated in some of his progeny, who lived as giants among men (see *Ramban, Genesis* 6:4). While Adam after the first sin may have lived a righteous life, we could not argue that his enormous physical powers ever slid into obscurity, relative to his spiritual ones. There was just too much there to go unnoticed.

After the Flood, Hashem narrowed the range within which physical phenomena expressed themselves (see *Ramban, Genesis* 5:4), giving Man a better chance at controlling his *yetzer hara,* his evil inclination. In effect, G-d retooled the laws of nature during the post-diluvian years of Noah's life (see *Malbim,* Genesis 8:23). Part of this program meant that Man's allotment of years was slashed. (The first stage of this had come before the Flood, when Man's life span was cut down to 120 [*Genesis* 6:3].) Noah was the first person to emerge into this new world, in which Man could truly render the physical unimportant relative to the spiritual.

the man of the earth.[14] This does not mean that he was coarser and earthier than others. To the contrary, it means that he was sufficiently *master* of the earth, that he was no longer inordinately drawn towards it.)

This generational transition spelled the difference between enforced vegetarianism and the right to eat meat. Taking the life of an animal and proceeding to consume it is a rather strong statement that negates the value of the animal relative to the consumer. Animals are not human, but we share much with them. Physiologically, there is more we have in common with them than divides us. We face similar challenges in nutrition, respiration, locomotion, and reproduction. The pathways that govern these processes on the chemical level are often even more similar. Looking at our form and function, it is difficult to argue that our worlds don't converge. Indeed, take a long hard look at the tangible, material aspects of people and animals, and the argument for a natural right to take their lives shrinks.

The stress is on "look." Consider, instead, what you cannot see, and the argument tilts in the other direction. Humans are not meant to be primarily physical beings. They are here to attach themselves to Divine *sechel.* That *sechel* should become so prominent in their every action that it can predominate, by far eclipsing their physical aspects.

Humans who rise above the physical need not take hold in high regard what they share with the animal world. They share nothing. They occupy a much higher plane, where it is apparent that the only use for the physical is as a handmaiden of loftier pursuits. Taking the life of an animal is not fundamentally different for them than using an inanimate object.

The *talmid chacham* makes the grade. So do those who are connected to him, whose lives are still defined by their attachment to a higher order of things. The *am ha'aretz,* however, knows nothing of transcendence. His life is not so different from that of the animal. To snuff out the life of an animal simply because he has the power to do so, is morally offensive. It represents the triumph of might, rather than merit. Hence, R' Elazar's pronouncement that the *am ha'aretz* is prohibited from eating meat.

---

14. *Genesis* 9:20.

⇜ The Living Cling to Life

R' Elazar also argues that others should not travel in the company of an *am ha'aretz*. Travel outside settled areas is fraught with danger. The more a person clings to life — through his merit and through his attitude — the better prepared he is to meet any challenge or danger.

The *am ha'aretz* might look robust, vital, and full of enthusiasm for life. In fact, though, he is dead inside. Had he any real regard for the value of life, it is impossible that he would not have connected with Torah, which gives us life. Torah is irrelevant to him because life has also lost its value and relevance. Essentially, he is already lifeless. Having abandoned responsibility for his own life, how can he be expected to value the life of his travel companion, should he require his assistance?

⇜ There is Nothing There

We can understand all the other statements in our passage as refinements of the theme we have developed. R' Shmuel bar Nachmani and R' Shmuel bar Yitzchak likened the *am ha'aretz* to a fish, which may be killed by merely tearing it, even from the back. This is an extension of the initial idea of this sequence. R' Elazar argued that the *am ha'aretz* was no better than an animal, and actually somewhat inferior. These sages further diminish the stature of the *am ha'aretz*. Animals, as a class, do require *shechitah,* while fish do not. Animals may be killed for Man's use, but the Torah stipulates the manner in which they are to be killed. We are not granted wholesale license to destroy them at will. The life of the animal has real value. There is some particular *aspect* of the animal that must bow to human need; this is reflected by limiting the way we slaughter it to a particular place on the body.

Fish are protected by no restrictions. The Torah places no restraints on Man's subjugation of them. The difference between them and humans is so stark that we assume no common ground. We find nothing so similar that we have to hesitate before we justify taking their lives. So it is with the *am ha'aretz*. There is nothing in him to suggest any commonality with human beings as they are supposed to be.

Moreover, they can be destroyed even from the back, the part of the body that normally gives structure and support to the skeleton. The back, more than any other part of the body, gives permanence to the organism. By emphasizing that the *am ha'aretz* can be destroyed even from the back, *Chazal* underscore his utter deficiency and lack of worth.[15]

The tension between physical and spiritual cuts both ways. When the *sechel* shines in its sterling grandeur, the physical associated with it loses all its prominence. On the other hand, from the standpoint of coarse physicality, it is the abstract, ethereal qualities of *sechel* which have no place in reality! A mindset rooted only in the pleasure of sensory stimulation and immediate titillation has no room for any existence that cannot be felt and enjoyed. It meets reports of such qualities with derision and scorn, seeing it as so much worthless pretension.

This was R' Akiva's autobiographical contribution. When he was an *am ha'aretz*, he completely rejected the value of the *talmid chacham*. He wished to bite him like a donkey, not like a dog. A dog's bite inflicts harm. The bone-crunching attack of the donkey destroys its victim. The *am ha'aretz* does not simply resent the *talmid chacham* and the life of enlightenment and *sechel* he lives. The hostility he feels does not come from competition between opponents within the same arena. The *am ha'aretz* finds no room for the *talmid chacham* to exist at all! It is as if the *talmid chacham* drifted in from a strange, alien universe where all the rules were different.

We have demonstrated that the words of *Chazal* are measured and precise, even when the message seems harsh and extreme. We have accounted for every difficult item in our passage. It will hopefully serve as an object lesson for all similar passages.

---

15. Again, we are looking only at the "net worth" of the *am ha'aretz* as measured by his level of accomplishment. The discussion is entirely theoretical. In practice, the Torah demands that we relate to human beings through focusing on their infinite potential. Killing or harming them, outside of the boundaries of court-ordered punishment, is unthinkable.

II. The *Am Ha'aretz* and Olam Haba

R' Elazar said, "*Amei ha'aretz* will not be resurrected, as it is stated, 'They are dead, never to live.'[16] I might assume [that this refers to] everyone? [For this reason the Torah] teaches, specifically stating, 'The still will not rise,' [showing that the verse speaks only] of one who stilled himself [was lax] in the study of the words of the Torah.'[17]

This passage is a painful thorn to many, since it denies the possibility of resurrection to all but the Torah scholar. Again, people criticize *Chazal* for a seemingly intemperate statement. This passage unfairly denies life's final hope[18] not only to non-Jews, but to many Jews as well. Many people feel that this prediction strips their lives of all value, and predicts an ultimate future that is no better than that of an animal.

There is no need for alarm. The author of the passage provides his own explanation and solution.

Since he [R' Elazar] saw that R' Yochanan was pained [by his remarks], he said to him, "Rebbi! I have a remedy for them [from a different verse] in the Torah: 'But you who cling to Hashem your G-d — you are all alive today.'[19] Now is it possible to cling to the *Shechinah*? Is it not written, 'For Hashem your G-d is a consuming fire'?[20] Rather, anyone who marries his daughter to a *talmid chacham,* or conducts trade on behalf of *talmidei chachamim,* or benefits *talmidei chachamim* from his property, the Torah regards him as if he clings to the *Shechinah.*"

---

16. *Isaiah* 26:14.

17. *Kesubos* 111b.

18. Unlike the *Rambam,* the *mekubalim* (Kabbalists) believe that resurrection is a prerequisite to entering *Olam Haba.* Denying *techias hameisim* (resurrection of the dead) to an individual insures that he has no place in eternity. This explains why the implications of our passage are so onerous. Maharal, of course, was a great kabbalist, and likely writes here from this perspective.

19. *Deuteronomy* 4:4.

20. Ibid. 4:24.

People completely misunderstand the place and purpose of Torah. So many think that life or G-d essentially "owes" them a place in the World to Come. Torah is somehow important to Hashem, and we should endeavor to do our best to observe it. If we do not, we will have to answer to Him, but He surely knows our limits. He will not deal too harshly with the multitudes who are neither perfectly consistent in their observance, nor thoroughly evil.

◈ The Single Road to the World to Come

This is a terrible mistake. Not being evil doesn't get you to *olam haba.* Torah does. If we can provide a chief reason for why Hashem gave us the Torah, it would be to provide us with eternal happiness. Torah is not an adjunct to the process of getting there. It is the only way to get there. Without Torah, an individual cannot earn[21] what Hashem surely wants him to have. Torah provides the wherewithal to achieve it; there are no alternatives!

It is simply incorrect to imagine that our passage depicts otherwise deserving people missing their eternal bliss on a technicality. Torah is no technicality. Meaning well will not allow you to drive a nail through a piece of wood with your fist. You need a hammer. Torah provides the only tools designed by Hashem to open the doors of eternity to mortal human beings.

Hashem, however, acted with great kindness to us. While it is impossible to achieve *olam haba* through any means other than Torah, Hashem left ample room for those who are not masters of Torah study to share in its blessing and power. Associating with and connecting to *talmidei chachamim* gives people a substantial stake in Torah.

The balance has shifted. The careless reader sees this passage slamming closed the gates of Heaven in front of the majority of people. Really, it does the opposite. The vast majority of people can participate

---

21. Maharal does not even hint at why this is so. Why can't a benevolent G-d simply give the gift of eternal life to those whom He created? Maharal may have considered the answer so basic to Jewish thought, that he perhaps saw no need to rehash it. Traditional approaches focus on ideas such as man not appreciating anything that he has not earned for himself. The reader is referred to *Derech Hashem* (available in translation as *The Way of G-d*) of R' Moshe Chaim Luzzatto, sections I:2:1-2, and Rabbi Aryeh Kaplan's essay "If You Were G-d."

in all aspects of Torah, be it observing the mitzvos or studying its complexity. Some people can do it on their own. Those who truly cannot, can still experience the fullness of Torah, and be molded and shaped by it. By attaching themselves to the *talmid chacham,* some of the eternal life-giving Torah is channeled to them. They, too, are transformed by the power of the Torah, meriting resurrection and *olam haba.*

An analogy will help you better understand this. Our bodies are made up of many different parts, organs and systems. We can sustain the loss of some without immediately changing our quality of life. Losing others affects us more severely, but life can continue. If the heart stops working, though, life ends. If you want to consider the heart a "chief" organ relative to the right big toe, no one will object.

⋅◈ The Single-body Model of the Jewish People

The Torah likens the Jewish people to a single person. In the life of the nation, some people assume specialized roles, and they become the analogue to different parts of the body. Thus, a community leader is often referred to as *rosh,* [22] which literally means "head." The *nasi* and the king rule over the people from a position of strength and elevated station. They occupy a niche in the structure of the nation that is similar to the way the head is perched atop the body. Wise men lead the community through their wisdom and Torah. The Torah calls them — particularly the *Sanhedrin* and other judges — *einei ha'am,* [23] the eyes of the nation, as their guidance is similar to the way the eyes guide the body on its way. Those *chachamim* who instruct and teach on the grass-roots level are appropriately enough called *lev ha'am,* the heart of the nation. Torah knowledge is as critical to the vitality of the people as the heart is to the body.

These are not mere figures of speech. Our Sages maintain that the Jewish nation *functions* as the individual body does. The *talmidei chachamim* who are the heart of the people are not just a most "important" group. They literally provide the same service to the rest of the people as the heart does, pumping life-giving power to remote parts of

---

22. See, for example, *Numbers* 13:3.

23. *Horayos* 5b takes the phrase *Im me'einei ha'edah* in *Numbers* 15:24 as a reference to the *Sanhedrin.*

the body. No person, nor any part of a person, can survive without receiving what the heart delivers.

Individuals who are weak in Torah are comparable to the many other limbs and components of the body. Without the benefit of the life-giving elixir of Torah, they have no real life of their own, at least not the life of ultimate significance that we call the world to come. Fortunately for them, this sweet fluid is available to them so long as they remain connected to the "heart." The *talmid chacham* has enough Torah to provide for himself, and to share and distribute it to others.

These others, though, do not benefit by the mere presence of the *talmid chacham* in the community. They must be close enough, connected enough to receive from him. Human tissue, arguably part of the body, becomes gangrenous if blood does not reach it. The mere presence of the heart in the chest cavity does not suffice. The benefit to distant organs is an *active* one, not a passive one.

The *talmid chacham* is not just a vital cog in the machine of the people. He is a siphon, a conduit. He actively channels some of his Torah to those who stand in close association to him. Many people do not adequately fill their personal portfolios with all the different aspects of Torah that they need for their own good. Hashem in His mercy provided a way to augment their earned holdings. The waters of Torah, when gathered in the proper receptacle, are available for others. The *talmid chacham* acts as a reservoir of its potency, readying it for those who are close enough to draw from it through their relationship with him.

An afterword. A charge of unfairness compelled this discussion. People argued that *Chazal* in this passage snatched away their right to resurrection and eternity. We have laid that charge to rest, by demonstrating that this was actually the opposite of what they said. Examination of other sources in *Chazal* will show that it was a baseless fear to begin with.

Firstly, *Chazal* do not even deny non-Jews the possibility of eternal life. Chazal clearly declare that the righteous of the nations of the earth have a place in the World to Come.[24] Is it conceivable that their view of *olam haba* is so inclusive that non-Jews are welcome, but ignorant Jews are not? Moreover, even when they had good reason to exclude certain classes of people, they balked at it. Thus, when Antoninus

---

24. See *Rambam, Melachim* 8:11 and commentaries.

asked *Rabbeinu HaKadosh* whether he (Antoninus) would find a place in *olam haba*, [25] his Jewish friend answered affirmatively. Even though a verse suggests that Romans, as descendants of Esav, are explicitly barred, ("There will be no survivor to the house of Esau"[26]), Rabbeinu HaKadosh insisted that the Torah only rejected those who clung to the *traits* of Esau.

The conclusion is inevitable. Everything depends on the quality of one's actions. No one is summarily or unfairly excluded from the opportunity to gain eternal life, an opportunity that Hashem made part of the human condition.

III. Relating to the Non-Jew

[A person is liable for damage inflicted by his animal on] "the animal of his friend"[27] — but not the animal of a non-Jew.[28]

Chazal stand accused of perverting justice regarding non-Jews, sanctioning theft and violence.

The charge is absurd. We will show that *Chazal* would not transgress boundaries of justice and propriety concerning any creature in the world.

◆§ The Three Groups of Men

According to the tradition our Sages received, humanity can be divided into three groups.

The first of these is the Jews, or those people who were chosen by G-d, including both the original generations, and their descendants.

---

25. *Avodah Zarah* 10b.

26. *Ovadiah* 1:18.

27. *Exodus* 21:35.

28. *Bava Kamma* 38a. The familiar text uses the word *Cana'ani,* or "Canaanite" in place of non-Jew. This is most likely a substitution for a different original text. It was meant to replace or obscure the original, which was either unfavorable (or appeared to be unfavorable) to non-Jews.

Through His servant Moses, they were given a Torah, and many rules and regulations.

The next group includes those who are not part of the Jewish people. They are not expected to observe all the laws of the Torah. They are, however, expected to stay within the limits of basic propriety — such as not serving something different than G-d. Members of this group still recognize and exclusively worship the Cause of all existence, to Whom all belongs. (For this reason, when *Chazal* speak of those who worship *avodah zarah* — worship that is foreign or strange — they do not use a term that we might have expected: *elilim*-worshipers, referring specifically to images and icons. This latter term more literally applies to idolaters, who were plentiful in the ancient world. *Chazal* deliberately used the former term to be more inclusive. They understood that serving *anything* besides Hashem is terribly destructive, whether the sun, moon, heavenly angels — or icons of wood and stone. Everything belongs to Him. Serving any other object or force — including intermediaries appointed by G-d Himself to serve His interests — is "foreign" and "strange" relative to His Essence.

When a non-Jew formally accepts[29] serving the First Cause alone, even though he does not practice the mitzvos, he is called a *ger toshav,* a kind of resident alien. The Torah and Gemara make many references[30] to this *ger toshav.* It is obvious that he is part of a whole class of people, all of whom reject the worship of any other being. A special provision of the Torah mandates that we, the Jewish community, must provide for their support when they are needy.

The third and last category includes people who serve any force or being besides Hashem. When the Torah uses the term *goy* without other explanation or embellishment, it means a member of this group.

---

29. Halachically, the formal acceptance must be in front of a Jewish court. (See *Kesef Mishneh, Melachim* 8:10 s.v., *vehamekabel.*) The *Ritva, Makkos* 9a s.v., *alma* creates another grouping because of this point. He assigns the name *ben Noah* to a Gentile whom we know to be faithful to the Torah's code of behavior for non-Jews, but who has not made a formal declaration of intent before the court. The treatment of the *ben Noah* varies from that of the *ger toshav* in several aspects, most notably that the community is not obligated to fully sustain the former.

30. Maharal cites several examples (*Leviticus* 25:35; *Chullin* 114b; *Bava Metzia* 71a and 111b). In each case he shows that the *ger toshav* is treated to some special law or privilege.

This is because all the nations[31] in Biblical times refused to give up other objects of devotion, and continued to serve other deities and beings besides G-d. (The familiar *Aleinu*[32] prayer is a reflection of this historical fact. Authored during Biblical times by Joshua, it praises Hashem for not making us like the *goyei ha'aratzos* — the "nations of the lands." The next lines make it clear why we direct our animus to these nations. "Therefore we put our hope in You . . . to remove detestable idolatry from the earth, and false gods will be utterly cut off, etc." Our hope is to eradicate *avodah zarah;* such worship was the common practice of all the surrounding nations that existed back then.)

To be comprehensive, we should mention that there is a fourth group. *Minim,* or heretics, occupy a notch below even the last group mentioned, and have no real place in the order of things. This will be explained later on,[33] but they needn't concern us here.

Know this. Wherever *Chazal* discuss non-Jews — whether their conduct, or the laws that apply to them — they refer to those in the third group.[34] This is a given, and can be relied upon as if it were explicitly stated.

⋖§ Sharing Space

While members of the second group are not our coreligionists, we still share a common, binding element in our service of the One G-d. We are connected through Him, as co-participants in a

---

31. *Goy* literally means "nation."

32. The *Aleinu* prayer frequently came under fire from Christian censors, who thought they detected some anti-Christian sentiment. Maharal here may have wished to seize the opportunity, and do what others did: protect the prayer (and the Jewish community) by assuring that the phraseology predated Christianity, and was aimed at ancient paganism.

33. See pg. 264-267.

34. Halachically, the application of this principle is complex, for a variety of reasons that Maharal chose not to discuss. The *Meiri* (*Avodah Zarah* 6a and other places) held that the people and religions he was familiar with ("nations civilized by religion") did not belong to this third category. Other *Rishonim* and later decisors were not so certain that all non-pagan groups could even theoretically be regarded as *gerei toshav*. See *Rambam, Avodah Zarah* 9:4 (uncensored ed. regarding *Notzrim*); *Pischei Teshuvah, Yoreh Deah,* 147:2 and Responsa *Yechaveh Da'as* 4:45 (discussion of the views of the *Rama* and *Noda BeYehuda* regarding *shituf,* or tainted monotheism); R' Zvi Hirsch *Chayes* (doubts about a formalized Islamic practice, even based on a pure monotheism).

common existence. The "place" we occupy is shaped not only by geographical parameters, but by cultural ones as well. People who live side by side, but share absolutely no cultural elements, may share an address, but truly do not share the same "space." No societal element is as important as a commitment to the true G-d. Where this commitment exists, there is a cultural basis that binds them to some degree.

The third group, however, has no place, no part in that existence. Its members are geographical neighbors, but not part of the same society. If you assume that you need some common cultural language to form a community — and that serving G-d is a basic part of its vocabulary — then these people live on the other side of the tracks.

The law described in our passage has everything to do with a common society. There are different types of laws. Some are absolute, and *a priori.* They reflect moral principles that are just so. Others, however, are generated by considerations of the cords that bind men together. They maintain societal cohesion and public good, rather than eliminate the morally outrageous.

It is entirely reasonable that we owe the idolater no restitution when our animals damage theirs. There is no compelling moral case against the owner of the offending animal. Generally, logic dictates that the damaged party is more responsible than the damager, at least when the cause of damage is well-known and identifiable. He should have anticipated the possibility of harm and taken precautions. You might object that he has no effective way of safeguarding his animal from damage without locking it up! Only by keeping his animal out of the common, public domain can he insure that other animals will not harm it. This, you will say, is terribly unfair, a deprivation of his right of unfettered access to public areas. Yet, the defendant has that same right of access! You greatly infringe on this right by holding him liable for damage! It is far more compelling to regard both parties as equally contributing to the mishap, and not to shift the onus of legal blame to one side.

Despite this reasoning, the Torah finds for the plaintiff. It may very well be that the plaintiff was no more in the "wrong" than his neighbor. One was negligent in preventing his animal from damaging; the other was lax in the vigilance that could have prevented the damage.

The issue is not who was wrong, or who was more in the wrong. The Torah's essential point is that in a society of people who are connected with each other, it is improper that anyone should sustain a loss because of the property of another. This is why the Torah underscores "the animal of his friend." It is the friendship, the commonality of all people in a single society that is compromised, weakened and endangered by tort cases of this sort, even without a surfeit of responsibility on one side.

The principle, then, that requires the owner to pay compensation is not one of clear moral weight. It somewhat artificially tilts the balance of responsibility in one direction. A public policy consideration drives it; it aims to bolster feelings of affinity that people should have for one another.

₪§ Pagans Need Not Apply

Members of the third group, however, cannot share these feelings and this common ground. They simply are not part of the same society. They should be dealt with simply on the basis of some overarching, *a priori* moral principle. That principle favors the plaintiff no more than the defendant. Case closed.

Looking carefully at the continuation of the passage, you will see that our argument is consistent with the explanation you will find there. The Gemara itself says that the reason that we do not compensate non-Jewish plaintiffs is that they transgress the seven Noahide laws. Hashem gave a code of conduct that all people are expected to uphold. It includes prohibitions against idolatry, blasphemy, murder, forbidden cohabitation, theft, and eating flesh torn from a living animal (because of the great cruelty involved[35]). It mandates setting up a court system to adjudicate and enforce these laws.

The non-Jews of long ago failed miserably in upholding this code. Hashem responded to their failure by exempting us from paying damages for harming their animals. But this is the only liberty that the Torah takes with their rights! We are still forbidden to steal from them.

Our reasoning above explains the difference. Stealing is a universal moral failing, and therefore we must avoid it. Avoiding theft is part of

---

35. Elsewhere (*Gevuros Hashem*, Ch. 66), Maharal gives a different reason for the prohibition of *ever min ha'chai*. He posits that people will not heed the other six laws unless they learn and practice restraint. The prohibition against torn flesh is an object lesson in self-control, teaching people that they must sometimes stop and wait.

a recognized moral principle, and is therefore expected in regard to all. The lowly, debased state of the victim never justifies the act of taking what does not belong to us. His flaw cannot become an excuse for one on our part.

Holding the damaging party blameless for damages is different. It is simply a reflection of the dynamic of legal wrangling, which results in a standoff between the claims of both plaintiff and defendant concerning who was at fault. When we resolve such issues in favor of the plaintiff, it is because of the common societal turf that we wish to protect. The denier of G-d walked away from it a long time ago.

You may point to a few other areas in which the non-Jew seems to be treated unfairly. Closer examination will quickly show you your error.

One passage in the Gemara[36] implies that the Torah's prohibition against monetary oppression applies only to transactions with other Jews.

ᴥᔌ A Higher Standard of Honesty

This is complete misreading. The Gemara actually deals with a single application of the laws of oppression. According to halachah, if a purchaser was either overcharged or undercharged one-sixth[37] of the usual market price, the difference must be refunded to whomever was disadvantaged. If the seller, for instance, charged the buyer $70 for an item that should be sold for $60, he must refund $10 to the buyer.

Now, this halachah applies even when the seller was unaware that he was overcharging the buyer. Fraudulent intent is simply not the issue. Whenever the buyer learns that he took one-sixth more than he should have, he is required to compensate the buyer.

---

36. The standard edition of Maharal cites *Bava Metzia,* without supplying a specific reference. This may be a printer's error. Although most of the Gemara's discussion of the laws of oppression occurs in *Bava Metzia,* it is *Bechoros* 13b that explicitly excludes non-Jews from protection under this statute. Furthermore, while *Bava Metzia* discusses many aspects of oppression, the *Bechoros* passage deals specifically with the point that Maharal talks about: returning the amount of payment in excess of the customary and usual.

37. Calculating the one-sixth is somewhat complicated. The law covers several permutations of the one-sixth rule, applying it to both the value of the object and the money expended. See *Choshen Mishpat* 227:2.

We are not dealing with a typical statute to prevent fraud. Obligating a refund is a great stringency beyond expected laws of honesty. It goes well beyond the comparable consumer protection statutes of other cultures. The Torah's law applies where there was no deliberate misrepresentation, and no hiding of information. Both the buyer and seller could have taken the time to check and double-check the market value of the object in question. Both could and should share in the responsibility for any mispricing. The two negotiated a deal that seemed fair to both, without either party knowingly lying or stretching the truth.

Apply a standard yardstick of fairness and propriety to such a deal, and most people will see no need for any refund. The Torah adheres to a higher standard, and demands compensation for the party that was "oppressed" — not by deliberate misrepresentation, but through ignorance. It makes perfect sense that the Torah demands such a higher standard only in regard to members of a close-knit inner circle: the community of Jews who are bound to each other through their commitment to Torah. In no way, though, would we ever deal with a non-Jew with less than common decency and fairness.

✑ All's Fair in War

The *Mechilta*[38] states, "Kill the best of the *goyim;* crush the head of the best of snakes." While we could argue that this *goy* is an evil idolater who seems to be a good person by all other indicators, the argument is not convincing. The plain sense of the passage is to destroy even those who are decent human beings, and not idolaters alone.

The proper explanation of this startling passage stares at us from its context. This line is a commentary on Pharaoh's pursuit of the Jewish people with 600 choice chariots. Where did Pharaoh find so many horses? The Egyptians lost all their livestock during the plague of hail, except for animals that had been sheltered indoors. And it was only the exemplary Egyptians — described by the Torah[39] as those "who feared the word of Hashem" — who took the precaution! These same

---

38. *Parashah* 1 (to *Exodus* 14:7).
39. Ibid. 9:20.

G-d-fearing Egyptians now offered their animals to Pharaoh so that he could pursue and run down a defenseless people!

How do we account for the discrepancy? The policy of the ancient Egyptians towards us — the relentless affliction, coupled with the wanton taking of our lives — amounts to warfare. Indeed, there is no greater warfare than this! The *Mechilta* warns us not to examine the moral credentials of our enemies *during a state of war*! War does not allow us to discriminate between the motivation and agenda of different soldiers. In battle, they are all potential threats. The best of them will still kill you in battle. If you hesitate to fire across the front because you know (and have regard for) some of the combatants on the other side, you may very well regret it later. He may not be as considerate to you if you fall into his hands.

A license to take the lives of non-Jews is incompatible with the sense of this passage, and contradictory to the black-letter law elsewhere in the works of *Chazal*. The Gemara considers an opportunity to do-in an idolater (not an ordinary non-Jew, but an established idolater!) through subterfuge, and without directly shedding his blood. May — or should — one find a pretext to lure him to the bottom of a storage pit, and then conveniently pull away the ladder? In other words, should or may Jews resort to self-help to rid the world of detested idolaters when the act will go undetected, and will not bring reprisals?

The Gemara's answer, fully accepted by the decisors as halachah, is an unequivocal "no." It is not for us to take human life, except as an outgrowth of official court procedure. Individuals simply may not do it, except in self-defense.

IV. Heretics and Sinners

"And for the slanderers may there be no hope. Let all the heretics be lost in an instant. May You quickly cut off the enemies of Your people. You should quickly uproot, smash, and cast down the arrogant sinners. . ."[40]

The critics we have been responding to level yet another accusation against *Chazal.* They fault some of the prayers *Chazal* authored, particularly passages like the one above that belittle governmental authorities.

This charge is spurious. If it were true, *Chazal* would do more than violate good taste. They would contradict their own teaching:

> "Pray for the welfare of the government, because if people did not fear it, a person would swallow his friend alive."[41]

We are instructed here to daven for a non-Jewish government. (If they meant only a Jewish government, they would not have to justify their request with a description of the anarchy that government prevents. The peace, greatness, and success of our people are all predicated on the welfare of our own rulers!)

We can readily understand the real sense of this *berachah.* Wherever *Chazal* speak of this segment of the *Shemonah Esrei,* they call it "the curse upon the heretics." It is aimed at those who negate and oppose our faith, not at cursing the political shackles of non-Jewish regimes.

Four groups oppose Torah faith. Each has its own reason and agenda; each is addressed in this *berachah.*

---

40. The *Amidah (Shemoneh Esrei).* Maharal clearly prefers a Sephardic version of the text, using the word *minim* in the second phrase, rather than the Ashkenazic *rishah.*

41. *Ethics of the Fathers* 3:2.

~§ Treachery in Four Forms

The first group[42] finds the requirements and demands of the Torah too difficult and burdensome. People in this group flee from its restrictions, preferring instead a personal autonomy that enables them to follow their own evil inclinations. About them our Torah says:

> ... Perhaps there is among you a man or a woman, or a family or tribe, whose heart turns away today from being with Hashem, our G-d, to go and serve the gods of those nations; perhaps there is among you a root flourishing with gall and wormwood. And it will be that when he hears the words of this imprecation, he will bless himself in his heart, saying, "Peace will be with me, though I walk as my heart sees fit. . ."[43]

Casting off the yoke of mitzvos, these people are then able to pursue whatever foreign path they choose. Note, though, that their decision is not born of an intellectual error. They make no mistake about the essence of Torah and its message. They simply do not want to be restricted by it. They are not firebrands. Nonetheless, they are

---

42. Contemporary *siddurim* begin this *berachah* with the word *v'lamalshinim,* and for the slanderers. This is how we presented it in the translation that opened this section. Maharal's explication of this *berachah,* however, seems to ignore the specific intent of the word "slanderer." The first group mentioned in this *berachah* according to our texts includes those who endanger the public welfare by informing on other Jews to the public authorities. Maharal, however, describes them as those who drop out of normative, halachic practice in order to enjoy themselves a bit more.

The Gemara (*Berachos* 28b) refers to the *berachah* as *Bircas Tzedokim* (Sadducees). A *Genizah* fragment, and the *siddurim* of R' Amram Gaon and R' Saadia Gaon, use the word *v'lamishumadim,* and for the apostates, to open the *berachah* (Jacobson, *Nesiv Binah,* p. 283). This is much closer to the treatment of the Maharal. Jewish apostates have always come in two varieties: those motivated by conviction, and those who "converted" out in order to create better living conditions for themselves. This text may have been assumed by Maharal in his commentary. Interestingly, Maharal cites most of the *berachah* in his piece, but never cites the opening word, leaving it to the imagination of the reader. It might be reasonable to speculate that Maharal gave his reader credit for understanding that censorship had exacted a heavy toll on the original text. (Christian censors assumed that the berachah expressed the animus of the organized Jewish community to Christendom.) He therefore left the word unspecified, assuming the reader would catch on.

43. *Deuteronomy* 29:17-18.

insidious to a Torah community, and we pray that we should be protected from the harmful effects of their presence in our midst. Small breaches in community standards always widen. Behaviors that flout normative rules remove the magic aura of authority. It makes it easier for anyone else to take these regulations lightly.

A second group of people departs from Torah practice as a matter of principle, not convenience. It seems to them that the Torah includes practical reasons for adhering to it. Torah suggests that every Jew will find his greatest personal happiness by fulfilling its demands and expectations. They disagree.

At the core of Torah is a rejection of all foreign gods. Man is instructed to extirpate from his heart all service and allegiance to false deities and the values associated with them, and to focus on Hashem alone.

These people are convinced that this is poor policy. The road to personal success and happiness, they think, requires us to travel on many non-Torah highways. Living in the fast lane requires precisely the opposite of this fundamental rule of the Torah. We will zip along quickest when we savor many different things, not only the G-dly.

◆§ Convenience and Ideology

These people differ markedly from the first group. The ease-centered members of the first group are not idealogues. They are interested in their own lives and comfort, and have no greater agenda. Their departure from Jewish norms is a quiet and personal one. They do not wish to make statements, but to be left alone. They make no claim about the good of the community, because they are really not interested in anything but their own good. This second group of people, however, carry their message to the world with missionary zeal. They are burdened by the gift of their imagined insight. Torah, they think, *blocks* human fulfillment and thwarts us from reaching goals of personal happiness. People must be liberated from it. Because they see themselves as good people, and good people wish to share their gifts with others, they conclude that they have a sacred trust to share their "illumination" with other Jews.

✎§ Universalists and Power-mongers

A different group worries about non-Jewish hostility towards our people. Judaism, they feel — not Jews — is the target of anti-Semitism. All peoples could join together as one integrated family of Man, if they would not stress the cultural differences that divide them from others[44] and others from them. The strict demands of Torah accentuate our differences from the rest of mankind when we should be underscoring our commonality. Torah is the great wedge between the Nation of Israel, and the welcoming embrace of the world community. We refer to them in this *berachah* as "the enemies of Your people," but we really mean "the enemies of the faith of Your people."[45] It is only our Torah that makes us a people; opposing our Torah is equivalent to opposing our peoplehood.

The last group also opposes the religion of Israel, but for baser motives. Universal brotherhood and global harmony do not inspire them, but simply their wish to extend human political power. When the law of G-d and the law of man conflict, the religious person will choose Heaven over earth. This is a thorn in the side of some temporal authorities. Power is so intoxicating that some rulers cannot abide any competition. Religious conviction represents an area of their potential kingdom that is hermetically sealed off from their influence. They legislate against religious observance, but not because of any real tension between the interests of Temple and State. The conflict is between the absolute power they crave, and the allegiance of the masses to a greater Power.[46] This government is called "arrogant" by *Chazal*. There can be no greater presumption than elevating human authority over that of G-d.

---

44. Manetho, a third-century B.C.E. Egyptian priest, wrote that Moses ordered in the Torah that Jews "should have no connection with any save members of their own confederacy." (Manetho was one of history's first recorded anti-Semites. He authored a particular slander about the Exodus which became a staple for anti-Semites for millennia to come. See Paul Johnson, *A History of the Jews*, pp. 29, 134.)

45. So it is Jews who are the object of derision here, not non-Jewish governments as the critics supposed.

46. Lenin, one of the worst abusers of absolute power in the history of mankind, wrote, "There can be nothing more abominable than religion." A contemporary histo-

ᴥ§ Balanced Response

Four phrases in our *berachah* address the four groups we mentioned, in precise order and measure. To the first group — those who think they will find more comfort and freedom unfettered from the bounds of Torah law — we say, "Let there be [for them] no hope." Their example weakens the resolve of the greater community. Of the next group we say, "Let all the *minim* (heretics) be lost in an instant." Notice that for the first, we only pray that their plans and aspirations be thwarted, that they utterly fail to achieve their personal goals, since their very success would invite others to imitate their deviancy.

We invoke far more upon the second. We urge that they be lost entirely. Their transgression, and their effect upon the community, is far more pernicious. Believing that other systems facilitate greater success, they urge replacing the Torah-centeredness of our lives with something foreign. Their neglect of the Torah is aggressive, not passive-benign, and they actively solicit fresh recruits. Thus they actually negate, not just weaken, parts of the Torah community.

The offense worsens with the next group. We ask that "the enemies of Your people be quickly cut off." Again, note that we could have phrased this simply and directly as a plea for Hashem's intervention against "our enemies," meaning all those who attempt to harm us. But that is not what we mean here. We invite Divine wrath against enemies of "Your people," those who oppose the single element that defines us as a people — our Torah. For the previous group, it sufficed that they simply be "lost." The world abounds with pitfalls that can (and in time, will) meet up with the person who walks through life without Divine protection. The sinner will be lost through one or more of the vicissitudes of life. More direct intervention against him is not needed. For those who move against our core peoplehood, though, we ask for more immediate relief. We ask that Hashem directly and efficiently "cut them off."

---

rian comments: "Lenin had no real feelings about corrupt priests, because they were easily beaten. The men he really feared and hated, and later persecuted, were the saints ... It was as though he recognized in the true man of G-d the same zeal and spirit which animated himself, and wished to expropriate it and enlist it in his cause" (Paul Johnson, *Modern Times,* Harper Perennial, 1991, p. 51).

We conclude the *berachah* with an imprecation against the fourth group, the power-intoxicated rulers. We call them arrogant, because it is their conceit alone that drives them. They bow before nothing; they refuse to subjugate themselves to anything but their own egos. This motivates them to use their power and influence to forcibly remove people from Torah. This is a frightful escalation beyond the previous group, because these people can marshal considerable resources to enforce their evil decrees. Accordingly, we do not merely ask for Hashem's swift intervention. Instead, we ask for Hashem's direct and quick blow against them, in an awful and multi-faceted response. Thus the prayer expands into a call for a complex reaction from G-d: that they be "uprooted, smashed, and cast down."

As happens so often, a deeper look at the profundity of *Chazal* yields a much different — and fuller — understanding than the superficial reading. Because our critics see nothing more in the *siddur* than the literary output of everyday authors, they miss all the nuance and sub-tlety, and conclude that this *berachah* is a diatribe against secular governments. We, on the other hand, have successfully shown that it is enemies of Torah within our own community who are targeted here, and that they are arrayed within the *berachah* in precise, hierarchical order. Moreover, we ask Hashem to deal with them in a manner completely appropriate to the danger they pose to the community, and the likelihood of their success.

Once studied in this way, it is difficult to avoid our conclusion that the *berachah* has nothing to do with foreign governments. Why do we retain this *berachah,* then, in an age when active campaigns to stamp out religious observance have disappeared? The answer, of course, is simple. We do not pray just for solutions to immediate problems. We catalog all the important ingredients and contingencies of our personal, communal, and national lives, and place all our needs on Hashem's doorstep. The *siddur* is a fixed response of the community, not one which varies from time to time. We often anticipate concerns and issues that may not concern us at the moment we stand in prayer.

All who study this *berachah* cannot help but be saddened and angered by the assault on the integrity of our Sages. The critics decry what they believe to be an unjustified attack on others, while it is really they who are unjustified in their criticism. We have shown that the negative sentiments that *Chazal* express in this *berachah* are both measured and warranted. Because of their shoddy scholarship, the critics missed the crucial points.

Their error is actually much greater yet. *Chazal* voice their abhorrence for inviting Divine Wrath even upon the fully guilty and deserving.

V. Evil vs. Evildoers

[Boorish people lived in R' Meir's neighborhood, and they caused him much anguish. He prayed for their demise. Beruriah his wife said to him:] "What is your reasoning [to pray for their deaths]? Because it is written, 'Let *chataim* cease from the earth'?[47] [But] is it then *chotim* [that is] written [in the verse? No!] [sinners]? The [word] written is *chataim* [i.e. it is sins which should cease]! Furthermore, go down to the end of the verse: — 'and let the wicked men be no more.' [Now is it the case that] once sinners cease [from the world] the wicked will be no more? Rather pray for mercy for them that they should repent, and there will be no more wicked." He prayed for mercy for them, and they repented.[48]

R' Meir accepted his wife's observation that the verse avoids calling for the death of the evil. Even the evil can repent. Why, therefore, pray for the destruction of a person, the cherished handiwork of Hashem? The verse asks for the cessation of sin, through the repentance of the sinners. In this way, there will be no more wicked since there will be no one sinning!

Chazal incorporated this ethic in our *berachah*. Using quite a few different phrases, they call for the obliteration of different forms of evil. All of them stop short of asking for the physical destruction of the

---

47. *Psalms* 104:35.
48. *Berachos* 10a.

wicked![49] We ask that "there be no hope" for those who break with tradition in the pursuit of ease and comfort. Their plans should not meet with success. Let their warped aspirations die a slow death — but not them!

The heretics should "be lost" — give them no place to run; remove their ideological refuge, when all heresy shrivels and disappears! We avoid the more obvious request of removing them surgically from the trunk of life.

Our enemies should be "cut off " — by finding no common group of Jew-haters with whom to share their enmity. We ask Hashem to "up-root, smash, and cast down" the arrogant governmental authorities. Eliminate the arrogance, not the governments! When they are humbled, they cease to be the targets of the *berachah.* Let them live and let them rule! Change must come! The imperious will that bows to nothing and no One must transform itself. Once tamed, we show them no animosity.

VI. Suppressing Criticism

We have shown how our critics are guilty of the very small-mindedness of which they accuse our Sages. We have further demonstrated how completely undeserving *Chazal* are of the charges leveled against them. We are left with one more criticism to answer.

They complain that *Chazal* openly and stridently criticize other faiths. It is bad form to attack the beliefs of others. Religious beliefs in particular go to the very core and essence of the person. Attacking such beliefs violates the dignity of other human beings.

The truth is that there simply are no such statements in the works of *Chazal.* Our critics have found passages that allow for such interpretation, and have been quick to understand them in the least generous way possible, never giving *Chazal* the benefit of the doubt. Where a

---

49. In the Ashkenazic siddur, the second phrase does not address heretics at all. Instead, two variant texts suggest either "evil-doers," or "evil." The Vilna Gaon preferred the latter, pointing to the thrust of the passage in *Berachos.* Interestingly, the Maharal obviates the need for any change. According to his approach, *Chazal* implicitly refer to the various sources of evil, and not those who practice them, regardless of who is named in the *berachah.*

prima facie case might be made against *Chazal,* our own scholars of previous generations, like *Tosafos,* [50] have already shown us how to correctly grasp the intent of the authors.

Although the offending passages have been with us for hundreds of years, none of the earlier commentaries met them with the same reaction. This can only be for one of two reasons.

One reason is that the passages simply do not say what they are purported to. A more careful reading of each passage always yields a different conclusion.

Another reason is that the earlier commentators simply disagreed with the premise of our critics. They did not believe that the forceful presentation of ideas in the public forum is offensive, even if these arguments struck deeply at treasured matters of the heart and soul. They strongly believed that open discussion of issues should never be suppressed. They would not accept the muting and stilling of opposing voices.[51] If they did, on occasion, attack foreign ideologies, they did so out of the conviction that all important propositions should bear the weight of public scrutiny.

Even non-Jewish thinkers understand the proper ethic of intellectual discourse. One of them[52] stressed the need to introduce his readers to the arguments of his opponents. Two benefits flowed from this, he claimed. Firstly, he could expose the weakness of their thinking. By contrasting their grasp of the arguments with his own, superior approach, his reader would realize that their conclusions were insupportable.

---

50. Maharal gives no citation. He perhaps refers to the comments of *Tosafos* regarding the Gemara's (*Yevamos* 61a) famous assertion that Jews are called Man, while non-Jews are not. For hundreds of years, anti-Semites offered this passage as proof that Jews treated their non-Jewish neighbors as subhuman vermin, and accorded their lives and property no meaning or significance. This argument figured in the infamous Beilis trial of the early 20th century.

51. It is likely that Maharal had in mind here the tragic history of "debate" forced upon us by the Church for hundreds of years in the medieval period. With very few exceptions, the Jewish representatives were never allowed to fully present their arguments and positions. They were mostly reduced to answering particular questions put to them from the other side, which was permitted, of course, to make their best case. A notable exception was the disputation at Barcelona, where *Ramban* secured permission from James of Aragon to speak more freely. Not surprisingly, this debate ended in a clear victory for the Jewish side.

52. Aristotle, *De Caelo,* Chapter 10, 279b.

Secondly, you make a far more favorable impression upon your audience when you go out of your way to present all sides of an issue. This is all the more so when you anticipate the counterarguments of your disputant, and attempt to refute them. He avers that it is important not to treat your opponent with contemptuous anger, but with civility and concern, conceding to him every privilege you would arrogate to yourself. He extends these courtesies even to those who dispute matters of faith. Do not cast aside the words of your opponent, even in areas of faith and religion, he urges. Instead, bring them close for careful consideration.

If you fail to do this, you show weakness, not strength. This is especially true in regard to those whose purpose is not to be disputatious, but simply to present their beliefs. Even where they dispute essentials of faith, it is wrong to silence them, muzzling their ability to speak. Rather, they should be encouraged to speak, so that they are unable to later claim that if they had been given the opportunity to present their views, they would have turned the tide of opinion in their own favor.

Thus, even if we discover a passage here and there which attacks the beliefs of other faiths, the truth-seeking spirit should welcome this. All the more so when you consider that we are discussing books, meant for calm, considered reading. We are not talking about stirring up the crowds with verbal diatribes and philippics, which is indeed offensive. The authors of instructional books are not given to polemics. They merely hope to teach, and it is inappropriate to stifle their expression.

Why do our critics not pour their fury upon some of the secular philosophers whom they cite? These ancient thinkers completely denied the notion of Creation, a position that is thoroughly repugnant even to our critics. This does not stop them from utilizing their works, and weighing their words and arguments, rather than dismissing them outright. This is the proper approach to take to those with whom you must disagree. Take their arguments seriously, and disprove them if you can! If *Chazal* present arguments against the positions of other faiths, then it behooves the adherents of those faiths to consider the arguments, and try to refute them.

By way of analogy, a mighty warrior does not demonstrate his prowess by fighting opponents whose arms have been tied. He makes his point only if his opponent fights with all his might, and he still vanquishes the challenger! Intellectual battles are no different. Silencing your opponent proves nothing but the weakness of your position.

If anything, the point is more crucial in intellectual matters than it is in the analogy. Masters of human behavior caution us to be more wary of those who hate us with unexpressed hostility. We cannot know what they really think in order to defend ourselves. We have a much easier time with those who openly speak about their reasons for disliking us. If we wish, we can attempt to answer their charges and complaints.

The same holds true of debate. We are far better off knowing the positions of our adversaries than being kept in the dark. If *Chazal* express the causes of their rejection of other groups, members of those groups ought to be appreciative.

As stated above, however, the entire premise of this discussion is likely inaccurate. There is nothing to prove that *Chazal* engaged in this sort of polemic altogether. There are alternative understandings of the passages in question. This should not be surprising. The Torah that Moses transmitted us is wide and deep enough that *Chazal* found it sufficient to deal with it and nothing more. We need not go elsewhere. We can never exhaust all the wondrous things we can talk about within our own Torah.

Glossary

Adam HaRishon — "the first man," or the biblical Adam.

aggadah [pl. *aggados*] — one (or the entire collection) of the homiletical, non-halachic teachings of the Sages.

Anshei Knesses HaGedolah — the Men of the Great Assembly, the chief body of Torah authority at the beginning of the Second Temple period.

Aron — ark, especially the Ark of the Law which housed the Tablets of the Ten Commandments in the Mishkan.

Aseres HaDibros — the Ten Commandments.

asur — prohibited.

aveirah — [pl. *aveiros*] transgression.

avodah — (a) work or service, hence (b) service of G-d, often expanded to *avodas* Hashem.

baheres — a type of *nega*. A bright spot appearing on skin, as described in Leviticus 13:2.

bas kol — a heavenly voice.

Beis Hillel — the House of Hillel; Hillel and his students and followers.

Beis Shammai — the House of Shammai; Shammai and his students and followers.

berachah [pl. *berachos*] — blessing. (a) a short formula for acknowledging a gift from G-d, whether material or spiritual; (b) an invocation of Divine favor, as in a blessing given by one person to another, or in a communication from G-d Himself.

Birkas HaMazon — the Grace After Meals.

Chacham [pl. *Chachamim*] — (a) a wise person; (b) particularly one of the Sages of the Talmudic period.

chas v'shalom — an idiom approximating "G-d forbid."

Chazal — an acronym for *Chachameinu Zichronom Livrachah,* or Our

Sages, of blessed memory. The term usually refers to the Rabbis of the Talmudic period.

Chumash — the Pentateuch; the first five Books of the Bible.

davening — prayer.

derabbanan — of the Rabbis. Said of laws originating in rabbinic decree, rather than Divine dictate, which is called *d'oraiso.*

derashah [pl. *derashos*] — lit., inquiry. A formalized way of extracting multiple levels of meaning from Biblical text, uncovering the intent of the Divine Author.

din — (a) law; (b) judgment.

d'oraiso — of Torah origin. Said of a law that is of Divine authorship, because it is either explicitly or implicitly demanded by Torah text. It contrasts with *derabbanan,* which admits to human derivation.

Erev Shabbos — the eve of the Sabbath.

Gan Eden — the Garden of Eden; the paradise in which Man was first created, and to which the deserving will return.

geder [pl. *gedarim*] — lit., fence. A rabbinic law that distances potential transgressors from transgression.

Gemara — the later (fourth and fifth centuries; Israel and Babylonia) and larger part of the Talmud. Written as a fuller explication of the Mishnah, it is the single most important redaction of the Oral Law.

Gehinnom — the place where souls are punished for their misdeeds during life; hell.

HaKadosh Baruch Hu — The Holy One, Blessed is He. A more evocative substitution for the word "G-d."

halachah — a point of law, or the entire collection of Jewish law. Its adjectival form is halachic.

Havdalah — the ceremony that formally divides between the holiness of Shabbos that has just ended and the new period of weekday activity.

heter — (a) that which is permissible; (b) a formal ruling that declares something permissible.

kedushah — holiness.

Klal Yisrael — the entire Jewish community, taken as a single entity.

kodashim — objects offered in the Temple service. Strict regulations govern who may partake of them, and the degree of *taharah* these people must enjoy before partaking of or touching them.

Kohen [pl. *Kohanim*] — member of the priestly family descended from Aaron. The Kohen is accorded special duties and privileges associated with the Temple service, and is bound by special laws of sanctity.

Kohen Gadol — the High Priest.

korban [pl. *korbanos*] — something brought close to the altar; a Temple offering, whether animal or vegetable.

Mashiach — Messiah, the awaited redeemer of Israel, who ushers in an era of universal recognition of the Kingship of Hashem.

melachah — creative activity forbidden on Shabbos by Torah law.

middah [pl. middos] — attribute or characteristic.

midrash — the product of rabbinic examination and explication of Biblical text.

mikveh — a body of standing water, collected naturally without direct human intervention, containing a legally prescribed volume. Among other things, a *mikveh* is used to purify an object or person which has become *tamei*.

milah — circumcision of males.

Mishkan — the Tabernacle, the movable Temple erected by the Jews in the Sinai Desert.

Mishnah — the first written redaction of the Oral Law, published under the direction of Judah the Prince in the third century.

mutar — permissible.

nega [pl. *negaim*] — changes in the appearance of human skin, articles of clothing, or walls of a house, as set forth in Leviticus chs. 13-14.

neshamah [pl. *neshamos*] — soul.

Olam Haba — the World to Come. A designation for the eternal afterlife.

pasuk [pl. pesukim] — sentence; particularly a Biblical verse.

Pesukei DeZimrah — Verses of Praise; a section of the morning prayer which sets the mood for the recitation of *Shema* and *Shemoneh Esrei* which follow.

pshat — the plain sense and meaning of a text.

R' — Rabbi.

rachamim — compassion.

Rishonim — lit. the first ones; the "early" commentators, who lived and wrote between the 11th and 15th centuries.

Rosh Chodesh — The first day of each lunar month. When the Temple stood, a special offering was brought beyond the mandated daily offering.

Sanhedrin — A court composed of a substantial number of jurists; used to differentiate the larger courts from the smallest panels of three judges.

Sanhedrin HaGadol — The highest court of the land.

sefiros [sing. *sefirah*] — in the mystical tradition, the ten "emanations," or patterns, through which the abstract Will of G-d ripples through the mystical worlds until taking concrete form. They "constitute the inner structure and makeup of the *Olamos* — universes," and "allow us to speak about what He does, without referring directly to what He is" (R' Aryeh Kaplan, Innerspace, pp. 37, 39).

Shacharis — the morning prayer.

sheid [pl. *sheidim*] — a demon, possessing properties of both physical and ethereal beings, and often harmful to humans.

Shema — the "Hear O Israel" declaration of faith recited each morning and evening.

Shemoneh Esrei — the eighteen blessings that form the central core of each weekday prayer service; the *Amidah*.

taharah — a halachically defined state of ritual purity; the absence of *tumah*- contamination.

tahor — person or object in a state of *taharah*.

talmidei chachamim — Torah scholars.

tamei — person or object that has been contaminated by *tumah*.

tefillah [pl. *tefillos*] prayer.

terumah — A portion of produce grown in Israel that must be separated and given to a Kohen. *Terumah* has special sanctity, and may only be eaten by a Kohen and his household, and only when *tahor*.

tumah — legally defined state of ritual impurity affecting certain people or objects.

tzaddik — a fully righteous person.

yetzer hara — The evil inclination. Man finds himself in a constant tension between this tendency, and the countervailing *yetzer tov,* or inclination to good.

zav — a male who has become *tamei* because of a specific type of unexpected seminal emission. See *Leviticus* 15:1-15.

zomemim — plotting witnesses. When witnesses are discredited through later testimony that places them where they could not possibly have observed the deed in question, they are punished by whatever consequences they plotted to inflict upon the defendant (*Deuteronomy* 19:19).

This volume is part of
THE ARTSCROLL SERIES®
an ongoing project of
translations, commentaries and expositions
on Scripture, Mishnah, Talmud, Halachah,
liturgy, history, the classic Rabbinic writings,
biographies and thought.

For a brochure of current publications
visit your local Hebrew bookseller
or contact the publisher:

Mesorah Publications, ltd

4401 Second Avenue
Brooklyn, New York 11232
(718) 921-9000